THE IRISH TIMES

Nealon's Guide
to the 31st Dáil & 24th Seanad

Edited by
Stephen Collins

Gill & Macmillan

Gill & Macmillan Ltd
Hume Avenue
Park West
Dublin 12
with associated companies throughout the world
www.gillmacmillan.ie

978 07171 50595

Original design concept by Elizabeth Fitz-Simon
Print origination by Carole Lynch
Index compiled by Dog's-ear Editing
Printed and bound in Italy by Printer Trento

*The paper used in this book is made from the wood pulp of managed forests.
For every tree felled, at least one tree is planted, thereby renewing natural resources.*

A catalogue record is available for this book
from the British Library.

1 3 5 4 2

Contents

Acknowledgments

Nealon's Guide to the 31st Dáil and 24th Seanad is the twelfth in the series started by Ted Nealon after the 1973 General Election. The series is a unique and accessible reference work which contains the election results, constituency by constituency, since that time. Equally important, it contains the essential biographical details of everybody elected to the Dáil and Seanad over the period.

There has been nothing like it in the history of the state. William Flynn's parliamentary companion, produced between 1923 and 1945, is the only comparable reference work, but it was more sporadic. It was not published after every election and it contained first count results only. Ted Nealon, noted journalist and politician, edited the Guides up to the 1997 General Election. Since then it has been produced by *The Irish Times* in conjunction with Gill & Macmillan.

I would like to thank two people in particular for their invaluable assistance in the production of this edition. Joe Joyce did a great deal of the hard work involved in assembling the detailed information that is an essential part of the volume; and his wise advice and guidance ensured that the project was completed on time. The copy-editor Emma Farrell was meticulous in her attention to detail. Her professionalism and good humour ensured that the Guide was produced to the highest standard with the minimum of fuss.

Thanks also to Mary Minihan and Paul Cullen of the *Irish Times* political staff, who gave a helping hand when the project threatened to slip behind schedule. Thanks to Mick Crowley in the systems department of *The Irish Times* for supplying the figures; and to Picture Editor Frank Miller and the photographic department for supplying the wonderful pictures.

Thanks are also due to Fergal Tobin, Publishing Director of Gill & Macmillan, and his team, including Fíodhna Ní Ghríofa of the editorial department and Ciara O'Connor of the marketing department.

Thanks to the staff of the Oireachtas for their assistance; and to the Oireachtas Library and Research Service for providing the maps. Finally, thanks to those members of the Dáil and Seanad and their staff who co-operated with the project and helped to ensure the accuracy of the information in the Guide.

STEPHEN COLLINS
September 2011

Foreword

An Taoiseach, Mr Enda Kenny TD

I would like to congratulate *The Irish Times* and Gill & Macmillan on the publication of the twelfth *Nealon's Guide to the Dáil and Seanad.*

This outstanding reference book has been published in the wake of every election since 1973 and has since that time been the central reference point for politicians and journalists, and indeed many others.

A renowned reference book, *Nealon's Guide* is incredibly useful in the first instance as a source of facts and figures; and it is greatly enhanced by quality contributions from the staff of *The Irish Times*, whose observations add much to its readability. This latest edition will form another chapter in what has become an invaluable stock of information for all those with an interest in Irish politics.

Election 2011 was nothing less than a democratic revolution at the ballot box. With 566 candidates seeking 166 seats, this election had real potential to sweep aside the old order and initiate a new era in Irish politics; and that is exactly what happened. A record total of 14 non-party TDs and 76 first-time TDs were elected; and Fine Gael, Labour and Sinn Féin each achieved their highest ever seat totals.

If anyone had any doubt about the power of people to effect seismic change through the exercise of their democratic franchise, the events of General Election 2011 provided a resounding answer. With each vote cast the Irish people's desire for change came closer to being realised. As ballot boxes around the country were opened and the tally men went to work, it quickly emerged just how fundamental that change in Irish politics would be.

The vigour with which the electorate embraced the chance to have their voices heard probably shouldn't have come as a surprise. A national turnout rate of 69.9% (with polling rates as high as 80% in some constituencies) was a clear statement of intent from the Irish people. Ireland was making a big decision and they wanted in. They were angry; and why wouldn't they be? They had been misled by the previous administration as to the gravity of the situation the country was facing; and misled again about its intentions on how to deal with the crisis the Government had done so much to create. The electorate craved leadership. They wanted and deserved a government with a plan to deal with the crisis the country faced and they demanded that the politicians they elected display the courage needed to implement that plan.

Watching voter after voter stride purposefully into polling stations around the country, a look of unwavering intent on their faces, it was as if they were saying, 'Today I will have my say; today my voice will be heard.' And when the votes were counted, there remained little ambiguity about the people's desire for real change.

It became very obvious to me both before and during the election that while the anger that existed amongst the electorate about past failures was deep, their desire for real and meaningful change was deeper. The volume of calls into my office since well before Christmas 2010 told me in no uncertain terms that an extensive plan to address the crisis would be required, and that voters wanted much more than a superficial affiliation to a different party. To put it simply: the people wanted us to lay our cards on the table. I was fully confident that Fine Gael was very well equipped to fulfil this requirement, due in no small part to the extensive policy programme we had developed over the previous months and years.

Never before at election time had I witnessed such a demand for specifics of policy or such a level of scrutiny of the party manifestos. The thirst for detail from members of the public was hugely encouraging and seemed to reflect a simple two-pronged question: 'What is your plan; and will it work?' We in Fine Gael, for example, received in excess of 4,000 policy queries through our website during the campaign. The people wanted evidence of a real plan.

Fine Gael had such a plan – one that was fair, costed and plausible. The people saw that it would work and ultimately they chose to place their faith in a Fine Gael–Labour coalition, a government which has the largest majority in the history of the state. The new coalition has given the people the stability they wanted and deserved and the new Government has already fulfilled many of the pledges outlined in our Programme for Government in what has been one of the busiest and most intense first Dáil sessions in generations.

Our most pressing priority on entering office was to restore our country's economy and international standing by addressing the key issues of restructuring the banks, correcting our public finances and investing in the creation of jobs. Our first major move was to radically restructure our banking system into two pillar banks, making the Irish banking system more focused, better funded and better capitalised. Making it, above all else, sustainable. Since the restructuring process began, private investors have made a €1 billion investment in Bank of Ireland, thus serving the dual benefit of reducing the burden of bank debt on the taxpayer as well as signaling to other investors that Ireland is open for business.

The jobs crisis dominated this election. Our chronic unemployment rate meant that this was the issue at the forefront of every voter's mind. Investing in the creation of jobs is something the new Government has already begun to do through the launch of the Jobs Initiative, our extensive stimulus plan aimed at stimulating job creation. Ultimately, this is a down-payment by this Government on its promise to put jobs and economic growth at the very top of the political agenda. Every Minister in my Government will work to deliver, and indeed to improve on, this employment forecast.

I stated clearly on 9 March 2011 that my fundamental goal on entering office would be to work relentlessly towards a future when Ireland will once again take charge of its own economic destiny and I am glad to report that we are on track in this regard. Also at the core of Fine Gael's election campaign was a promise to renegotiate the rescue package with our three external partners. I welcome the fact that, following intensive campaigning from the Government, a significantly lower interest rate

has been agreed to by our Eurozone partners as part of a more flexible overall deal easing the burden on our economy to the tune of at least €800 million annually.

Political reform was another huge issue during this election, as the electorate made it very clear that sacrifice should start at the top. It was a view that I shared; and on the day I became Taoiseach I reduced my own pay and that of the cabinet significantly. This was only the first in a litany of changes to the political system to which the new Government has committed, including: an increase in the number of Dáil sitting days, a referendum on the Seanad in 2012, and the holding of two referenda in October.

The new Government has also signalled its intention to place families and children at the heart of everything we do and my decision to establish a dedicated Department of Children, as well as the position I took in the wake of the publication of the Cloyne Report, is evidence of this commitment.

On 9 March 2011 I entered a covenant with the Irish people. I made a commitment to work hard to rescue our economy, to resuscitate our reputation and to restore our society. I am glad to report that we have made a strong start, but in truth our work has only just begun.

I have been clear in my ambition that by 2016 Ireland will be the best small country in the world in which to do business, the best country in which to raise a family, and the best in which to grow old with dignity and respect.

I have been given the honour as Taoiseach of leading Ireland on the road to recovery. I will ensure that this Government faces into this formidable crisis until ultimately we face it down. It is a collective journey involving every citizen of the state. Our goals and objectives can be achieved and we can dare to hope again.

Enda Kenny

The Election Background

Stephen Collins

The general election of 2011 was one of the great transformational contests in Irish political history. Fianna Fáil, the party that had dominated the state for almost 80 years, lost three-quarters of its Dáil seats in an unprecedented rout that changed the face of Irish politics.

The last time anything on a similar scale happened was in 1918 when the Irish Parliamentary Party was swept into the dust-heap of history by the rise of Sinn Féin. The election of 1932 was another transformational contest that brought Fianna Fáil to power for the first time but the change in party fortunes was on nothing like the scale of 2011. The question now is whether the result heralds a new epoch in Irish politics.

The scale of the change that took place in February 2011 was seismic. One of Ireland's leading political scientists, the late Peter Mair, pointed out that the contest was not only one of the most volatile in Irish democratic history but was one of the most volatile elections in Europe since 1945. 'In fact, the Irish election emerges as the third most volatile in western Europe since 1945, being surpassed only by Italy in 1994, when the Christian Democrats and Socialists collapsed and Berlusconi's Forza Italia first came to power; and by the Netherlands in 2002, when Pim Fortuyn led the first Dutch populist revolt,' wrote Mair.

What made the Irish result unique was that it did not involve a new party storming onto the scene, as happened in Italy and the Netherlands. It showed the electorate turning to one party that last enjoyed dominance almost 80 years ago and to another that was founded in 1912, before the state even existed. The scale of the changes is still difficult to comprehend. Fianna Fáil lost an astonishing 58 seats, while Fine Gael gained 25 and the Labour Party gained 16. The Green Party lost all 6 seats while Sinn Féin gained 10 and Independents 14.

So why was it such a watershed election? Long- and short-term considerations combined to bring about an election at the worst possible time for Fianna Fáil and its coalition allies and the best possible moment for the Opposition parties and Independents.

The slide in the Government's fortunes began in the summer of 2008, shortly after Brian Cowen succeeded Bertie Ahern as Taoiseach and leader of Fianna Fáil. The loss of the first Lisbon Treaty referendum in June 2008 was a sign that the electorate was weary of a party that had won a third successive term in the 2007 election.

In fact, beginning in 1987, Fianna Fáil had taken power after six elections in a row. The only break in almost a quarter of a century of Fianna Fáil hegemony before 2011 was the 1994–97 rainbow coalition, led by John Bruton, which achieved office without an election in the middle of a Dáil term.

The 2007 election victory was simply a bridge too far. Fianna Fáil appeared headed for failure for most of that campaign but snatched victory from the jaws of defeat on the basis that it was the party most capable of dealing with an economic downturn. It was not long before Fianna Fáil TDs began to curse their luck. Their Fine Gael counterparts quickly recovered from their disappointment in defeat to count their blessings. Enda Kenny proved himself to be a lucky general by losing a battle that positioned him to win the war.

Shortly after the Lisbon referendum defeat it became clear that the public finances were heading for trouble in 2008 with a sharp decline in tax revenue. On top of that an unprecedented banking crisis began to unfold, leaving new Minister for Finance Brian Lenihan (appointed in May 2008) facing a truly appalling vista. Lenihan quipped shortly after taking his appointment that he had 'the misfortune' to become Minister for Finance just as the building boom came to 'a shuddering end'. The media criticised him for an alleged gaffe but he never spoke a truer word. His efforts to deal with the bust that followed the boom of the Celtic Tiger years saw the Government's popularity plummet. Tough budget decisions, the blanket bank guarantee and the subsequent bailout, the establishment of the National Asset Management Agency (NAMA) and a precipitous slide in tax revenues combined to make that government the most unpopular in the history of the state.

By the time of the local and European elections of 2009 Fianna Fáil was on the ropes. It was pushed into second place as Fine Gael became the biggest party in local government for the first time in its history. While the second Lisbon Treaty referendum was carried in the autumn of 2009, with a massive effort on the part of the three major parties and a range of civic society groups, there was no revival in the Government's fortunes.

Instead Fianna Fáil began to sink lower and lower in the polls as the economic and banking crises worsened. After the local elections of 2009, which showed Fianna Fáil on 25 per cent, political pundits wondered if the party could really do as badly as that in a general election. A year later, with the party dropping below 20 per cent in the polls, the question was whether that figure might make some kind of floor.

In the autumn of 2009, Ceann Comhairle John O'Donoghue resigned after a row over his expenses. That was followed in early 2010 by the resignation of two cabinet Ministers, Willie O'Dea and Martin Cullen, for very different reasons. They combined to give the impression that events were spinning out of the Government's control.

By the summer of 2010 the Labour Party had taken the lead in the polls ahead of Fine Gael and Fianna Fáil. Party leader Eamon Gilmore had become the star performer in the Dáil for his attacks on Cowen and Fianna Fáil. 'Gilmore for Taoiseach' became the slogan as the party looked forward to challenging the two bigger Dáil parties for top place in the forthcoming election.

The surge in Labour support reignited doubts in Fine Gael about Enda Kenny's ability to connect with the public and a leadership heave was launched with the backing of most of his front bench. Kenny dug in and fired his challenger Richard Bruton along with the majority of his front bench. It was a bold strategy and it paid off as he routed his opponents.

Meanwhile the pressure on the Government continued unabated. Later in the summer of 2010, as the International Monetary Fund warned that the austerity measures already in place might not be enough, some Fianna Fáil and Green Party politicians wondered privately if it might not be best to seek a mandate from the electorate at that stage for further tough action.

Fianna Fáil Ministers knew they were on the way to defeat but one senior figure wanted to stage a Dunkirk-like election, where they could salvage between 40 and 50 seats and go into Opposition, rather than soldier on and accept whatever fate awaited.

However, Brian Cowen was determined to keep going and the Government began working on a four-year recovery plan in conjunction with the European Commission. The Commissioner for Economic and Monetary Affairs Olli Rehn visited Dublin in November 2010 to try and soften public opinion and encourage the Opposition to accept the necessity for the plan.

By that stage, though, events were spinning out of control. The international money markets lost confidence in the ability of the Irish state to repay the enormous sums being swallowed up by the banking bailout. Strong pressure was applied by the European Central Bank on the Irish Government to accept a recovery programme financed by the European institutions and the International Monetary Fund.

The Government's handling of the episode destroyed whatever remaining credibility it had. Negotiations on the terms of a bailout were in progress even as Ministers protested that media reports on the issue were 'fiction'. On top of the ignominy arising from the loss of sovereignty, the Government had to contend with Opposition taunts that it had lied to the public.

It was a political and economic shambles and the Greens had had enough. On 22 November party leader John Gormley announced that they would withdraw from Government once the budget and the Finance Bill had been passed in late January or early February of 2011.

There was drama in early December over the budget, but it was passed by the Dáil with the support of Independents. Cowen seemed to have earned a little breathing space and Fianna Fáil Ministers insisted that the election would not take place before April or even May, giving the party some time to plan a campaign.

Even that strategy fell apart in January when Cowen came under pressure to explain previously unknown contacts with disgraced Anglo-Irish Bank boss Seán Fitzpatrick in 2008. Amid rumours of a leadership heave, Cowen put down a motion of confidence in himself and took on his internal critics. Most of those who had been privately critical of his leadership backed off, but Minister for Foreign Affairs Micheál Martin mounted a challenge. Cowen survived and Martin resigned from the cabinet.

Scarcely was the contest over when Cowen tried a manoeuvre to bring fresh talent into the cabinet through a reshuffle following the acceptance of resignations of four Ministers who did not intend to run again. The Greens, who had not been told of the Taoiseach's intentions, expressed unease and tried to have the decision reversed. By that stage the resignations had gone to President McAleese and there was no going back. Gormley apparently suggested that the Áras be contacted to establish if the President had accepted the resignations but the suggestion prompted a firm response from Brian Lenihan. 'You can bully Fianna Fáil but you won't bully the President.'

The following morning, 20 January, Cowen led his depleted cabinet into the Dáil and announced that a general election would be held on 11 March. Two days later he resigned as Fianna Fáil leader saying he would continue on as Taoiseach until after the election. Martin won the contest to succeed him, seeing off Brian Lenihan, Éamon Ó Cuív and Mary Hanafin.

In the meantime the Greens pulled out of Government ahead of a Labour confidence motion. The Finance Bill was passed by the Dáil but Cowen realised there was no point trying to continue in office so he came into the chamber and dissolved the Dáil on St Brigid's Day, naming 25 February as the date of the election.

After the helter skelter of the previous three months, the election campaign itself was a relatively sedate affair. Fine Gael kicked off its formal campaign with a Five-point Plan and refused to be drawn into detailed arguments with the Government over its economic strategy for the years ahead.

The tactic worked like a dream and Enda Kenny became the star of the election campaign. Dubbed the 'Val Doonican of Irish politics' because he suddenly appeared to be a popular figure after 35 years as a politician, he criss-crossed the country campaigning in towns and villages in every constituency. Kenny had the confidence to dictate timing of the television debates, which were his perceived weakness with the media. He refused to take part in a TV3 debate, saying bluntly: 'I will not participate in any programme that Vincent Browne has anything to do with.' Dire consequences for this refusal were widely predicted in the media but the public had no problem with Kenny's decision. He participated in the first three-way debate in Irish and then in a five-way debate involving the smaller parties and

The Election Background

finally in a three-way debate on RTÉ. He performed well on all the debates and laid to rest his reputation as a weak media performer.

For Eamon Gilmore the election campaign was a different experience. He performed well in all the television debates but the Labour campaign did not catch the public imagination in the way the Fine Gael one did.

Possibly lulled into a false sense of confidence by the media talk of a 'Gilmore Gale', the Labour campaign was not as well organised or focused as Fine Gael's. On just the third day of the campaign, Gilmore raised serious questions about his own political judgement in the course of a press conference in which he said the election was about whether the budget would be decided by the European Central Bank in Frankfurt or by the democratically elected government of the Irish people. 'It's Frankfurt's way or Labour's way,' declared Gilmore, who went on to describe the chairman of the ECB, Jean Claude Trichet, as 'a mere civil servant'.

The remarks rebounded on Gilmore because, whatever the public feeling about the austerity programme associated with the EU/IMF bailout, most voters were capable of a realistic assessment of the options. In any case public ire was directed at Fianna Fáil and the Greens and not at Frankfurt.

As the opinion polls showed support for Fine Gael and Kenny rising and that for Labour and Gilmore declining, Labour began to attack its potential coalition partner. Fine Gael refused to get involved in a row and started to dream of an overall majority for the first time in the party's history.

Fianna Fáil was in a unique position, fighting the election campaign with Micheál Martin as leader while Brian Cowen remained in the Taoiseach's office. The party kicked off well enough with a hastily assembled manifesto but as the polls began to come in it was clear that there was no revival in sight. The party scraped along with around 15 per cent of the vote and it became clear that the only question was the scale of the beating it

would endure. Brian Hayes of Fine Gael summed it up well in the middle of the campaign. 'We are feasting over the carcass of Fianna Fáil. This isn't an election between us and Fianna Fáil. It's between Fine Gael and Labour,' he said.

Fianna Fáil's coalition partners, the Greens, were in an even worse position. Whether the party could hang on to one or two seats or face a total wipe out was the issue. While Gormley and his cabinet colleague Eamon Ryan campaigned as hard as they could they were in an impossible position.

A number of left-wing groups came together as the United Left Alliance and put in a fighting campaign. Socialist MEP Joe Higgins was the group's biggest star but there were a number of other experienced left-wing campaigners who were presented with an ideal opportunity to make a breakthrough.

Independents also proliferated. Long time senator Shane Ross ran a storming campaign in Dublin South while builder/developer Mick Wallace, who owed the banks €40 million, did something similar in Wexford.

From day one a change of government was inevitable. As the campaign drew to a close the big question was whether Fine Gael might pull off the impossible dream and win an overall majority or whether the long expected outcome of a Fine Gael–Labour coalition would become a reality.

In the event the surge to Fine Gael was halted in the final days of the campaign and Labour recovered some ground. Still, with 36 per cent of the vote going to Fine Gael it was a damned close-run thing. Director of elections Phil Hogan masterminded a daring strategy that eked out every last possible seat. The party's share of the vote, at 36.1 per cent, was not quite as good as its previous best ever performance in 1982 but it won 76 seats compared with 70 in 1982. More to the point, it became by far the biggest party in the 31st Dáil.

The way in which Fine Gael managed to win 46 per cent of the seats on 36 per cent of

the vote was due in some part to the fact that the party was transfer-friendly, but it was also down to superb vote management. Winning four seats out of five in Mayo and three seats of out five in constituencies such as Dublin South, Wicklow, Cavan–Monaghan and Carlow–Kilkenny depended on vote-sharing arrangements that could easily have gone wrong, resulting in high-profile TDs losing their seats. A combination of good management and good luck paid huge dividends. While there was some disappointment in Fine Gael at the failure to achieve an overall majority, it is arguable that it would have needed well over 40 per cent of the national vote to deliver that objective.

The Labour Party had its best election ever in 2011 with 19.4 per cent of the vote, a marginal improvement of 0.1 per cent on its previous best in 1992. In terms of seats the record was more clear–cut, with the party winning its highest ever total of 37, compared with 33 in 1992. However, when the votes and seats of Democratic Left, which subsequently merged with Labour are added into the mix, the 2011 result was slightly behind that of 1992.

The disappointment at coming in well behind Fine Gael in terms of seats was tempered by the fact that Labour is now the second largest party in the state, well ahead of Fianna Fáil. That represents another fundamental change in the nature of Irish politics.

The Fianna Fáil result was nothing short of a disaster. The collapse from 78 seats in 2007 to just 20 meant that there are large swathes of the country where the party is now unrepresented in the Dáil. Traditional party heartlands such as Kerry and Tipperary now do not have a single Fianna Fáil TD. In Dublin and its suburbs, the party has been reduced to just one. The survivor was Minister for Finance Brian Lenihan.

Fianna Fáil dynasties tumbled. The two Andrews cousins lost their Dublin seats, while two of the three Lenihans in the Dáil lost out. Seán Haughey, son of Charles and grandson of Seán Lemass, lost his seat, as did Tánaiste Mary Coughlan.

On a strictly proportional share, Fianna Fáil should have got 29 seats on the basis of its first preference, but it garnered only 20 because it failed to attract transfers in any significant quantity.

The Greens, Fianna Fáil's coalition partners, suffered parliamentary extinction. The party lost all six seats it won in 2007 and obtained a paltry 1.7 per cent of the vote. The party has been represented in the Dáil since 1989, when Roger Garland won its first seat, in Dublin South. While the Greens will survive as a movement, their experience of government ended in disaster and getting back into national politics will be difficult.

Sinn Féin won a record 9.9 per cent of the vote and 14 seats. While its vote was up only 3 percentage points from 2007, its return in terms of seats was far better, with a gain of 10 since the last time. The party had a much better return for its votes than Fianna Fáil and its seat return was close to its percentage share of the vote.

The United Left Alliance (ULA) won 2.6 per cent of the vote with a handsome return of five Dáil seats for its share of the vote while the remainder of the Independents and Others had 12.6 per cent of the vote and took 14 seats.

Only time will tell how significant and long lasting is the shift represented by the 2011 election result but it has the potential to shape the course of Irish politics for decades to come.

HOUSES OF THE OIREACHTAS
Address
Leinster House, Kildare Street, Dublin 2

Telephone
National: (01) 618 3000.
International: + 353 1 618 3000.
Dáil Éireann LoCall: 1890 337 889;
Outside the Dublin (01) area only:
1890 DEPUTY.
Seanad Éireann LoCall: 1890 732 623;
Outside the Dublin (01) area only:
1890 SEANAD.

Email
Oireachtas email addresses follow the format:
firstname.surname@oireachtas.ie.

KEY TO ABBREVIATIONS
FG	Fine Gael
Lab	Labour
FF	Fianna Fáil
SF	Sinn Féin
ULA	United Left Alliance
GP	Green Party
Ind	Independent
PBPA	People Before Profit Alliance
SP	Socialist Party
WP	Workers' Party
PD	Progressive Democrats
*	Outgoing

The Campaign

Miriam Lord

On the first day of spring the 30th Dáil was dissolved.

It had been a long winter and the time was ripe for a new beginning.

A very angry public determined to deliver it.

This general election was never going to be a cliff-hanger – everybody knew the departing Fianna Fáil would be kicked, with great force, over the edge. The only question was how far they could fall.

In the end, their dispatch was brutal and the descent catastrophic. The electorate showed no mercy, coldly erasing decades of pre-eminence and presumption. The humbling of mighty Fianna Fáil emerged as the big story of election 2011.

Such has been the party's dominance in Irish society, the scale of its meltdown almost overshadowed Fine Gael's historic installation as the biggest political party in the country. Together with coalition partners Labour, they took power with the largest majority in the history of the state.

Ominiously, while they left Leinster House embracing the promise of spring, they returned on Ash Wednesday facing a long and difficult road ahead.

The lead up to the election seemed to go on forever. Brian Cowen's government could do nothing right, staggering through its final year in a fug of mishaps, mistakes and mismanagement.

As the economy continued to nosedive, the public looked on with growing dismay: confidence seemed to ebb from the coalition, there was a lack of communication, a sense of drift had set in.

The Green Party, weakened by its association with an increasingly unpopular senior partner, was uneasy with the arrangement but incapable of making a break. Like their senior partners, they overstayed their welcome and suffered as a result.

The cover photograph on the 2007 edition of *Nealon's Guide* features incoming Taoiseach Bertie Ahern, Green Party leader Trevor Sargent and Mary Harney of the Progressive Democrats. By the time that Dáil met, Trevor Sargent had already resigned as Green Party leader, replaced by John Gormley. The party had six TDs, two of them Ministers. It has no seats in the 31st Dáil.

Mary Harney remained a senior Minister throughout the turbulent Ahern/Cowen years, ending her political career as an Independent deputy after the Progressive Democrats formally disbanded.

She didn't contest this election.

Bertie Ahern, mired in controversy, stepped down as Taoiseach and Fianna Fáil leader a year after that photo was taken, leaving Brian Cowen with a country on the brink of ruin.

On the backbenches, Ahern wasn't averse to making occasional comments to the media about how he would handle the economic situation if he were still running the Government. He also visited a number of third world countries to lecture them on his role in creating The Celtic Tiger while taking on a sports column for the now defunct *News of the World*.

His hapless successor, publicly loyal to a fault, could have done without Ahern popping up as a constant reminder of how Fianna Fáil governments enthusiastically facilitated the construction and property bubble that brought the country to its knees.

The former Taoiseach, still a TD, appeared in a light-hearted television advert for his newspaper column, speaking from inside a kitchen cupboard surrounded by vegetables and biscuits. The public reacted badly: another outrage to bolster the election revenge list.

Brian Cowen's government staggered towards the polls in complete disarray. Embarrassing revelations about him enjoying dinner and a round of golf with former Anglo-Irish Bank boss, Seán Fitzpatrick, just two months before the blanket bank guarantee, came on the heels of the so-called 'Garglegate' controversy.

After socialising into the early hours at a Fianna Fáil think-in, the Taoiseach sounded far from fresh in the morning when he surfaced for an important *Morning Ireland* interview. During the uproar that followed, his Ministers explained he had been suffering from 'congestion'. Fine Gael frontbencher Simon Coveney tweeted that the Taoiseach 'sounded halfway between drunk and hung-over'. The incident attracted global media attention, including a gag on *The Tonight Show with Jay Leno*.

Once again, there was talk of a heave against Cowen. Once again, he pledged to up his game. The Government muddled on while Fine Gael, Labour and Sinn Féin prepared for the election.

When the state was forced to seek a bailout from the IMF, the ECB and the EU, the Government's humiliation was complete and the public's anger was palpable. During a memorable television encounter which struck a chord with many voters, former Labour Party leader Pat Rabbitte lost his temper with Minister Pat Carey who was trying to put a vaguely positive gloss on his Government's capitulation to the IMF. 'You ought to be ashamed of yourself,' roared Rabbitte, berating Carey for 'comin' on here with your aul' palaver'. He told the astonished Minister: 'You should be ashamed to show your face in the studio after you have brought our country to penury, and the damage that you have done to people's livelihoods ... You have destroyed this economy. You denied it and then you went on to pretend it was Ireland coming to the rescue of Europe. It's about time you went, because you can do no more damage to this country.'

In another example of the foot in mouth disease that afflicted the cabinet, the Minister for Agriculture Brendan Smith caused a minor furore by proudly announcing – the day after Brian Lenihan unveiled €6 billion in budget cuts – that 53 tonnes of fresh cheddar would be distributed around the country. He unwittingly gave the impression that the free cheese scheme, which has been going for decades, was a new initiative to help 'the needy'. With people losing jobs and struggling to pay the mortgage on homes in negative equity, this 'let them eat cheese' gesture was interpreted as a further example of a government out of touch with the people.

In the dying days of a dysfunctional administration, five Fianna Fáil Ministers suddenly resigned in a move designed to allow the Taoiseach 'refresh' his front bench before the election. (The thinking was that voters may have been less annoyed by the sight of some unfamiliar faces.)

But the party's stock had fallen so badly, Junior Ministers and backbenchers – trying to distance themselves from association with their toxic government – didn't want promotion. They viewed the move as an ill-judged stroke which wouldn't fool the electorate one bit. Most were already trying to sell themselves to constituents as political sole traders.

Having survived a confidence vote in the wake of the Fitzpatrick golf revelation the week before, this botched reshuffle proved the final straw for the parliamentary party. Cowen took soundings and resigned the leadership, remaining on as caretaker Taoiseach. In the ensuing contest, Micheál Martin, who had voted against his leader in the confidence motion, won the unenviable task of leading his party to certain electoral defeat.

When Enda Kenny took over Fine Gael in 2002, he also inherited a party in decline. Back then, he was in a similar – though some might say not so critical – position to the one Deputy Martin finds himself in now. Over the years, Kenny rebuilt and re-energised Fine Gael, yet questions remained about his leadership abilities and popularity with the public. As the possibility of a return to power became more and more likely, elements within the party worried that Kenny would drag them down. Eamon Gilmore of Labour regularly outshone his Fine Gael counterpart at Leaders' Questions and was consistently ahead of him in opinion polls. Kenny's standing was particularly bad in Dublin.

In 2010, Richard Bruton and a group of mainly younger, urban deputies mounted a heave. They appeared to have the numbers, but were outmanoeuvred by the more experienced Kenny camp. Despite the continuing reservations of some, he emerged with his reputation enhanced, assured of leading his party into the general election.

Meanwhile, in an effort to capitalise on his position as most popular leader of the Opposition, Labour pushed the idea of 'Gilmore for Taoiseach'. They chose the wrong strategy, discovering too late that personality politics may have worked in Bertie Ahern's time, but now, with cuts biting and the IMF/ECB in town, a scared electorate wanted policies and direction.

Fine Gael delivered it with brain-deadening monotony in the form of its 'Five-point Plan'. Enda Kenny plugged it relentlessly, saying it would give 'light, clarity and direction to what will be a difficult journey to a better future ahead'.

And the people bought it. In time, they bought into Enda Kenny too.

Up to the start of the election campaign, with Fine Gael riding high in the opinion polls, the majority of voters still couldn't envisage Kenny as their leader, dismissing him as a nice man, but lightweight. 'I'd vote for Fine Gael but not with that Enda Kenny in charge' became a familiar refrain.

The party leader fought an energetic campaign – he's a natural on the campaign trail – all the while plugging that Five-point Plan. As the election unfolded, it became clear that Fine Gael was unassailable. Labour began going backwards in the opinion polls, only halting the slide and fighting back in the final week. Those 'Gilmore for Taoiseach' mugs and t-shirts became collectors' items. Meanwhile, Enda Kenny was beginning to look more prime ministerial by the day.

On the last two weekends, you could see it: on city walkabouts, people sought him out to discuss their problems, called him 'Enda' and asked what he was going to do when in the top job. Touring his Mayo heartland, his handlers were careful not to allow any displays of whooping local triumphalism, lest it should upset the sensitivities of the recently converted.

Fine Gael romped home, with Kenny bringing in an unprecedented three running mates in Mayo. Labour more than doubled their seats, Eamon Gilmore happily settled for the job of Tánaiste and Sinn Féin, with Gerry Adams topping the poll in Louth, returned with 14 deputies. The combined number of Independents fell just one short of the tally achieved by Fianna Fáil.

The Campaign

Twenty seats were all the party could manage – just one of them in Dublin. That seat was won by the former Minister for Finance, Brian Lenihan, who was diagnosed with pancreatic cancer late in 2009 but continued on tirelessly with his work. Despite the public criticism of his government's management of the economy, he was hugely popular on a personal level. When he died in June 2011 at the age of 52, he was fondly remembered as a man of courage and integrity.

The political geography has changed. It's there for all to see in the Dáil chamber, where deputies from Fine Gael and Labour spill across the benches, taking up over two-thirds of the seats. Fianna Fáil, the former giant of Irish parliamentary politics, now look anonymous in the middle of a colourful blend of Independents and busy Sinn Féiners. They are still trying to come to terms with their reduced circumstances.

Enda the Underestimated waited a long time to become Taoiseach; clocking up the mileage, working hard and fighting his corner.

He finally got his wish. And on 17 March, hardly a week in the job, it was Taoiseach Enda Kenny who travelled to The White House to present the traditional bowl of shamrock to Barack Obama.

Who'd have thought it?

Enda always did.

The Opinion Polls

Damian Loscher

The most extreme weather, it seems, is rarely predicted. And extreme weather, when forecast, often turns out to be not all that extreme. The 2011 General Election was a political hurricane, but so well signposted by opinion polls that the shock was easily absorbed by voters and the media, if not by politicians.

A change in government had been signalled well in advance of the 2011 General Election. By May 2009 confidence in the Government had collapsed to just 10 per cent as the great recession drove down activity in the economy and drove up unemployment. In parallel with a drop in Government confidence, support for Fianna Fáil reached new lows.

And if there was any lingering uncertainty about a change of government, it was wiped away by the December 2010 *Irish Times*/Ipsos MRBI poll, conducted two months before the election and following the Government's acceptance of an IMF/ECB/EU bailout. It showed that just 8 per cent of voters were satisfied with how the Government was managing the economy.

Support for Fianna Fáil, the main party of Government, had fallen so far in the December 2011 poll (to a low of 17 per cent) that all the party could hope for in the upcoming election was to mitigate the damage and try to maintain enough seats to be able to offer an effective opposition. A similar fate awaited the other party of Government, the Green Party, who had also seen their support shrink by more than half since going into coalition with Fianna Fáil.

Pre-election polls also tracked a shift to the left in Irish politics, as the economic situation deteriorated and trust in conventional politics and convenient responses began to wane.

Whereas historically a clear majority of Irish voters would vote for parties of the right (Fianna Fáil, Fine Gael), by the middle of 2010 the majority were leaning left. Come the day of the election, some of the steam had gone out of the left rally, but still Sinn Féin, Labour and Independents were all positioned for a stronger election performance than they delivered in 2007.

From a long way out the polls had signposted not just a change of government, they also proved highly informative as to the likely composition of the next government. A Fine Gael–Labour coalition was always the most likely outcome. And while the parties did not campaign together, they were clearly willing to work together. Of course if Fine Gael were to achieve an overall majority, or come near to achieving it, coalition would look far less attractive. And while support for Fine Gael surged in the final weeks, it was never enough. The final *Irish Times*/Ipsos MRBI poll indicated Fine Gael would not win the required number of seats to form a single-party government.

On election day the hurricane rolled in and, by and large, it reshaped our political landscape in the way the polls had predicted it would. Once again, the final *Irish Times*/Ipsos MRBI poll provided a remarkably accurate indication as to the final election result.

While the final election poll varied only marginally from the election result (and well within acceptable levels of statistical variation), these minor variations are worth exploring further. Two parties, Sinn Féin and Fine Gael, were marginally overstated in the pre-election poll.

In 2011, the Sinn Féin overstatement was just one point. In 2007, the *Irish Times*/Ipsos MRBI pre-election poll also overstated Sinn Féin, on that occasion by two points. If this overstatement is systemic, the cause may be the likelihood of Sinn Féin supporters to actually vote.

In our pre-election poll, Ipsos MRBI recorded whether or not voters had voted in the previous election, seeking an indication of their likelihood to vote in the forthcoming election. This poll revealed that just 71 per cent of Sinn Féin voters claimed to have actually voted in the 2007 General Election, seven points below the national average, thereby giving rise to the notion that Sinn Féin supporters may have turned out in lower numbers on election day.

As to the Fine Gael overstatement, again by just one point, timing may hold the answer. The final *Irish Times*/Ipsos MRBI poll was conducted one week in advance of election day. During the campaign the Fine Gael vote surged and it would not be unreasonable to conclude the party's vote may have peaked in advance of the election, at about the time of the final *Irish Times*/Ipsos MRBI polls. In the final analysis, polls can only provide a measure of support at the time of polling.

Interestingly, support for Fianna Fáil was understated in the *Irish Times*/Ipsos MRBI pre-election poll. In previous general elections the tendency was for voters to overstate Fianna Fáil support, most likely as a result of the prominence the party had built over many decades as the dominant power in Irish politics. That said, an understatement of the Fianna Fáil vote had been predicted by some commentators on the basis that Fianna Fáil had fallen so far out of favour over their handling of the economy, voters may not have wanted to admit to being a Fianna Fáil voter. And this may very well have been the reason for their understatement in the polls. If understatement was a function of social embarrassment, it is likely that this will fade in time and will not be a factor in the next election.

Once again opinion polls proved enormously informative, providing an independent backdrop to the 2011 General Election and

The Opinion Polls

giving the voter a voice to compete with the spin that is a feature of every campaign. When viewed in context and over time they help us to understand what drove, and what drives, public opinion and voting intentions.

And while they only provide a snapshot of party support at a particular point in time, they have been shown time and again to accurately measure voting intentions.

Damian Loscher is Managing Director of Ispos MRBI

PRE-ELECTION POLL FINDINGS VS. ELECTION OUTCOME

	Final *Irish Times*/Ipsos MRBI Poll	Election Result 2011
Fine Gael	37	36
Labour	19	19
Fianna Fáil	16	17
Independents/Others	15	15
Sinn Féin	11	10
Green Party	2	2

Ballot boxes for the Dublin constituencies at the Dublin City Count Centre in the RDS. Photograph: Cyril Byrne.

The number of TDs returned to the 31st Dáil from 43 constituencies for each party was:

Fine Gael	76
Labour	37
Fianna Fáil	20
Sinn Féin	14
United Left Alliance	5
Others	14

Deputy	Party	Constituency
• Adams, Gerry	SF	Louth
Bannon, James	FG	Longford–Westmeath
Barrett, Sean	FG	Dún Laoghaire
• Barry, Tom	FG	Cork East
• Boyd Barrett, Richard	ULA	Dún Laoghaire
Breen, Pat	FG	Clare
Broughan, Thomas P.	Lab	Dublin North-East
Browne, John	FF	Wexford
Bruton, Richard	FG	Dublin North-Central
Burton, Joan	Lab	Dublin West
• Butler, Ray	FG	Meath West
• Buttimer, Jerry	FG	Cork South-Central
Byrne, Catherine	FG	Dublin South-Central
+Byrne, Eric	Lab	Dublin South-Central
Calleary, Dara	FF	Mayo
• Cannon, Ciarán	FG	Galway East
Carey, Joe	FG	Clare
• Coffey, Paudie	FG	Waterford
• Collins, Áine	FG	Cork North-West
• Collins, Joan	ULA	Dublin South-Central
Collins, Niall	FF	Limerick
• Colreavy, Michael	SF	Sligo–North Leitrim
• Conaghan, Michael	Lab	Dublin South-Central
• Conlan, Sean	FG	Cavan–Monaghan
• Connaughton Jnr, Paul	FG	Galway East
• Conway, Ciara	Lab	Waterford
Coonan, Noel	FG	Tipperary North
•Corcoran Kennedy, Marcella	FG	Laois–Offaly
Costello, Joe	Lab	Dublin Central
Coveney, Simon	FG	Cork South-Central
• Cowen, Barry	FF	Laois–Offaly
Creed, Michael	FG	Cork North-West
Creighton, Lucinda	FG	Dublin South-East
+Crowe, Seán	SF	Dublin South-West
• Daly, Clare	ULA	Dublin North
• Daly, Jim	FG	Cork South-West
Deasy, John	FG	Waterford
Deenihan, Jimmy	FG	Kerry North–Limerick West
• Deering, Pat	FG	Carlow–Kilkenny
Doherty, Pearse	SF	Donegal South-West
• Doherty, Regina	FG	Meath East
• Donnelly, Stephen	Ind	Wicklow
• Donohoe, Paschal	FG	Dublin Central
Dooley, Timmy	FF	Clare
• Dowds, Robert	Lab	Dublin Mid-West
Doyle, Andrew	FG	Wicklow
Durkan, Bernard	FG	Kildare North
• Ellis, Dessie	SF	Dublin North-West
English, Damien	FG	Meath West
• Farrell, Alan	FG	Dublin North
Feighan, Frank	FG	Roscommon–South Leitrim
• Ferris, Anne	Lab	Wicklow
Ferris, Martin	SF	Kerry North–Limerick West
+Fitzgerald, Frances	FG	Dublin Mid-West
• Fitzpatrick, Peter	FG	Louth
Flanagan, Charles	FG	Laois–Offaly
• Flanagan, Luke 'Ming'	Ind	Roscommon–South Leitrim
Flanagan, Terence	FG	Dublin North-East
Fleming, Seán	FF	Laois–Offaly
• Fleming, Tom	Ind	Kerry South
Gilmore, Eamon	Lab	Dún Laoghaire
Grealish, Noel	Ind	Galway West
• Griffin, Brendan	FG	Kerry South
• Halligan, John	Ind	Waterford
• Hannigan, Dominic	Lab	Meath East
• Harrington, Noel	FG	Cork South-West
• Harris, Simon	FG	Wicklow
Hayes, Brian	FG	Dublin South-West
Hayes, Tom	FG	Tipperary South
+Healy, Seamus	ULA	Tipperary South
• Healy-Rae, Michael	Ind	Kerry South
• Heydon, Martin	FG	Kildare South
+Higgins, Joe	ULA	Dublin West
Hogan, Phil	FG	Carlow–Kilkenny
Howlin, Brendan	Lab	Wexford
• Humphreys, Heather	FG	Cavan–Monaghan
• Humphreys, Kevin	Lab	Dublin South-East
• Keating, Derek	FG	Dublin Mid-West
• Keaveney, Colm	Lab	Galway East
Kehoe, Paul	FG	Wexford
Kelleher, Billy	FF	Cork North-Central
• Kelly, Alan	Lab	Tipperary North
Kenny, Enda	FG	Mayo

+Kenny, Sean	Lab	Dublin North-East	
Kirk, Séamus	FF	Louth	
(Ceann Comhairle, returned automatically)			
Kitt, Michael P.	FF	Galway East	
• Kyne, Seán	FG	Galway West	
• Lawlor, Anthony	FG	Kildare North	
Lenihan, Brian	FF	Dublin West	
Lowry, Michael	Ind	Tipperary North	
Lynch, Ciarán	Lab	Cork South-Central	
Lynch, Kathleen	Lab	Cork North-Central	
• Lyons, John	Lab	Dublin North-West	
• McCarthy, Michael	Lab	Cork South-West	
• McConalogue, Charlie	FF	Donegal North-East	
• McDonald, Mary Lou	SF	Dublin Central	
McEntee, Shane	FG	Meath East	
• McFadden, Nicky	FG	Longford–Westmeath	
McGinley, Dinny	FG	Donegal South-West	
McGrath, Finian	Ind	Dublin North-Central	
McGrath, Mattie	Ind	Tipperary South	
McGrath, Michael	FF	Cork South-Central	
McGuinness, John	FF	Carlow–Kilkenny	
McHugh, Joe	FG	Donegal North-East	
• McLellan, Sandra	SF	Cork East	
• McLoughlin, Tony	FG	Sligo–North Leitrim	
• McNamara, Michael	Lab	Clare	
• Mac Lochlainn, Pádraig	SF	Donegal North-East	
• Maloney, Eamonn	Lab	Dublin South-West	
Martin, Micheál	FF	Cork South-Central	
• Mathews, Peter	FG	Dublin South	
Mitchell, Olivia	FG	Dublin South	
• Mitchell O'Connor, Mary	FG	Dún Laoghaire	
Moynihan, Michael	FF	Cork North-West	
• Mulherin, Michelle	FG	Mayo	
+Murphy, Catherine	Ind	Kildare North	
• Murphy, Dara	FG	Cork North-Central	
• Murphy, Eoghan	FG	Dublin South-East	
• Nash, Gerald	Lab	Louth	
Naughten, Denis	FG	Roscommon–South Leitrim	
Neville, Dan	FG	Limerick	
• Nolan, Derek	Lab	Galway West	
Noonan, Michael	FG	Limerick City	
• O'Brien, Jonathan	SF	Cork North-Central	
Ó Caoláin, Caoimhghín	SF	Cavan–Monaghan	
Ó Cuív, Éamon	FF	Galway West	
O'Dea, Willie	FF	Limerick City	
O'Donnell, Kieran	FG	Limerick City	
• O'Donovan, Patrick	FG	Limerick	
O'Dowd, Fergus	FG	Louth	
Ó Fearghaíl, Seán	FF	Kildare South	
O'Mahony, John	FG	Mayo	
• O'Reilly, Joe	FG	Cavan–Monaghan	
• Ó Ríordáin, Aodhán	Lab	Dublin North-Central	
Ó Snodaigh, Aengus	SF	Dublin South-Central	
O'Sullivan, Jan	Lab	Limerick City	
O'Sullivan, Maureen	Ind	Dublin Central	
Penrose, Willie	Lab	Longford–Westmeath	
Perry, John	FG	Sligo–North Leitrim	
• Phelan, Ann	Lab	Carlow–Kilkenny	
• Phelan, John Paul	FG	Carlow–Kilkenny	
• Pringle, Thomas	Ind	Donegal South-West	
Quinn, Ruairí	Lab	Dublin South-East	
Rabbitte, Pat	Lab	Dublin South-West	
Reilly, James	FG	Dublin North	
Ring, Michael	FG	Mayo	
• Ross, Shane	Ind	Dublin South	
• Ryan, Brendan	Lab	Dublin North	
Shatter, Alan	FG	Dublin South	
Sherlock, Sean	Lab	Cork East	
Shortall, Róisín	Lab	Dublin North-West	
Smith, Brendan	FF	Cavan–Monaghan	
• Spring, Arthur	Lab	Kerry North–Limerick West	
Stagg, Emmet	Lab	Kildare North	
• Stanley, Brian	SF	Laois–Offaly	
Stanton, David	FG	Cork East	
Timmins, Billy	FG	Wicklow	
• Tóibín, Peadar	SF	Meath West	
• Troy, Robert	FF	Longford–Westmeath	
Tuffy, Joanna	Lab	Dublin Mid-West	
+Twomey, Liam	FG	Wexford	
Varadkar, Leo	FG	Dublin West	
Wall, Jack	Lab	Kildare South	
• Wallace, Mick	Ind	Wexford	
• Walsh, Brian	FG	Galway West	
• White, Alex	Lab	Dublin South	

The 31st Dáil has 166 deputies, the same number as the previous Dáil. Of these, 82 were members of the 30th Dáil, 8 were previously members (denoted by +) but not of the 30th Dáil, and 76 are new deputies (denoted by •).

Enda Kenny gets a cup of tea in the office of Simon Harris during a canvass in the Wicklow area. Photograph: David Sleator.

The 2011 General Election was called on 1 February when President Mary McAleese dissolved the Dáil on the advice of Taoiseach Brian Cowen. Polling took place on 25 February and the 31st Dáil met for the first time on 9 March.

A total of 566 candidates contested the election for 165 seats. Eighty-six of the candidates (15 per cent) were women. The 166th seat was occupied by the Ceann Comhairle Seamus Kirk of Fianna Fáil, who was returned automatically in his constituency of Louth.

Among the changes in parties were the disappearance of the Progressive Democrats (disbanded since the previous general election) and the appearance of the United Left Alliance banner, which included the Socialist Party and the People Before Profit Alliance. A total of 238 candidates failed to win the quarter of a quota in their constituencies, which is required to claim reimbursement of election expenses up to €8,700.

State of the Parties

Election	FG	Lab	FF	SF	ULA	GP	SP	PD	Others
2011	**76**	**37**	**20***	**14**	**5**	–	–	–	**14**
2007	51	20	78	4	–	6	–	2	5
2002	31	21	81	5	–	6	1	8	13
1997	54	17	77	1	–	2	1	4	10
1992	45	33	68	–	–	1	–	10	9
1989	55	15	77	–	–	1	–	6	12
1987	51	12	81	–	–	–	–	14	8

*Including Ceann Comhairle, who was automatically returned.

Line-up

Election	Electorate	Candidates	Seats
2011	**3,209,244**	**566**	**166**
2007	3,066,517	466	166
2002	2,994,642	463	166
1997	2,741,262	484	166
1992	2,557,036	481	166
1989	2,448,813	370	166
1987	2,445,515	466	166

First-Preference Votes

Election	FG		Lab		FF		SF		ULA		GP		PD		Others	
2011	801,628	36.10%	431,796	19.45%	387,358	17.45%	220,661	9.94%	57,139	2.6%	41,039	1.85%	–	–	280,738	12.6%
2007	564,438	27.32%	209,175	10.13%	858,593	41.56%	143,410	6.94%	–	–	96,936	4.69%	56,396	2.73%	136,912	6.63%
2002	417,653	22.48%	200,138	10.77%	770,846	41.49%	121,039	6.51%	–	–	71,480	3.85%	73,628	3.96%	203,329	10.94%
1997	499,936	27.95%	186,044	10.40%	703,682	39.33%	–	–	–	–	–	2.8%	83,765	4.68%	315,558	17.64%
1992	422,106	24.47%	333,013	19.31%	674,650	39.11%	–	–	–	–	–	1.4%	80,787	4.68%	214,297	12.42%
1989	485,307	29.29	156,989	9.48%	731,472	44.15%	–	–	–	–	–	1.5%	91,013	5.49%	192,032	11.59%
1987	481,127	27.07%	114,551	6.44%	784,547	44.15%	–	–	–	–	–	–	210,583	11.85%	186,357	10.49%

Turnout

Election	Total Poll		Spoiled Votes		Valid Poll	
2011	**2,243,176**	**69.90%**	**22,817**	**1.02%**	**2,220,359**	**69.19%**
2007	2,065,320	67.35%	19,491	0.95%	2,045,829	66.71%
2002	1,878,393	62.73%	20,280	1.08%	1,858,113	62.05%
1997	1,807,016	65.92%	18,031	1.00%	1,789,985	65.26%
1992	1,751,351	68.49%	26,498	1.51%	1,724,853	67.46%
1989	1,677,592	68.51%	20,779	1.24%	1,656,813	67.66%
1987	1,793,406	73.33%	16,241	0.91%	1,777,165	72.69%

Regional First-Preference Percentages by Euro Constituencies

Constituency	FG		Lab		FF		SF		ULA		GP		Others	
Ireland North-West (Connacht–Ulster)	175,662	40.1%	38,282	8.7%	82,846	18.9%	64,785	14.8%	0	0.00%	3,703	0.8%	73,165	16.7%
Dublin	163,023	29.9%	159,709	29.3%	67,836	12.5%	44,525	8.2%	38,808	7.1%	19,529	3.6%	51,279	9.4%
Ireland East (Rest of Leinster)	217,354	36.6%	114,011	19.2%	115,542	19.5%	61,906	10.4%	2,437	0.4%	9,716	1.6%	72,240	12.2%
Ireland South (Munster)	245,589	38.1%	119,794	18.6%	121,134	18.8%	49,445	7.7%	15,894	2.5%	8,091	1.3%	84,054	13.1%

Taoiseach Enda Kenny and President Mary McAleese with newly appointed members of the cabinet at Áras an Uachtaráin after presentation of their seals of office, on 9 March 2011.

From left to right
Front:
Brendan Howlin, Michael Noonan, Enda Kenny, President Mary McAleese, Eamon Gilmore, Ruairí Quinn and Richard Bruton.

Back:
Joan Burton, Pat Rabbitte, James Reilly, Jimmy Deenihan, Frances Fitzgerald, Simon Coveney, Alan Shatter, Leo Varadkar, Phil Hogan, Willie Penrose, Paul Kehoe and Máire Whelan SC, Attorney General.

The Government (appointed 9 March 2011)

Taoiseach	Enda Kenny
Tánaiste and Minister for Foreign Affairs and Trade	Eamon Gilmore
Minister for Finance	Michael Noonan
Minister for Education and Skills	Ruairí Quinn
Minister for Public Expenditure and Reform	Brendan Howlin
Minister for Jobs, Enterprise and Innovation	Richard Bruton
Minister for Social Protection	Joan Burton
Minister for Arts, Heritage and the Gaeltacht	Jimmy Deenihan
Minister for Communications, Energy and Natural Resources	Pat Rabbitte
Minister for the Environment, Community and Local Government	Phil Hogan
Minister for Justice, Equality and Defence	Alan Shatter
Minister for Agriculture, Marine and Food	Simon Coveney
Minister for Children and Youth Affairs	Frances Fitzgerald
Minister for Health	James Reilly
Minister for Transport, Tourism and Sport	Leo Varadkar

Ministers of State

Department	Special Responsibilities	Name
Taoiseach; Defence	Government Chief Whip	Paul Kehoe
Environment	Housing and Planning	Willie Penrose
Arts, Heritage and Gaeltacht	Gaeltacht Affairs	Dinny McGinley
Health	Primary Care	Róisín Shortall
Jobs, Enterprise and Innovation	Small Business	John Perry
Transport, Tourism and Sport	Tourism and Sport	Michael Ring
Foreign Affairs and Trade	Trade and Development	Jan O'Sullivan
Health; Justice, Equality and Defence	Disability, Older People, Equality and Mental Health	Kathleen Lynch
Environment; Communications	NewEra Project	Fergus O'Dowd
Public Expenditure; Finance	Public Service Reform and the Office of Public Works	Brian Hayes
Agriculture, Fisheries and Food	Food, Horticulture and Food Safety	Shane McEntee
Taoiseach; Foreign Affairs	European Affairs	Lucinda Creighton
Jobs and Enterprise; Education	Research and Innovation	Sean Sherlock
Education and Skills	Training and Skills	Ciarán Cannon
Transport, Tourism and Sport	Public and Commuter Transport	Alan Kelly

Carlow–Kilkenny

Statistics

Seats	5
Electorate	105,449
Total Poll	74,564
Turnout	70.7%
Spoiled	821
Total Valid Poll	73,743
Quota	12,291
Candidates	19

Party Share of Vote

1st Preferences	Number	%	Gain/Loss
Fine Gael	28,924	39.22	9.61
Labour	11,980	16.25	6.90
Fianna Fáil	20,721	28.10	-19.60
Sinn Féin	7,033	9.54	5.74
United Left Alliance	1,135	1.54	1.54
Green Party	2,072	2.81	-5.15
Others	1,878	2.55	2.55

	Quotas	Seats
Fine Gael	2.4	3
Labour	1	1
Fianna Fáil	1.7	1
Sinn Féin	0.6	–
United Left Alliance	0.1	–
Green Party	0.2	–
Others	0.2	–

FG gain 2, Lab gain 1; from FF and GP.

Ann Phelan (Lab)

Home Address
Brandondale, Graignamanagh, Co. Kilkenny.
Constituency Office
18 Patrick Street, Kilkenny.
Contact Details
Home: (059) 972 4310. Mobile: (086) 329 4420.
Email: annmphelan@eircom.net.
Website: www.labour.ie/annphelan.
Twitter: @annphelan1.
Birth Place/Date
Graignamanagh, September 1961.
Marital Status
Married to Kieran Phelan. One son, two daughters.
Education
Brigidine Convent, Goresbridge. Duiske College, Graignamanagh.
Occupation
Public representative.

Ann Phelan is a new deputy.

Elected in her first attempt. Previously elected to Kilkenny County Council 2004 and re-elected in 2009. Deputy Chairperson of Kilkenny County Council 2010.

John McGuinness (FF)

Home Address
Windsmoor, Brooklawn, Ballyfoyle Road, Kilkenny.
Constituency Office
11 O'Loughlin Road, Kilkenny.
Contact Details
Constituency Office: (056) 777 0672/3;
Fax: (056) 777 0674. Mobile: (087) 285 5834.
Email: john@johnmcguinness.ie.
Website: www.johnmcguinness.ie.
Birth Place/Date
Kilkenny, 15 March 1955.
Marital Status
Married to Margaret Redmond. Three sons, one daughter.
Education
Kilkenny CBS. Diploma in Business Management.
Occupation
Full-time public representative.

Chairman of the Public Accounts Committee and Fianna Fáil frontbench spokesperson on Business and Regulatory Reform.

Minister of State for Trade and Commerce 2007–09.

First elected in 1997. He served on the Joint Oireachtas Committees for Enterprise and Small Business, European Affairs, and Justice, Equality and Women's Rights. Re-elected in 2002 and served as the Vice-Chairperson of the Public Accounts Committee and a member of the Finance and Public Service Committee.

Author (with Naoise Nunn) of *The House Always Wins* (Gill & Macmillan, 2010).

Member of Kilkenny Corporation 1979–2003. Mayor of Kilkenny, 1996–97 (third generation of family to serve as Mayor of the Borough). Member, Kilkenny County Council 1991–2003.

John Paul Phelan (FG)

Home Address
Smithstown, Tullogher, via Mullinavat,
Co. Kilkenny.
Constituency Office
25 Market Street, Thomastown, Co. Kilkenny.
Contact Details
Constituency Office: (056) 779 3210.
Email: johnpaul.phelan@oireachtas.ie.
Website: www.johnpaulphelan.ie.
Birth Place/Date
Waterford, 27 September 1978.
Marital Status
Single.
Education
Good Council College, New Ross. Waterford
Institute of Technology. King's Inns.
Occupation
Full-time public representative.

John Paul Phelan is a new deputy.

Senator from 2002 and re-elected to the
Agricultural Panel in 2007 after narrowly failing
to win a Dáil seat. Contested 2009 European
Parliament elections in Ireland East
constituency.

Member of Kilkenny County Council
1999–2003.

Phil Hogan (FG)

Home Address
Grovine, Kilkenny.
Constituency Office
New Street, Kilkenny.
Contact Details
Constituency Office: (056) 777 1490;
Fax: (056) 777 149. Email:
philip.hogan@oireachtas.ie. Website:
www.philhogan.ie. Facebook: PhilHoganTD.
Birth Place/Date
Kilkenny, 4 July 1960.
Marital Status
Separated. One son.
Education
St Joseph's College, Freshford. St Kieran's
College, Kilkenny. UCC (BA, HDipEd).
Occupation
Government Minister.

Phil Hogan was appointed Minister for the
Environment, Community and Local
Government on 9 March 2011. He was
National Director of Elections for Fine Gael in
2011. First elected to the Dáil in 1989, he has
retained his seat in all subsequent elections.

Minister of State at the Department of
Finance, with special responsibility for Public
Expenditure and the Office of Public Works, in
December 1994. He resigned in February
1995 after controversy about a budget leak.

Fine Gael spokesperson on Environment,
Heritage and Local Government in September
2007. Political Director of Fine Gael and a
member of the party's front bench since
1997. Chairman of the Parliamentary Party,
1995–2001. Director of Organisation from
2002 until June 2007.

Senator on the Industrial and Commercial Panel,
1987–89. Member of Kilkenny County Council,
1982–2003 (Chairman, 1985–86 and 1998–99);
South-Eastern Health Board 1991–99.

Member, Gaelic Athletic Association; Kilkenny
Archaeological Society; Castlecomer Golf Club.

Pat Deering (FG)

Home Address
Ballyoliver, Rathvilly, Co. Carlow.
Constituency Office
16 Old Dublin Road, Carlow.
Contact
Constituency Office: (059) 917 3446.
Mobile: (087) 947 0736. Email:
pat.deering@oireachtas.ie;
patdeering67@gmail.com. Website:
www.patdeering.ie.
Birth Place/Date
Carlow, 2 February 1967.
Marital Status
Married to Paula Byrne. One daughter, one
son.
Education
St Patrick's N.S., Rathvilly; Patrician College,
Ballyfin; Community School, Tullow, Kildalton
Agricultural College, Piltown, Co. Kilkenny.
Occupation
Farmer; public representative.

Pat Deering is a new deputy.

Elected to Carlow County Council in 2009,
taking the seat held by his father Michael for
more than forty years. Deeply involved in local
GAA. Chairman of Carlow County Board since
2005. Chairman Carlow County Development
Board from 2009; Chairman Transport &
Infrastructure Strategic Policy Committee
from 2009.

Carlow–Kilkenny

Seats 5
Quota 12,291

COUNT		1	Distribution of **Dalton, Walsh** votes	2	Distribution of **Murphy** votes	3	Distribution of **Leahy** votes	4	Distribution of **O'Hara** votes	5	Distribution of **Couchman** votes	6
AYLWARD, Bobby*	(FF)	6,762	(+10)	6,772	(+3)	6,775	(+11)	6,786	(+10)	6,796	(+1)	6,797
CASSIN, John	(SF)	2,958	(+1)	2,959	(+7)	2,966	(+4)	2,970	(+33)	3,003	(+31)	3,034
COUCHMAN, Johnny	(Ind)	384	(+6)	390	(+20)	410	(+13)	423	(+48)	471		
DALTON, John	(Ind)	70										
DEERING, Pat	(FG)	7,470	(+4)	7,474	(+9)	7,483	(+8)	7,491	(+11)	7,502	(+95)	7,597
FUNCHION, Kathleen	(SF)	4,075	(+14)	4,089	(+12)	4,101	(+20)	4,121	(+23)	4,144	(+18)	4,162
HOGAN, Phil*	(FG)	10,525	(+12)	10,537	(+3)	10,540	(+18)	10,558	(+7)	10,565	(+22)	10,587
HURLEY, Des	(Lab)	3,908	(+2)	3,910	(+9)	3,919	(+9)	3,928	(+24)	3,952	(+26)	3,978
KELLY, Stephen	(Ind)	601	(+24)	625	(+21)	646	(+35)	681	(+53)	734	(+86)	820
LEAHY, Ramie	(Ind)	256	(+16)	272	(+5)	277						
MACLIAM, Conor	(ULA)	1,135	(+9)	1,144	(+13)	1,157	(+22)	1,179	(+21)	1,200	(+17)	1,217
MCGUINNESS, John*	(FF)	9,531	(+12)	9,543	(+5)	9,548	(+35)	9,583	(+12)	9,595	(+17)	9,612
MURNANE O'CONNOR, Jennifer	(FF)	4,428	(+3)	4,431	(+3)	4,434	(+1)	4,435	(+18)	4,453	(+40)	4,493
MURPHY, David	(Ind)	195	(+12)	207								
O'HARA, John	(Ind)	253	(+17)	270	(+57)	327	(+18)	345				
PHELAN, Ann	(Lab)	8,072	(+13)	8,085	(+13)	8,098	(+27)	8,125	(+28)	8,153	(+18)	8,171
PHELAN, John Paul	(FG)	10,929	(+10)	10,939	(+10)	10,949	(+26)	10,975	(+18)	10,993	(+24)	11,017
WALSH, Noel G	(Ind)	119										
WHITE, Mary*	(GP)	2,072	(+5)	2,077	(+5)	2,082	(+16)	2,098	(+8)	2,106	(+29)	2,135
NON-TRANSFERABLE				19		12		14		31		47

Distribution of **Kelly, MacLiam** votes		Distribution of **White** votes		Distribution of **Cassin** votes		Distribution of **Hurley** votes		Distribution of **Murnane O'Connor** votes		Distribution of **Funchion** votes		Distribution of **Phelan A** surplus	
7		**8**		**9**		**10**		**11**		**12**		**13**	
(+70)	6,867	(+61)	6,928	(+33)	6,961	(+44)	7,005	(+1,063)	8,068	(+401)	8,469	(+141)	8,610
(+182)	3,216	(+98)	3,314										
(+57)	7,654	(+310)	7,964	(+274)	8,238	(+670)	8,908	(+1,059)	9,967	(+368)	10,335	(+151)	10,486
(+300)	4,462	(+111)	4,573	(+1,885)	6,458	(+301)	6,759	(+332)	7,091				
(+185)	10,772	(+162)	10,934	(+34)	10,968	(+152)	11,120	(+87)	11,207	(+563)	11,770	(+227)	11,997
(+113)	4,091	(+207)	4,298	(+385)	4,683								
(+155)	9,767	(+172)	9,939	(+60)	9,999	(+109)	10,108	(+1,697)	11,805	(+825)	12,630		
(+40)	4,533	(+225)	4,758	(+307)	5,065	(+571)	5,636						
(+355)	8,526	(+536)	9,062	(+124)	9,186	(+2,447)	11,633	(+433)	12,066	(+2,094)	14,160		
(+166)	11,183	(+233)	11,416	(+51)	11,467	(+112)	11,579	(+132)	11,711	(+506)	12,217	(+357)	12,574
(+143)	2,278												
271		163		161		277		833		2,334		993	

Cavan–Monaghan

Statistics

Seats	5
Electorate	99,178
Total Poll	72,142
Turnout	72.7%
Spoiled	867
Total Valid Poll	71,275
Quota	11,880
Candidates	14

Party Share of Vote

1st Preferences	Number	%	Gain/Loss
Fine Gael	28,199	39.56	8.36
Labour	4,011	5.63	4.42
Fianna Fáil	14,360	20.15	-17.63
Sinn Féin	18,452	25.89	5.88
United Left Alliance	0	0.00	0.00
Green Party	530	0.74	-2.88
Others	5,723	8.03	1.85

	Quotas	Seats
Fine Gael	2.4	3
Labour	0.3	–
Fianna Fáil	1.2	1
Sinn Féin	1.6	1
United Left Alliance	0	–
Green Party	0.04	–
Others	0.5	–

FG gain 2 from FF.

Caoimhghín Ó Caoláin (SF)

Home Address
14 Mullaghdun, Monaghan.
Constituency Office
21 Dublin Street, Monaghan.
Contact Details
Constituency Office: (047) 82917;
Fax: (047) 71849. Email:
caoimhghin.ocaolain@oireachtas.ie.
Birth Place/Date
Monaghan, 18 September 1953.
Marital Status
Married to Briege McGinn. Four daughters,
one son.
Education
St Mary's CBS, Monaghan.
Occupation
Full-time public representative. Formerly bank
official.

Sinn Féin spokesperson on Health and
Children. First elected a Dáil deputy in 1997,
the first Sinn Féin representative to be elected
after the party abandoned the policy of
abstentionism; has retained his seat in all
subsequent general elections. Sinn Féin
Leader in the Dáil 2002–11.

Member, Monaghan County Council
1985–2003. Member, Sinn Féin Ard
Chomhairle since 1983 and of the negotiating
committee during the talks which led to the
Good Friday Agreement; Sinn Féin delegation
to the Forum for Peace and Reconciliation.

Election agent for hunger striker Kieran
Doherty, who was elected to the Dáil during
the H-Block hunger strikes in 1981. General
Manager of *An Phoblacht/Republican News*
1982–85.

Brendan Smith (FF)

Home Address
3 Carrickfern, Cavan.
Constituency Office
75 Church Street, Cavan.
Contact Details
Constituency Office: (049) 436 2366;
Fax: (049) 436 2367. Dáil Office: (01) 618 3376.
Email: brendan.smith@oireachtas.ie.
Website: www.brendansmith.ie.
Birth Place/Date
Cavan, June 1956.
Marital Status
Married to Anne McGarry.
Education
St Camillus College, Killucan, Co. Westmeath.
UCD (BA).
Occupation
Full-time public representative.

First elected to the Dáil in 1992, Brendan
Smith is Fianna Fáil spokesperson on
Education and Skills.

He was Minister for Agriculture, Fisheries and
Food from May 2008–March 2011; Minister
for Justice and Law Reform, January
2011–March 2011; Minister for Children, June
2007–May 2008; Minister of State at the
Department of Agriculture and Food, with
special responsibility for Food and
Horticulture, September 2004–June 2007.

Government Whip on Oireachtas Joint
Committee on Foreign Affairs in 28th Dáil.
Former Co-Chairman of British–Irish Inter-
Parliamentary Body. Member, Dáil Committee
on Procedure and Privileges 2002–04.

Joe O'Reilly (FG)

Home Address
2 The Willows, Chapel Road, Bailieborough,
Co. Cavan.
Constituency Office
11 Rossa Place, Teach Fine Gael, Cavan
Town.
Contact Details
Office: (049) 436 5853; (01) 618 3721.
Mobile: (086) 244 4321.
Email: joe.oreilly@oireachtas.ie.
Website: www.joeoreilly.ie.
Facebook: joeoreilly. Twitter: @senjoeoreilly.
Birth Place/Date
Cavan, 14 April 1955.
Marital Status
Married to Mary Tully. Three sons.
Education
St Aidan's Comprehensive, Cootehill.
UCD (BA, MA). St Patrick's Training College,
Drumcondra. TCD (HDipEd). Incorporated Law
Society (FE1).
Occupation
Public representative; teacher.

Joe O'Reilly is a new deputy.

Senator, 1989–92 on Cultural and Educational
Panel and 2007–11 on Industrial and
Commercial Panel. Narrowly missed election
to the Dáil in 2007.

First elected to Cavan County Council in 1985;
Cathaoirleach of council 2004–05.

Sean Conlan (FG)

Home Address
Main Street, Ballybay, Co. Monaghan.
Constituency Office
Main Street, Ballybay, Co. Monaghan
Contact Details
Constituency Office: (042) 975 5500.
Dáil Office: (01) 618 3154.
Mobile: (087) 667 9306.
Email: seanconlanfg@yahoo.ie;
sean.conlon@oireachtas.ie.
Birth Place/Date
Dublin, 1975.
Marital Status
Single.
Education
Ballybay N.S. St Macartan's College,
Monaghan. UCD (BA in Economics).
Incorporated Law Society.
Occupation
Solicitor; publican; public representative.

Sean Conlon is a new deputy.

Elected to Ballybay Town Council 2009.
Former Chairperson of Young Fine Gael while
a student at UCD.

Heather Humphreys (FG)

Home Address
Dernaroy, Newbliss, Co. Monaghan.
Constituency Office
Unit 2, Mall Road, Monaghan.
Contact Details
Constituency Office: (047) 71911.
Dáil Office: (01) 618 3408.
Email: heather.humphreys@oireachtas.ie.
Facebook: heather.humphreysfg.
Birth Place/Date
Drum, Co. Monaghan.
Marital Status
Married to Eric Humphreys. Two daughters.
Education
St Aidan's Comprehensive, Cootehill.
Occupation
Full-time public representative. Formerly
credit union manager.

Heather Humphreys is a new deputy.

The first woman to be elected for Fine Gael in
Cavan–Monaghan and only the second
woman ever to represent the constituency.
She took the final seat in the 2011 General
Election, securing a historic three seats for
Fine Gael.

Co-opted to Monaghan County Council in
2003 and elected in 2004 and 2009. Mayor of
council in 2010.

She worked for Ulster Bank in Cavan,
Ballyconnell and Swanlinbar before becoming
manager of Cootehill Credit Union.

Cavan–Monaghan

Seats 5 Quota 11,880		COUNT 1	Distribution of **Duffy, Lonergan** votes and **Ó Caoláin** surplus		Distribution of **McGuirk** votes		Distribution of **Forde** votes	
COUNT		**1**		**2**		**3**		**4**
CONLAN, Seán	(FG)	7,864	(+60)	7,924	(+301)	8,225	(+94)	8,319
CONLON, Margaret*	(FF)	4,658	(+45)	4,703	(+114)	4,817	(+62)	4,879
DUFFY, Joseph	(Ind)	129						
FORDE, Caroline	(Ind)	1,912	(+81)	1,993	(+174)	2,167		
HOGAN, Liam	(Lab)	4,011	(+133)	4,144	(+129)	4,273	(+254)	4,527
HUMPHREYS, Heather	(FG)	8,144	(+57)	8,201	(+173)	8,374	(+147)	8,521
LONERGAN, Darcy	(GP)	530						
MCGUIRK, John	(Ind)	1,708	(+52)	1,760				
MCVITTY, Peter	(FG)	3,858	(+23)	3,881	(+31)	3,912	(+295)	4,207
Ó CAOLÁIN, Caoimhghín*	(SF)	11,913						
O'REILLY, Joe	(FG)	8,333	(+28)	8,361	(+51)	8,412	(+187)	8,599
REILLY, Kathryn	(SF)	6,539	(+85)	6,624	(+234)	6,858	(+431)	7,289
SMITH, Brendan*	(FF)	9,702	(+32)	9,734	(+83)	9,817	(+275)	10,092
TREANOR, Seamus	(Ind)	1,974	(+33)	2,007	(+372)	2,379	(+279)	2,658
NON-TRANSFERABLE				30		98		143

Distribution of **Treanor** votes		Distribution of **McVitty** votes		Distribution of **Hogan** votes		Distribution of **Conlon** votes		Distribution of **Smith** surplus	
	5		6		7		8		9
(+409)	8,728	(+434)	9,162	(+733)	9,895	(+728)	10,623	(+555)	11,178
(+173)	5,052	(+18)	5,070	(+209)	5,279				
(+266)	4,793	(+205)	4,998						
(+365)	8,886	(+679)	9,565	(+612)	10,177	(+348)	10,525	(+336)	10,861
(+39)	4,246								
(+80)	8,679	(+1,813)	10,492	(+709)	11,201	(+104)	11,305	(+129)	11,434
(+597)	7,886	(+438)	8,324	(+1,303)	9,627	(+257)	9,884	(+456)	10,340
(+157)	10,249	(+521)	10,770	(+467)	11,237	(+3,430)	14,667		
	572		138		965		412		1,311

Clare

Statistics

Seats	4
Electorate	82,745
Total Poll	58,495
Turnout	70.7%
Spoiled	579
Total Valid Poll	57,916
Quota	11,584
Candidates	16

Party Share of Vote

1st Preferences	Number	%	Gain/ Loss
Fine Gael	24,524	42.34	7.13
Labour	8,572	14.80	13.22
Fianna Fáil	12,804	22.11	-21.92
Sinn Féin	0	0.00	-3.42
United Left Alliance	0	0.00	0.00
Green Party	1,154	1.99	-3.08
Others	10,862	18.75	9.50

	Quotas	Seats
Fine Gael	2.1	2
Labour	0.7	1
Fianna Fáil	1.1	1
Sinn Féin	0	–
United Left Alliance	0	–
Green Party	0.1	–
Others	0.9	–

Lab gain 1 from FF.

Pat Breen (FG)

Home Address
Lisduff, Ballynacally, Co. Clare.
Constituency Office
Parkview House, Lower Market Street Car Park, Ennis; The Square, Kilrush.
Contact Details
Home: (065) 683 8229.
Constituency Office: (065) 686 8466;
Fax: (065) 686 8486.
Mobile: (087) 242 2136.
Email: pat.breen@oireachtas.ie.
Website: www.patbreen.ie.
Birth Place/Date
Ennis, 21 March 1957.
Marital Status
Married to Anne McInerney. Two sons.
Education
Lisheen N.S. St Flannan's College, Ennis. Limerick Technical College.
Occupation
Public representative; farmer. Formerly architectural technician.

Pat Breen was first elected in 2002. Fine Gael deputy spokesperson on Foreign Affairs with responsibility for Human Rights and Overseas Development Aid in last Dáil. Vice-Chairman of the Joint Committee on Enterprise and Small Business 2002–04.

Previously deputy spokesperson on Enterprise, Trade and Employment, with special responsibility for EU Internal Market Development and Small and Medium Enterprises, and deputy spokesperson for Transport and Infrastructure.

Member, Clare County Council 1999–2003.

Michael McNamara (Lab)

Home Address
Scariff, Co.Clare.
Constituency Office
New Road, Ennis; Skycourt, Shannon.
Contact
Constituency Offices: (065) 689 3639 (Ennis); (061) 479 020 (Shannon).
Email: michael.mcnamara@oireachtas.ie.
Website: www.michaelmcnamara.ie.
Birth Place/Date
Clare, 1 March 1974.
Marital Status
Single.
Education
Scariff Community College. St Flannan's College, Ennis. UCC. King's Inns. KU Leuven.
Occupation
Barrister; farmer.

Michael McNamara is a new deputy.

Elected at his first attempt to win a Dáil seat. Stood as an Independent in Ireland West constituency in the European Parliament elections in 2009.

Has worked as a legal and electoral expert with international organisations including the UN and OSCE in countries such as Afghanistan, Iraq, Yemen and Pakistan. Legal adviser to RTÉ's *Prime Time* 1997–2000.

Joe Carey (FG)

Home Address
3 Thomond Villas, Clarecastle, Co. Clare.
Constituency Office
Francis Street, Ennis.
Contact Details
Home: (065) 682 9191.
Constituency Office: (065) 689 1199.
Website: www.joecarey.ie.
Twitter: @joecareytd.
Birth Place/Date
Clarecastle, 24 June 1975.
Marital Status
Married to Grace Fitzell. One daughter.
Education
Clarecastle N.S., Ennis. St Flannan's College, Ennis. Galway IT. Athlone IT.
Occupation
Full-time public representative.

First elected to the Dáil in 2007. Appointed Fine Gael spokesperson on Juvenile Justice in October 2007. Fine Gael Assistant Chief Whip in July 2010.

Member of Joint Oireachtas Committees on Social Protection, and Justice, Defence and Women's Rights in 30th Dáil. Member, Clare County Council 1999–2007.

He is a son of Donal Carey, Fine Gael TD for Clare 1982–2002, Senator 1981–82 and Minister of State at the Department of the Taoiseach, the Department of Arts Culture and the Gaeltacht 1995–97.

Timmy Dooley (FF)

Home Address
8 The Old Forge, Tulla, Co. Clare.
Constituency Office
8 Mill Road, Ennis.
Contact Details
Home: (065) 683 1732.
Constituency Office: (065) 689 1115.
Dáil Office: (01) 616 3514.
Email: timmy.dooley@oireachtas.ie.
Website: www.timmydooley.ie.
Birth Place/Date
Limerick, 13 February 1969.
Marital Status
Married to Emer McMahon. Two children.
Education
Mountshannon N.S. Scariff Community College, Co. Clare. UCD.
Occupation
Full-time public representative. Formerly businessman.

First elected to the Dáil in 2007 following a term in the Seanad as elected member of the Administrative Panel. Party spokesperson on Transport, Tourism and Sport.

Chairman of the Kevin Barry Cumann of Fianna Fáil in UCD 1989. Founder member of the National Youth Committee 1990–93. Member, Fianna Fáil National Executive. Member, National Forum on Europe.

Clare

COUNT	1	Distribution of **Brassil** votes 2	Distribution of **McCabe** votes 3	Distribution of **Ferrigan** votes 4	Distribution of **Walshe** votes 5

Seats 4
Quota 11,584

Candidate		1	2		3		4		5	
BRASSIL, Patrick	(Ind)	175								
BREEN, James	(Ind)	6,491	(+55)	6,546	(+37)	6,583	(+16)	6,599	(+63)	6,662
BREEN, Pat*	(FG)	9,855	(+10)	9,865	(+14)	9,879	(+17)	9,896	(+21)	9,917
CAREY, Joe*	(FG)	7,840	(+19)	7,859	(+17)	7,876	(+12)	7,888	(+18)	7,906
CONNOLLY, Jim	(Ind)	978	(+24)	1,002	(+13)	1,015	(+16)	1,031	(+44)	1,075
CRONIN, Ann	(Ind)	419	(+10)	429	(+11)	440	(+57)	497	(+24)	521
DOOLEY, Timmy*	(FF)	6,789	(+6)	6,795	(+11)	6,806	(+7)	6,813	(+10)	6,823
FERRIGAN, Sarah	(Ind)	252	(+8)	260	(+5)	265				
HILLERY, Dr John	(FF)	6,015	(+5)	6,020	(+24)	6,044	(+9)	6,053	(+13)	6,066
MARKHAM, Brian	(Ind)	1,543	(+4)	1,547	(+18)	1,565	(+20)	1,585	(+52)	1,637
MCALEER, Madeline	(Ind)	428	(+1)	429	(+21)	450	(+37)	487	(+22)	509
MCCABE, John Joseph	(Ind)	248	(+4)	252						
MCNAMARA, Michael	(Lab)	8,572	(+9)	8,581	(+34)	8,615	(+44)	8,659	(+38)	8,697
MEANEY, Brian	(GP)	1,154	(+4)	1,158	(+5)	1,163	(+9)	1,172	(+15)	1,187
MULCAHY, Tony	(FG)	6,829	(+3)	6,832	(+29)	6,861	(+5)	6,866	(+15)	6,881
WALSHE, Gerry	(Ind)	328	(+4)	332	(+8)	340	(+12)	352		
NON-TRANSFERABLE				9		5		4		17

Distribution of **Cronin, McAleer** votes		Distribution of **Connolly** votes		Distribution of **Meaney** votes		Distribution of **Markham** votes		Distribution of **Hillery** votes		Distribution of **Mulcahy** votes		Distribution of **Breen** surplus	
6		**7**		**8**		**9**		**10**		**11**		**12**	
(+133)	6,795	(+234)	7,029	(+107)	7,136	(+542)	7,678	(+1,054)	8,732	(+622)	9,354	(+166)	9,520
(+32)	9,949	(+135)	10,084	(+123)	10,207	(+272)	10,479	(+509)	10,988	(+2,346)	13,334		
(+47)	7,953	(+75)	8,028	(+132)	8,160	(+174)	8,334	(+283)	8,617	(+2,344)	10,961	(+1,528)	12,489
(+141)	1,216												
(+35)	6,858	(+48)	6,906	(+57)	6,963	(+108)	7,071	(+3,526)	10,597	(+368)	10,965	(+56)	11,021
(+27)	6,093	(+68)	6,161	(+81)	6,242	(+226)	6,468						
(+188)	1,825	(+239)	2,064	(+93)	2,157								
(+174)	8,871	(+200)	9,071	(+513)	9,584	(+401)	9,985	(+567)	10,552	(+1,331)	11,883		
(+79)	1,266	(+73)	1,339										
(+51)	6,932	(+48)	6,980	(+126)	7,106	(+122)	7,228	(+210)	7,438				
123		96		107		312		319		427		0	

Cork East

Statistics

Seats	4
Electorate	83,651
Total Poll	57,459
Turnout	68.7%
Spoiled	526
Total Valid Poll	56,933
Quota	11,387
Candidates	13

Party Share of Vote

1st Preferences	Number	%	Gain/Loss
Fine Gael	20,847	36.62	5.76
Labour	17,563	30.85	9.94
Fianna Fáil	9,642	16.94	-21.03
Sinn Féin	6,292	11.05	4.23
United Left Alliance	0	0.00	0.00
Green Party	635	1.12	-1.81
Others	1,954	3.43	2.91

	Quotas	Seats
Fine Gael	1.8	2
Labour	1.5	1
Fianna Fáil	0.8	–
Sinn Féin	0.6	1
United Left Alliance	0	–
Green Party	0.1	–
Others	0.2	–

FG gain 1, SF gain 1; from FF.

Sean Sherlock (Lab)

Home Address
Blackwater Drive, Mallow, Co. Cork.
Constituency Office
Davis (Fleming's) Lane, Mallow, Co. Cork.
Contact Details
Constituency Office: (022) 53523.
Mobile: (087) 740 2057.
Email: sean.sherlock@oireachtas.ie;
sean.sherlock@deti.ie.
Website: www.seansherlock.ie.
Twitter: @seansherlocktd.
Birth Place/Date
Cork, 6 December 1972.
Marital Status
Single.
Education
Patrician Academy, Mallow. College of Commerce, Cork. NUI Galway (BA Economics and Politics).
Occupation
Public representative; Minister of State.

Sean Sherlock was appointed Minister of State with responsibility for Research and Innovation at the Departments of Enterprise, Jobs and Innovation, and of Education and Skills on 10 March 2011.

First elected to the Dáil in 2007. Labour Party spokesperson on Agriculture in last Dáil.

He was co-opted to Cork County Council and Mallow Town Council in 2003 and elected to both in 2004. Mayor of Mallow, 2004. Former assistant to Labour Party president and MEP Proinsias de Rossa.

Sean Sherlock is a son of Joe Sherlock, Sinn Féin/The Workers' Party TD for Cork East 1981–82, Workers' Party TD 1987–92, Labour Party TD 2002–07, and member of the Labour Panel of the Seanad 1993–97.

David Stanton (FG)

Home Address
Coppingerstown, Midleton, Co. Cork.
Constituency Office
29 St Mary's Road, Midleton, Co. Cork.
Contact Details
Constituency Office: (021) 463 2867.
Dáil Office: (01) 618 3181.
Mobile: (087) 234 9662.
Email: david.stanton@oireachtas.ie.
Website: www.stanton.ie
Birth Place/Date
Cork, 15 February 1957.
Marital Status
Married to Mary Lehane. Four sons.
Education
St Colman's Vocational School, Midleton. Sharman Crawford Technical Institute, Cork. UCC (BA, MEd, Diploma in Career Guidance, Diploma in Educational Administration).
Occupation
Full-time public representative. Formerly teacher; career guidance counsellor.

Elected to the Dáil in 1997 at his first attempt and re-elected at each subsequent election.

Has been Fine Gael spokesperson on Defence, and Social and Family Affairs; deputy spokesperson on Education and Science, and Labour Affairs, Consumer Rights and Trade.

Served as a commissioned officer in An Fórsa Cosanta Áitiúil. Director and former public relations officer of Midleton and District Day Care Centre Ltd, and member of the Chambers of Commerce at Cobh, Youghal and Midleton.

Tom Barry (FG)

Home Address
Monanimy Upper, Kilmallock, Mallow, Co. Cork.
Contact Details
Constituency Office: (022) 26816; (022) 26800.
Mobile: (087) 754 0438.
Email: tom.barry@oireachtas.ie.
Website: www.tombarry.ie.
Birth Place/Date
Cork, 10 October 1968.
Marital Status
Married to Dr Kathy Quane. Two sons, one daughter.
Education
De La Salle College, Waterford. UCC (BSc [Hons] Biochemistry).
Occupation
Full-time public representative.

Tom Barry is a new deputy.

Elected to Cork County Council, 2009. Member of audit and joint policing committees. Founder member of a steering committee working towards the reintroduction of the sugar beet industry in Ireland. He is a member of the Teagasc Tillage Commodity Group, which plans the future strategy for the tillage sector in Ireland.

Founder and managing director of agri-business TB Warehousing.

Sandra McLellan (SF)

Home Address
Ardrath, Youghal, Co. Cork.
Contact Details
Dáil Office: (01) 618 3122.
Mobile: (086) 375 2944.
Email: sandra.mclellan@oireachtas.ie
Birth Place/Date
Youghal, May 1961.
Marital Status
Married to Liam McLellan. Three children.
Education
Loreto Convent, Youghal.
Occupation
Full-time public representative. Former SIPTU representative in electronics factory.
Sandra McLellan is a new deputy.

Sinn Féin spokesperson on Arts, Heritage, Tourism and Sport. She contested the 2007 General Election unsuccessfully. Elected to Cork County Council in 2009 and to Youghal Town Council in 2004 and 2009. Mayor of Youghal, 2009.

Cork East

Seats 4 Quota 11,387			Distribution of **Sherlock** surplus		Distribution of **Bulman, Burke, Cullinane, Harty, O'Neill** votes
COUNT		1	2		3
AHERN, Michael*	(FF)	4,618	(+16)	4,634	(+164)	4,798
BARRY, Tom	(FG)	5,798	(+90)	5,888	(+209)	6,097
BULMAN, Patrick	(Ind)	212	(+1)	213		
BURKE, Paul	(Ind)	176	(+1)	177		
CULLINANE, Claire	(Ind)	510	(+3)	513		
HARTY, Malachy	(GP)	635	(+5)	640		
MCLELLAN, Sandra	(SF)	6,292	(+53)	6,345	(+532)	6,877
MULVIHILL, John	(Lab)	5,701	(+172)	5,873	(+515)	6,388
O'DRISCOLL, Pa	(FG)	5,030	(+56)	5,086	(+150)	5,236
O'KEEFFE, Kevin	(FF)	5,024	(+42)	5,066	(+79)	5,145
O'NEILL, Paul	(Ind)	1,056	(+8)	1,064		
SHERLOCK, Sean*	(Lab)	11,862				
STANTON, David*	(FG)	10,019	(+28)	10,047	(+571)	10,618
NON-TRANSFERABLE			0		387	

Distribution of **Ahern** votes		Distribution of **O'Driscoll** votes		Distribution of **Stanton** surplus		Distribution of **Mulvihill** votes	
4		**5**		**6**		**7**	
(+300)	6,397	(+2,501)	8,898	(+828)	9,726	(+1,724)	11,450
(+326)	7,203	(+325)	7,528	(+58)	7,586	(+2,199)	9,785
(+402)	6,790	(+186)	6,976	(+121)	7,097		
(+208)	5,444						
(+2,666)	7,811	(+590)	8,401	(+77)	8,478	(+658)	9,136
(+463)	11,081	(+1,390)	12,471				
433		452		0		2,516	

Cork North-Central

Statistics

Seats	4
Electorate	75,302
Total Poll	52,709
Turnout	70.0%
Spoiled	572
Total Valid Poll	52,137
Quota	10,428
Candidates	15

Party Share of Vote

1st Preferences	Number	%	Gain/Loss
Fine Gael	13,669	26.22	-1.35
Labour	13,801	26.47	14.14
Fianna Fáil	7,896	15.14	-20.60
Sinn Féin	7,923	15.20	7.04
United Left Alliance	4,803	9.21	9.21
Green Party	524	1.01	-2.54
Others	1,954	3.43	2.91

	Quotas	Seats
Fine Gael	1.3	1
Labour	1.3	1
Fianna Fáil	0.8	1
Sinn Féin	0.8	1
United Left Alliance	0.5	–
Green Party	0.1	–
Others	0.3	–

SF gain 1 from FF.

Jonathan O'Brien (SF)

Home Address
11 Fairfield Green, Farranree, Cork City.
Constituency Office
52 Shandon Street, Cork City.
Contact Details
Constituency Office: (021) 421 2233.
Mobile: (085) 213 3907.
Email: jonathan.obrien@oireachtas.ie.
Twitter: @jobrien_sf.
Birth Place/Date
Cork City, December 1971.
Marital Status
Married to Gillian. Four children.
Education
North Monastery secondary school.
Occupation
Public representative.

Jonathan O'Brien is a new deputy.

First Sinn Féin TD elected in Cork City since before the Civil War. Party spokesperson on Justice, Equality and Defence.

Co-opted to the party's only seat on Cork City Council in 2001, he was re-elected in 2004 and 2009. Unsuccessfully contested general elections in 2002 and 2007.

Director of Cork City Football Club, which is now owned by its fans.

Kathleen Lynch (Lab)

Home Address
Farrancleary, 5 Assumption Road, Blackpool, Cork.
Contact Details
Office: (021) 439 9930; (021) 421 2463.
Email: kathleen.lynch@oireachtas.ie;
kathleen_lynch@health.gov.ie.
Website: www.labour.ie/kathleenlynch.
Facebook: kathleen-lynch.
Twitter: @kathleenlynchtd.
Birth Place/Date
Cork, 6 July 1953.
Marital Status
Married to Bernard Lynch. Three daughters, one son.
Education
Blackpool School, Cork.
Occupation
Full-time public representative.

Appointed Minister of State at the Department of Health, and Department of Justice, Equality and Defence, with responsibility for Disability, Older People, Equality and Mental Health on 10 March 2011.

Member of Joint Oireachtas Committee on Health in 30th Dáil and on Joint Committee on Justice, Equality, Defence and Women's Rights during 29th Dáil.

First elected to the Dáil in 1994 as a Democratic Left candidate in the Cork North Central by-election caused by the death of Labour TD Gerry O'Sullivan. She lost her seat in the 1997 General Election and was re-elected in 2002 (following the merger of Democratic Left with Labour) and in 2007.

Member of Cork City Council 1985–2003.

Kathleen Lynch is a sister-in-law of Ciarán Lynch, new TD for Cork South-Central.

Billy Kelleher (FF)

Home Address
Ballyphilip, White's Cross, Glanmire, Co. Cork.
Constituency Office
28A Ballyhooley Road, Dillon's Cross, Cork.
Contact Details
Home: (021) 482 1045. Constituency Office:
(021) 450 2289. Mobile: (087) 258 0521.
Email: billykelleher@eircom.net;
billy.kelleher@oireachtas.ie.
Website: www.billykelleher.com.
Birth Place/Date
Cork, 20 January 1968.
Marital Status
Married to Liza Davis. Three children.
Education
Sacred Heart College, Carrignavar, Co. Cork.
Pallaskenry Agricultural College, Limerick.
Occupation
Public representative; farmer.

Fianna Fáil spokesperson on Health, Billy
Kelleher was Minister of State for Trade and
Commerce, and Minister of State for Labour
Affairs during the last Dáil.

First elected to the Dáil in 1997 and re-elected
at each subsequent election. Former Member
of Joint Committees on: Agriculture, Food and
the Marine; Environment and Local
Government; and Tourism, Sport and
Recreation.

He was a Senator, Taoiseach's nominee,
1992–97. He was a candidate in the 1992
General Election in Cork North-Central, losing
out on the last seat by 25 votes. He was also
a candidate in the same constituency in the
by-election caused by the death of Gerry
O'Sullivan (Lab) in 1994.

Dara Murphy (FG)

Home Address
Gardener's Hill, St Luke's Cross, Cork.
Constituency Office
1 Herbert Park, Gardiner's Hill, Cork.
Contact Details
Dáil Office: (01) 618 3862.
Mobile: (086) 253 3729.
Email: dara.murphy@oireachtas.ie.
Birth Place/Date
Cork, December 1969.
Marital Status
Married to Tanya. Three daughters.
Education
Christian Brothers, Cork. UCC.
Occupation
Public representative. Formerly owner of
catering business.

Dara Murphy is a new deputy.

He was elected to Cork City Council on his
second attempt in 2004 and re-elected in
2009. Lord Mayor of Cork, 2009–10.

Cork North-Central

Seats 4
Quota 10,428

COUNT		1	Distribution of **Ashu-Arrah, O'Rourke** votes	2	Distribution of **Adams** votes	3	Distribution of **Rea** votes	4	Distribution of **Walsh** votes	5
ADAMS, John	(Ind)	282	(+31)	313						
ASHU-ARRAH, Benjamin	(Ind)	161								
BARRY, Mick	(ULA)	4,803	(+23)	4,826	(+50)	4,876	(+27)	4,903	(+37)	4,940
BURTON, Pat	(FG)	7,072	(+32)	7,104	(+13)	7,117	(+38)	7,155	(+85)	7,240
CONWAY, Kevin B	(Ind)	958	(+11)	969	(+27)	996	(+24)	1,020	(+9)	1,029
GILROY, John	(Lab)	6,125	(+9)	6,134	(+20)	6,154	(+4)	6,158	(+87)	6,245
KELLEHER, Billy*	(FF)	7,896	(+37)	7,933	(+8)	7,941	(+40)	7,981	(+42)	8,023
LYNCH, Kathleen*	(Lab)	7,676	(+20)	7,696	(+38)	7,734	(+15)	7,749	(+98)	7,847
MURPHY, Dara	(FG)	6,597	(+18)	6,615	(+27)	6,642	(+40)	6,682	(+86)	6,768
O'BRIEN, Jonathan	(SF)	7,923	(+19)	7,942	(+36)	7,978	(+44)	8,022	(+31)	8,053
O'ROURKE, Fergus	(Ind)	95								
O'SULLIVAN, Padraig	(Ind)	1,020	(+30)	1,050	(+35)	1,085	(+51)	1,136	(+47)	1,183
REA, Harry	(CSP)	324	(+2)	326	(+5)	331				
TYNAN, Ted	(WP)	681	(+7)	688	(+19)	707	(+17)	724	(+17)	741
WALSH, Ken	(GP)	524	(+6)	530	(+19)	549	(+9)	558		
NON-TRANSFERABLE				11		16		22		19

Distribution of **Tynan** votes		Distribution of **Conway, O'Sullivan** votes		Distribution of **Barry** votes		Distribution of **O'Brien** surplus		Distribution of **Gilroy** votes		Distribution of **Lynch** surplus	
6		**7**		**8**		**9**		**10**		**11**	
(+191)	5,131	(+188)	5,319								
(+23)	7,263	(+322)	7,585	(+193)	7,778	(+38)	7,816	(+637)	8,453	(+780)	9,233
(+4)	1,033										
(+58)	6,303	(+356)	6,659	(+497)	7,156	(+137)	7,293				
(+34)	8,057	(+327)	8,384	(+158)	8,542	(+32)	8,574	(+609)	9,183	(+412)	9,595
(+106)	7,953	(+283)	8,236	(+1,268)	9,504	(+411)	9,915	(+4,173)	14,088		
(+41)	6,809	(+229)	7,038	(+233)	7,271	(+85)	7,356	(+1,011)	8,367	(+1,148)	9,515
(+201)	8,254	(+313)	8,567	(+2,564)	11,131						
(+47)	1,230										
36		245		406		0		863		1,320	

Cork North-West

Statistics

Seats	3
Electorate	62,870
Total Poll	46,194
Turnout	73.5%
Spoiled	454
Total Valid Poll	45,740
Quota	11,436
Candidates	9

Party Share of Vote

1st Preferences	Number	%	Gain/Loss
Fine Gael	22,321	48.80	10.38
Labour	6,421	14.04	9.13
Fianna Fáil	11,390	24.90	-28.15
Sinn Féin	3,405	7.44	7.44
United Left Alliance	1,552	3.39	3.39
Green Party	651	1.42	-2.20
Others	0	0.00	0.00

	Quotas	Seats
Fine Gael	2	2
Labour	0.6	–
Fianna Fáil	1	1
Sinn Féin	0.3	–
United Left Alliance	0.1	–
Green Party	0.1	–
Others	0	–

FG gain 1 from FF.

Michael Creed (FG)

Home Address
1 Sullane Weirs, Macroom, Co. Cork.
Constituency Office
Main Street, Macroom, Co. Cork.
Contact Details
Home: (026) 42944. Constituency Office:
(026) 41835. Dáil Office: (01) 618 3525.
Mobile: (087) 242 4631.
Email: michael.creed@oireachtas.ie.
Birth Place/Date
Cork, 29 June 1963.
Marital Status
Married to Sinead. Two sons, one daughter.
Education
St Colman's College, Fermoy, Co. Cork. De La
Salle College, Macroom. UCC (BA, HDipEd).
DIT (Diploma in Legal Studies).
Occupation
Public representative; businessman.

First elected in 1989 but lost his seat in 2002
General Election and regained it in 2007. Fine
Gael's spokesperson on European Affairs
from October 2010 to March 2011 and
spokesperson on Agriculture, Fisheries and
Food 2007–10.

He was Chairman of the Dáil's Small Business
and Services Committee 1995–97. Chairman:
Fine Gael Parliamentary Party Committee on
Enterprise and Economic Strategy 1993–94;
Committee on Health 1989–93. Front bench
spokesperson on: Education, and Arts,
Culture and Gaeltacht, 1994; Health, 1989–93;
and Youth and Sport, 1993–94.

Co-opted to Cork County Council in 1987 and
elected until 2007. Chairperson, Cork County
Council 2005–06.

Son of Donal Creed, TD for Mid Cork 1965–81
and Cork North-West 1981–89. Minister of
State, Department of Health, June–November
1981; at the Department of the Environment
1981–82; at the Department of Education
from 1982–86.

Michael Moynihan (FF)

Home Address
Meens, Kiskeam, Mallow, Co. Cork.
Constituency Office
Percival Street, Kanturk, Co. Cork; Lower
Main Street, Charleville, Co. Cork.
Contact Details
Home: (029) 76200. Constituency Offices:
(029) 51299 (Kanturk); (063) 21088
(Charlevlle); Fax: (029) 51300.
Dáil Office: (01) 618 3595.
Mobile: (087) 274 5810.
Birth Place/Date
Cork, 12 January 1968.
Marital Status
Married to Bríd O'Sullivan. One daughter.
Education
Boherbue Comprehensive School, Mallow.
Occupation
Full-time public representative; farmer.

Michael Moynihan is Fianna Fáil
spokesperson on Agriculture. First elected to
the Dáil in 1997. Chairman of the Joint
Committee on Education and Science
2004–07. Member of the Committees on
Heritage and the Irish Language, and
Agriculture, Food and the Marine during the
28th Dáil.

Life member, Kiskeam GAA Club. Vice-
Chairman, Kiskeam Seán Moylan
Commemoration Committee.

Áine Collins (FG)

Home Address
Laught, Rathcoole, Mallow, Co. Cork.
Constituency Office
Fairfield, Millstreet, Co. Cork; New Line,
Charleville, Millstreet, Co. Cork.
Contact Details
Constituency Office: (029) 71845.
Mobile: (087) 232 6945.
Email: aine.collins@oireachtas.ie;
collinsaine@eircom.net.
Birth Place/Date
Cork, 9 September 1969.
Marital Status
Married to Paul. Two daughters, one son.
Education
Millstreet Community School. Certified Public
Accountant.
Occupation
Public representative; business consultant.

Áine Collins is a new deputy.

From a Fine Gael family, she never previously
contested an election. She is a founding
member of Millstreet Development
Association and a member of Millstreet
Community Council and she runs a business
consultancy from the town.

Cork North-West

Seats 3 Quota 11,436		COUNT	Distribution of **Collins, Foley** votes		Distribution of **O Donnabháin** votes		Distribution of **O'Grady** votes		Distribution of **Canty** votes		Distribution of **Creed** surplus	
		1		**2**		**3**		**4**		**5**		**6**
CANTY, Derry	(FG)	4,325	(+145)	4,470	(+234)	4,704	(+388)	5,092				
COLLINS, Áine	(FG)	7,884	(+339)	8,223	(+122)	8,345	(+393)	8,738	(+1,796)	10,534	(+708)	11,242
COLLINS, Mark	(GP)	651										
COUGHLAN, Martin	(Lab)	6,421	(+645)	7,066	(+189)	7,255	(+1,697)	8,952	(+966)	9,918	(+210)	10,128
CREED, Michael*	(FG)	10,112	(+152)	10,264	(+162)	10,426	(+371)	10,797	(+1,618)	12,415		
FOLEY, Anne	(ULA)	1,552										
MOYNIHAN, Michael*	(FF)	8,845	(+164)	9,009	(+1,690)	10,699	(+409)	11,108	(+254)	11,362	(+61)	11,423
O DONNABHÁIN, Daithi	(FF)	2,545	(+88)	2,633								
O'GRADY, Des	(SF)	3,405	(+511)	3,916	(+136)	4,052						
NON-TRANSFERABLE				159		100		794		458		0

Willie O'Dea watches as his team knocks on doors while canvassing in Limerick. Photograph: David Sleator.

Cork South-Central

Statistics

Seats	5
Electorate	91,619
Total Poll	64,664
Turnout	70.6%
Spoiled	624
Total Valid Poll	64,040
Quota	10,674
Candidates	17

Party Share of Vote

1st Preferences	Number	%	Gain/Loss
Fine Gael	22,225	34.70	6.29
Labour	11,869	18.53	9.28
Fianna Fáil	17,936	28.01	-16.27
Sinn Féin	5,250	8.20	3.09
United Left Alliance	0	0.00	0.00
Green Party	1,640	2.56	-5.81
Others	5,120	8.00	6.13

	Quotas	Seats
Fine Gael	2.1	2
Labour	1.1	1
Fianna Fáil	1.7	2
Sinn Féin	0.5	–
United Left Alliance	0	–
Green Party	0.2	–
Others	0.5	–

No change.

Micheál Martin (FF)

Home Address
Lios Laoi, 16 Silver Manor, Ballincollig, Cork.
Constituency Office
137 Evergreen Road, Turner's Cross, Cork.
Contact Details
Constituency Office: (021) 432 0088.
Dáil Office: (01) 618 4350. Email:
michealmartintd@eircom.net.
Website:www.michealmartin.ie. Facebook:
michealmartintd. Twitter: @fiannafailparty.
Birth Place/Date
Cork, 1 August 1960.
Marital Status
Married to Mary O'Shea. Young family.
Education
Coláiste Chríost Rí, Cork. UCC (BA, HDipED,
MA Political History).
Occupation
Public representative; Uachtarán Fhianna Fáil.
Formerly secondary school teacher.

Elected eighth leader of Fianna Fáil on 26
January 2011 in a four-way contest to
succeed Brian Cowen. He defeated party
colleagues Éamon Ó Cuív, Brian Lenihan and
Mary Hanafin. Became Leader of the
Opposition in the Dáil on 10 March 2011.

Resigned as Minister for Foreign Affairs on 19
January 2011 after challenging Taoiseach
Brian Cowen's leadership. Had been Minister
for Foreign Affairs since 2008; Minister for
Enterprise, Trade and Employment 2004–08;
Minister for Health and Children 2000–04; and
Minister for Education 1997–2000.

First elected to the Dáil in 1989 and at all
subsequent general elections. Fianna Fáil
front bench spokesperson on Education and
the Gaeltacht 1995–97. Former Chairman of
the Oireachtas All Party Committee on the
Irish Language. Former member of the Dáil
Committee on Crime, and the Dáil Committee
on Finance and General Affairs.

First elected to Cork Corporation in 1985 and
Lord Mayor of Cork from 1992–93. He is a
former member of the Governing Body UCC
and of the Governing Body RTC, and a former
member of the ASTI.

Ciarán Lynch (Lab)

Home Address
31 Yewlands, Maryborough Woods, Douglas,
Co. Cork.
Constituency Office
29 St Patrick's Mills, Douglas.
Contact Details
Constituency Office: (021) 436 6200.
Mobile: (086) 603 3923.
Email: ciaran.lynch@oireachtas.ie.
Website: www.ciaranlynch.ie.
Birth Place/Date
Cork, 13 June 1964.
Marital Status
Married to Bernadette Long. One daughter,
one son.
Education
UCC (Social Studies). Waterford IT
(Humanities).
Occupation
Public representative; adult literacy organiser.

Ciarán Lynch was first elected in 2007.

He contested the local elections in 1997 and
was elected to Cork City Council 2004.
Chairman of Labour Party, Cork South-Central
Constituency.

Member: Teachers' Union of Ireland; Adult
Literacy Organisers' Association; National
Executive; National Adult Literacy Agency;
City of Cork VEC Adult Education Board; Cork
City Library Committee; Kinsale Road Dump
Action Group; Carr's Hill Famine Cemetery
Commemorative Committee.

He is a brother-in-law of Kathleen Lynch, TD
for Cork North-Central 1994–97 and 2002 to
date.

Simon Coveney (FG)

Home Address
The Rock, Carrigaline, Co. Cork.
Constituency Office
Main Street, Carrigaline, Co. Cork.
Contact Details
Office: (021) 437 4200.
Email: simon.coveney@oireachtas.ie.
Website: www.simoncoveney.ie.
Birth Place/Date
Cork, 16 June 1972.
Education
Clongowes Wood College, Co. Kildare. UCC.
Gurteen Agricultural College. Royal Agriculture
College, Gloucestershire (BSc in Agriculture
and Land Management).
Occupation
Government Minister; farmer.

Appointed Minister for Agriculture, Marine
and Food on 9 March 2011.

Fine Gael spokesperson on Transport during
the 30th Dáil and chaired the party's Policy
Development Committee in the run-up to the
2011 General Election.

First elected to the Dáil in a by-election for Cork
South-Central in October 1998 following the
death of his father. Elected to the European
Parliament for the Ireland South constituency in
2004 but gave up the seat in June 2007 in
order to remain in domestic politics.

Member of the Foreign Affairs Committee
and the Internal Market and Consumer
Protection Committee in the European
Parliament, and author of the parliament's
Annual Report on Human Rights in the World
for 2004 and 2006.

Member, Cork County Council and Southern
Health Board, 1999–2003. Former Chairperson
of Joint City and County Committee.

A keen fan of all competitive sport, he played
Rugby for Garryowen, Cork Constitution and
Crosshaven Rugby Club. In 1997–98 he led the
Sail Chernobyl Project, which involved sailing
30,000 miles around the world for charity.

Jerry Buttimer (FG)

Home Address
25 Benvoirlich Estate, Bishopstown, Co. Cork.
Constituency Office
4A Glasheen Road, Cork.
Contact Details
Constituency Office: (021) 484 0652.
Mobile: (086) 235 6892.
Email: jerry.buttimer@oireachtas.ie.
Website: www.jerrybuttimer.ie
Birth Place/Date
Cork, 18 March 1967.
Marital Status
Single.
Education
Scoil an Spioraid Naoimh Buachaillí.
Farranferris Secondary School. NUI Maynooth.
UCC (HDipEd).
Occupation
Full-time public representative. Formerly
secondary school teacher.

Jerry Buttimer is a new deputy. Elected to the
Seanad in 2007 after unsuccessfully
contesting that year's general election about
which he wrote a memoir, *Candidate: The
Diary of an Election Candidate* (Gill &
Macmillan, 2007).

Member, Cork City Council 2004–07. Former
Youth and Development Officer, Cork County
GAA Board. Member, Croke Park marketing
committee. Chairman, Bishopstown GAA
Club.

Michael McGrath (FF)

Home Address
4 North Lawn, Carrig na Curra, Carrigaline,
Co. Cork.
Constituency Office
Kilmoney Road, Carrigaline, Co. Cork.
Contact Details
Office: (021) 437 6699.
Website: www.michaelmcgrath.ie.
Birth Place/Date
Cork, 23 August 1976.
Marital Status
Married to Sarah O'Brien. Five children.
Education
St Peter's Community College, Passage
West, Co. Cork. UCC (BComm).
Occupation
Public representative; chartered accountant.

Michael McGrath is the Fianna Fáil
spokesperson on Finance, appointed in
August 2011.

First elected to the Dáil in 2007. Previously
unsuccessful candidate for the Seanad in
2002.

Elected to Cork County Council in the local
elections in 2004, topping the poll in his
electoral area at the first attempt. Member,
Passage West Town Council 1999 and re-
elected in 2004; Chairperson of the council
2000–01.

Resigned as Head of Management
Information and Systems in UCC in 2005 to
concentrate on constituency work.

Cork South-Central

Seats 5
Quota 10,674

COUNT	1	Distribution of Martin surplus		Distribution of Isherwood, Linehan, O'Driscoll votes		Distribution of Dunphy votes		Distribution of Ó Cadhla votes	
	1	**2**		**3**		**4**		**5**	
BOYLE, Dan (GP)	1,640	(+1)	1,641	(+9)	1,650	(+22)	1,672	(+36)	1,708
BUTTIMER, Jerry (FG)	7,128	(+2)	7,130	(+20)	7,150	(+23)	7,173	(+21)	7,194
CLUNE, Deirdre* (FG)	5,650	(+2)	5,652	(+20)	5,672	(+17)	5,689	(+20)	5,709
COVENEY, Simon* (FG)	9,447	(+3)	9,450	(+21)	9,471	(+50)	9,521	(+37)	9,558
DESMOND, Paula (Lab)	3,388	(+1)	3,389	(+23)	3,412	(+43)	3,455	(+44)	3,499
DUNPHY, Sean (Ind)	448	(+)	448	(+33)	481				
FINN, Mick (Ind)	2,386	(+1)	2,387	(+53)	2,440	(+100)	2,540	(+57)	2,597
ISHERWOOD, Eric (Ind)	193	(+)	193						
LINEHAN, Gerard (Ind)	90	(+)	90						
LYNCH, Ciarán* (Lab)	8,481	(+3)	8,484	(+32)	8,516	(+27)	8,543	(+50)	8,593
MARTIN, Micheál* (FF)	10,715								
MCCARTHY, David (Ind)	880	(+)	880	(+37)	917	(+35)	952	(+85)	1,037
MCGRATH, Michael* (FF)	7,221	(+27)	7,248	(+26)	7,274	(+53)	7,327	(+23)	7,350
NEVILLE, Ted (Ind)	523	(+)	523	(+24)	547	(+34)	581	(+58)	639
Ó CADHLA, Diarmaid (Ind)	508	(+)	508	(+23)	531	(+32)	563		
O'LEARY, Chris (SF)	5,250	(+1)	5,251	(+40)	5,291	(+28)	5,319	(+95)	5,414
O'DRISCOLL, Finbar (Ind)	92	(+)	92						
NON-TRANSFERABLE		0		14		17		37	

Distribution of **McCarthy, Neville** votes		Distribution of **Boyle** votes		Distribution of **Finn** votes		Distribution of **Desmond** votes		Distribution of **Lynch** surplus		Distribution of **Clune** votes		Distribution of **Buttimer** surplus	
6		**7**		**8**		**9**		**10**		**11**		**12**	
(+92)	1,800												
(+133)	7,327	(+226)	7,553	(+269)	7,822	(+210)	8,032	(+378)	8,410	(+4,686)	13,096		
(+94)	5,803	(+179)	5,982	(+142)	6,124	(+240)	6,364	(+326)	6,690				
(+154)	9,712	(+264)	9,976	(+193)	10,169	(+362)	10,531	(+341)	10,872				
(+110)	3,609	(+268)	3,877	(+250)	4,127								
(+285)	2,882	(+78)	2,960										
(+217)	8,810	(+408)	9,218	(+703)	9,921	(+2,644)	12,565						
(+134)	7,484	(+151)	7,635	(+276)	7,911	(+209)	8,120	(+273)	8,393	(+632)	9,025	(+998)	10,023
(+274)	5,688	(+108)	5,796	(+667)	6,463	(+256)	6,719	(+549)	7,268	(+372)	7,640	(+547)	8,187
183		118		460		206		24		1,000		877	

Cork South-West

Statistics

Seats	3
Electorate	62,967
Total Poll	46,048
Turnout	73.1%
Spoiled	390
Total Valid Poll	45,658
Quota	11,415
Candidates	13

Party Share of Vote

1st Preferences	Number	%	Gain/Loss
Fine Gael	22,162	48.54	12.54
Labour	6,533	14.31	4.67
Fianna Fáil	10,787	23.63	-18.95
Sinn Féin	3,346	7.33	2.27
United Left Alliance	0	0.00	0.00
Green Party	765	1.68	-5.05
Others	2,065	4.52	4.52

	Quotas	Seats
Fine Gael	1.9	2
Labour	0.6	1
Fianna Fáil	0.9	–
Sinn Féin	0.3	–
United Left Alliance	0	–
Green Party	0.1	–
Others	0.2	–

Lab gain 1 from FF.

Jim Daly (FG)

Home Address
5 Millgrove, Clonakilty, Co. Cork.
Constituency Office
Fernhill Road, Clonkilty; 7 South Main Street, Bandon.
Contact Details
Constituency Office: (023) 884 3868;
(023) 885 8770. Email: jim.daly@oireachtas.ie.
Website: www.jimdaly.ie.
Twitter: @jimdalytd.
Birth Place/Date
Cork, 20 December 1972.
Marital Status
Married to Virge. Four sons.
Education
Coláiste Muire, Cobh. NUI Maynooth (BA in Gaeilge & Philosophy). Mary Immaculate College Limerick (Dip Primary Education).
Occupation
Full-time public representative. Formerly primary teacher.

Jim Daly is a new deputy.

First elected to Cork County Council in 2004 and re-elected for Skibbereen electoral area in 2009. Chairman, Clonakilty District Chamber of Tourism. Member, Clonakilty District Chamber of Commerce formation committee.

Former principal Gaelscoil Dr M Uí Shúilleabháin, Skibbereen 2002–05. Full-time politician since 2005.

Noel Harrington (FG)

Home Address
Bank Place, Castletownbere, Co. Cork.
Constituency Office
High Street, Bantry, Co. Cork; Townsend Street, Skibbereen, Co. Cork.
Contact Details
Constituency Office: (027) 56222.
Dáil Office: (01) 618 3956.
Mobile: (086) 856 7178.
Email: noel.harrington@oireachtas.ie.
Website: www.noelharrington.com.
Twitter: @nharrington2.
Birth Place/Date
Castletownbere, 24 December 1970.
Marital Status
Married to Catherine. Two sons, one daughter.
Education
Castletownbere N.S. Beara Community School.
Occupation
Public pepresentative; postmaster.

Noel Harrington is a new deputy.

Elected to Cork County Council for the Bantry electoral area in 1999 and re-elected in 2004 and 2009. Mayor of Cork County in 2008.

Missed election to the Industrial and Commercial Panel of the Seanad by less than one vote on the 24th count in 2007.

Michael McCarthy (Lab)

Home Address
Mileenananig, Clonakilty Road, Dunmanway, Co. Cork.
Constituency Office
Market Square, Dunmanway, Co. Cork.
Contact Details
Constituency Office: (023) 885 5705.
Dáil Office: (01) 618 3844.
Email: michael.mccarthy@oireachtas.ie.
Website: www.labour.ie/michaelmccarthy.
Twitter: @mmccarthytd.
Birth Place/Date
Bantry, Co. Cork, 15 November 1976.
Marital Status
Married to Nollagh McCarthy. Two children.
Education
St Mary's Primary School, Dunmanway. St Patrick's Boys N.S., Dunmanway. Coláiste Chairbre, Dunmanway.
Occupation
Full-time public representative. Formerly pharmaceutical company employee.

Michael McCarthy is a new deputy.

Elected to Seanad in 2002 and re-elected in 2007 after contesting general elections in both years. Labour Party spokesperson on the Marine in last Seanad.

Elected to Cork County Council for the Skibbereen electoral area in 1999.

Cork South-West

Seats 3 Quota 11,415		Distribution of **Butler, Doonan, Kearney, McCaughey, McInerney, O'Sullivan** votes		Distribution of **Hayes** votes		Distribution of **O'Sullivan** votes		Distribution of **Murphy** votes		Distribution of **Daly** surplus votes	
COUNT	1		2		3		4		5		6
BUTLER, Edmund (Ind)	330										
DALY, Jim (FG)	8,878	(+377)	9,255	(+441)	9,696	(+812)	10,508	(+2,734)	13,242		
DOONAN, Paul (Ind)	239										
HARRINGTON, Noel (FG)	6,898	(+314)	7,212	(+267)	7,479	(+189)	7,668	(+1,900)	9,568	(+1,536)	11,104
HAYES, Paul (SF)	3,346	(+397)	3,743								
KEARNEY, John (Ind)	772										
MCCARTHY, Michael (Lab)	6,533	(+724)	7,257	(+1,452)	8,709	(+503)	9,212	(+1,327)	10,539	(+215)	10,754
MCCAUGHEY, Kevin (GP)	765										
MCINERNEY, David (Ind)	493										
MURPHY, Kevin (FG)	6,386	(+279)	6,665	(+252)	6,917	(+295)	7,212				
O'DONOVAN, Denis (FF)	5,984	(+224)	6,208	(+273)	6,481	(+2,972)	9,453	(+626)	10,079	(+76)	10,155
O'SULLIVAN, Christy* (FF)	4,803	(+155)	4,958	(+257)	5,215						
O'SULLIVAN, Michael (Ind)	231										
NON-TRANSFERABLE			360		801		444		625		0

Micheál Martin announces members of his front bench, including John Curran, Mary Hanafin, Averil Power and Mary Fitzpatrick, before the election. Photograph: Bryan O'Brien.

Donegal North-East

Statistics

Seats	3
Electorate	59,084
Total Poll	38,324
Turnout	64.9%
Spoiled	406
Total Valid Poll	37,918
Quota	9,480
Candidates	11

Party Share of Vote

1st Preferences	Number	%	Gain/Loss
Fine Gael	11,987	31.61	9.01
Labour	4,090	10.79	8.96
Fianna Fáil	6,613	17.44	-32.82
Sinn Féin	9,278	24.47	7.00
United Left Alliance	0	0.00	0.00
Green Party	206	0.54	-0.81
Others	5,744	15.15	8.65

	Quotas	Seats
Fine Gael	1.3	1
Labour	0.4	–
Fianna Fáil	0.7	1
Sinn Féin	1	1
United Left Alliance	0	–
Green Party	0	–
Others	0.6	–

SF gain 1 from FF.

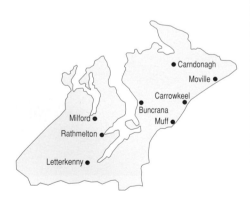

Pádraig Mac Lochlainn (SF)

Home Address
13 The Meadows, Buncrana, Co. Donegal.
Constituency Office
28 Lower Main Street, Buncrana,
Co. Donegal.
Contact Details
Office: (074) 932 2697.
Dáil Office: (01) 618 4061.
Mobile: (087) 277 1958.
Email: padraig.maclochlainn@oireachtas.ie.
Facebook: Pádraig Mac Lochlainn.
Birth Place/Date
Leeds, England, 12 June 1973.
Marital Status
Partner. One son and one stepson.
Education
Diploma in Social Studies.
Occupation
Full-time public representative.

Pádraig Mac Lochlainn is a new deputy. He
stood unsuccessfully in the 2002 and 2007
general elections and in the European
Parliament elections in 2009.

Co-opted onto Buncrana Town Council 2002
and elected to Donegal County Council 2004.

National director of Sinn Féin campaign
against the Lisbon Treaty 2008. Member of
Sinn Féin Ard Chomhairle.

Joe McHugh (FG)

Home Address
Claggan, Carrigart, Letterkenny, Co. Donegal.
Constituency Office
Grier House, Lower Main Street, Letterkenny,
Co. Donegal.
Contact Details
Office: (074) 916 4787; (01) 618 4242.
Email: joe.mchugh@oireachtas.ie.
Website: www.donegalmatters.com.
Facebook: joemchughtd.
Birth Place/Date
Letterkenny, 16 July 1971.
Marital Status
Married to Olwyn Enright. Two children.
Education
Umlagh N.S., Carrigart. Loreto Convent,
Milford. St Patrick's College, Maynooth (BA
Economics & Social Science; HDipEd).
Occupation
Public representative. Formerly geography
and maths teacher; community worker.

First elected to the Dáil in 2007. Fine Gael
spokesperson on North–South Co-operation
during the 30th Dáil.

Member of the Seanad 2002–07. Member of
Donegal County Council, 1999–2003.

A geography and maths teacher in Loreto
College Letterkenny from 1993–95, he also
taught in Dubai from 1995–96, where he set
up the first GAA club in the area. Former
member of Carrigart Boxing Club; Donegal
league soccer player; and Gaelic footballer.

He is married to Olwyn Enright, Fine Gael TD
for Laois–Offaly 2002–11.

Charlie McConalogue (FF)

Home Address
Carrowmore, Gleneely, Carndonagh,
Co. Donegal.
Constituency Office
Chapel Street, Carndonagh, Co. Donegal.
Contact Details
Dáil Office: (01) 618 3199.
Mobile: (086) 816 1078. Email:
charlie.mcconalogue@oireachtas.ie.
Birth Place/Date
Letterkenny, October 1977.
Marital Status
Single.
Education
UCD (History and Politics).
Occupation
Public representative; farmer.

Charlie McConalogue is a new deputy.

Fianna Fáil spokesperson on Children. Elected
to Donegal County Council in 2009. Deputy
Mayor of Donegal 2009–10. Formerly a
political organiser for Fianna Fáil in Leinster,
before returning to Donegal.

Donegal North-East

Seats 3 Quota 9,480		COUNT 1	Distribution of **Murphy, Stewart** votes 2		Distribution of **Holmes** votes 3		Distribution of **Mac Lochlainn** surplus 4	
BLANEY, Dara	(Ind)	1,228	(+21)	1,249	(+68)	1,317	(+10)	1,327
HARTE, Jimmy	(Lab)	4,090	(+72)	4,162	(+139)	4,301	(+18)	4,319
HOLMES, Betty	(Ind)	1,150	(+47)	1,197				
MAC LOCHLAINN, Pádraig	(SF)	9,278	(+72)	9,350	(+235)	9,585		
MCCONALOGUE, Charlie	(FF)	6,613	(+48)	6,661	(+134)	6,795	(+21)	6,816
MCGARVEY, Ian	(Ind)	1,287	(+9)	1,296	(+103)	1,399	(+10)	1,409
MCHUGH, Joe*	(FG)	7,330	(+38)	7,368	(+145)	7,513	(+11)	7,524
MURPHY, Humphrey	(GP)	206						
RYAN, John	(FG)	4,657	(+53)	4,710	(+161)	4,871	(+13)	4,884
SHIELS, Dessie	(Ind)	1,876	(+27)	1,903	(+160)	2,063	(+22)	2,085
STEWART, Ryan	(Ind)	203						
NON-TRANSFERABLE				22		52		0

Distribution of **Blaney** votes		Distribution of **McGarvey** votes		Distribution of **Shiels** votes		Distribution of **Ryan** votes		Distribution of **McHugh** surplus	
5		6		7		8		9	
(+216)	4,535	(+266)	4,801	(+845)	5,646	(+485)	6,131	(+1,088)	7,219
(+248)	7,064	(+191)	7,255	(+256)	7,511	(+734)	8,245	(+731)	8,976
(+244)	1,653								
(+138)	7,662	(+485)	8,147	(+584)	8,731	(+3,318)	12,049		
(+66)	4,950	(+26)	4,976	(+105)	5,081				
(+214)	2,299	(+306)	2,605						
201		379		815		544		750	

Donegal South-West

Statistics

Seats	3
Electorate	64,568
Total Poll	43,595
Turnout	67.5
Spoiled	332
Total Valid Poll	43,263
Quota	10,816
Candidates	9

Party Share of Vote

1st Preferences	Number	%	Gain/Loss
Fine Gael	8,589	19.85	-3.15
Labour	2,209	5.11	2.32
Fianna Fáil	9,745	22.53	-28.00
Sinn Féin	14,262	32.97	11.73
United Left Alliance	0	0.00	0.00
Green Party	527	1.22	-0.26
Others	7,931	18.33	17.36

	Quotas	Seats
Fine Gael	0.8	1
Labour	0.2	–
Fianna Fáil	0.9	–
Sinn Féin	1.3	1
United Left Alliance	0	–
Green Party	0	–
Others	0.7	1

Ind gains 1 from FF.

Pearse Doherty (SF)

Home Address
Machaire Chlochair, Na Doiri Beaga, Leitir Ceanainn.
Constituency Office
Ard Na gCeapari, Middletown, Derrybeg, Co. Donegal
Contact Details
Constituency Office: (074) 953 2832.
Dáil Office: (01) 618 3960.
Mobile: (086) 381 7747.
Email: pearse.doherty@oireachtas.ie.
Website: www.pearsedoherty.ie.
Birth Place/Date
Glasgow, 6 July 1977.
Marital Status
Married to Róisín. Two sons.
Education
Pobal Scoil Gaoth Dobhair. DIT (Certificate in Civil Engineering).
Occupation
Full-time public representative.

Pearse Doherty is Sinn Féin's spokesperson on Finance.

He was first elected to the Dáil at a by-election in November 2010 which was forced on the then Fianna Fáil–Green Party government by a High Court case by him. He had previously contested the 2002 and 2007 general elections and the European Parliament election in 2004.

Elected to the Agricultural Panel of the Seanad in 2007, becoming the first Sinn Féin senator. Elected to Donegal County Council 2004.

Dinny McGinley (FG)

Home Address
Bunbeg, Co. Donegal.
Contact Details
Constituency Office: (074) 953 1025.
Dáil Office: (01) 618 3452.
Mobile: (087) 241 4809.
Email: dinny.mcginley@oireachtas.ie.
Birth Place/Date
Gweedore, Co. Donegal, 27 April 1945.
Marital Status
Single.
Education
Coláiste Íosagáin, Ballyvourney, Co. Cork. St Patrick's Teachers' Training College, Drumcondra, Dublin. UCD (BA, HDipEd).
Occupation
Full-time public representative. Formerly national school teacher/principal.

Dinny McGinley was appointed Minister of State for Gaeltacht Affairs on 10 March 2011.

He has been re-elected at every election since 1982 and was Fine Gael deputy spokesperson on Community, Equality and Gaeltacht Affairs in the last Dáil.

Chairperson, Joint Oireachtas Committee on the Irish Language 1995–97. Member, British–Irish Parliamentary Body 1993–97. Former member of the Joint Oireachtas Committees on Social Affairs, and Small Business.

Member, Donegal Vocational Education Committee 1991–99. Member of the Irish National Teachers' Organisation since 1965. Member of Comhairle Raidió na Gaeltachta 1977–80.

Thomas Pringle (Ind)

Home Address
151 Church Road, Killybegs, Co. Donegal.
Constituency Office
Connolly House, Bridge Street, Killybegs.
Contact Details
Constituency Office: (074) 974 1880.
Dáil Office: (01) 618 3038.
Email: thomas.pringle@oireachtas.ie.
Website: www.thomaspringle.ie.
Birth Place/Date
Dublin, August 1967.
Marital Status
Married. Three children.
Education
St Catherine's Vocational School, Killybegs.
Letterkenny Institute of Technology.
Occupation
Public representative. Formerly employee of
Donegal County Council.

Thomas Pringle is a new deputy.

Elected to Donegal County Council in 1999 as
an Independent. Subsequently joined Sinn
Féin and re-elected to council for Sinn Féin in
2004. Independent again in 2007 and re-
elected in 2009. Contested the 2002 general
election and 2010 by-election without
success.

Donegal South-West

Seats 3
Quota 10,816

COUNT	1	Distribution of **Doherty** surplus 2		Distribution of **Duffy, Sweeney** votes 3		Distribution of **McBrearty, McCahill** votes 4		Distribution of **Coughlan** votes 5	
COUGHLAN, Mary* (FF)	4,956	(+216)	5,172	(+87)	5,259	(+396)	5,655		
DOHERTY, Pearse* (SF)	14,262								
DUFFY, John (GP)	527	(+141)	668						
MCBREARTY, Frank (Lab)	2,209	(+673)	2,882	(+121)	3,003				
MCCAHILL, Stephen (Ind)	1,831	(+206)	2,037	(+104)	2,141				
MCGINLEY, Dinny* (FG)	8,589	(+539)	9,128	(+159)	9,287	(+1,300)	10,587	(+782)	11,369
Ó DOMHNAILL, Brian (FF)	4,789	(+358)	5,147	(+89)	5,236	(+488)	5,724	(+3,110)	8,834
PRINGLE, Thomas (Ind)	5,845	(+1,186)	7,031	(+333)	7,364	(+1,775)	9,139	(+1,036)	10,175
SWEENEY, Ann (Ind)	255	(+127)	382						
NON-TRANSFERABLE			0		157		1,185		727

Pat Rabbitte in Korky's shoe shop, Grafton Street, where the Labour Party had a press conference to draw attention to their proposals for supporting the retail sector. Photograph: Bryan O'Brien.

Dublin Central

Statistics

Seats	4
Electorate	56,892
Total Poll	35,069
Turnout	61.6%
Spoiled	457
Total Valid Poll	34,612
Quota	6,923
Candidates	16

Party Share of Vote

1st Preferences	Number	%	Gain/Loss
Fine Gael	6,903	19.94	10.41
Labour	9,787	28.28	15.71
Fianna Fáil	5,141	14.85	-29.60
Sinn Féin	4,526	13.08	3.89
United Left Alliance	0	0.00	0.00
Green Party	683	1.97	-3.79
Others	7,572	21.88	3.93

	Quotas	Seats
Fine Gael	1	1
Labour	1.4	1
Fianna Fáil	0.7	–
Sinn Féin	0.7	1
United Left Alliance	0	–
Green Party	0.1	–
Others	1.1	1

FG gain 1, SF gain 1; from FF.

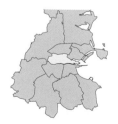

Paschal Donohoe (FG)

Home Address
86 Shandon Park, Phibsborough, Dublin 7.
Contact Details
Dáil Office: (01) 618 3907.
Mobile: (087) 281 6868.
Email: paschal.donohoe@gmail.com.
Birth Place/Date
Dublin, 19 September 1974.
Marital Status
Married to Justine. Two children.
Education
St Declan's CBS Cabra. TCD (Economics and Politics).
Occupation
Public representative. Formerly sales manager with multinational company.

Paschal Donohoe is a new deputy.

Elected to the Administrative Panel of the Seanad in 2007 after running unsuccessfully for the Dáil in Dublin Central. Party spokesperson on Transport in the Seanad 2007–11.

Member of Dublin City Council for Cabra/Glasnevin electoral area 2004–07.

Joe Costello (Lab)

Home Address
66 Aughrim Street, Dublin 7.
Constituency Office
334 North Circular Road, Dublin 7.
Contact Details
Home: (01) 838 5355. Constituency Office: (01) 830 8182. Dáil Office: (01) 618 3896.
Mobile: (087) 245 0777.
Email: joe.costello@oireachtas.ie;
joecostellotd@gmail.com.
Website: http://joecostellotd.blogspot.com.
Birth Place/Date
Sligo, 13 July 1945.
Marital Status
Married to Emer Malone.
Education
Summerhill College, Sligo. St Patrick's College, Maynooth. UCD.
Occupation
Public representative. Formerly secondary school teacher.

Joe Costello was first elected to the Dáil in 1992, lost his seat in 1997 and re-gained it in 2002. He was Labour Party spokesperson on European Affairs and Human Rights (from 2007 to June 2010) and on Transport (June 2010–11) in the last Dáil.

Member: Dáil Sub-Committee on the Barron Report on the Dublin and Monaghan Bombings of 1974; Dáil Select Committee on European Affairs 2006–07. Senator, Administrative Panel, 1989–92. Party leader in Seanad 1997–2002. Spokesperson on: Education; Science; Trade and Employment; Sport; and Finance. Member, Joint Committee on Family, Community and Social Affairs.

Former Vice-Chairman, Parliamentary Labour Party. Member, British–Irish Inter-Parliamentary Body.

Member, Dublin City Council 1991–2003. Deputy Lord Mayor 1991–92. Former President of Association of Secondary Teachers of Ireland. Prisoners' Rights Organisation 1973–87 (Chairman 1975–85).

His wife, Councillor Emer Costello, was Lord Mayor of Dublin 2009–10.

Maureen O'Sullivan (Ind)

Home Address
39 Fairfield Avenue, East Wall, Dublin 3.
Contact Details
Dáil Office: (01) 618 3488; Fax: (01) 618 4195.
Mobile: (087) 055 0223.
Email: maureen.osullivan@oireachtas.ie.
Website: www.maureenosullivan.ie
Birth Place/Date
Dublin, 10 March 1951.
Marital Status
Single.
Education:
Sisters of Charity, King's Inn Street, Dublin 1.
UCD (BA, HDipEd). Dip Guidance Counselling.
Occupation
Full-time public representative. Formerly
secondary school teacher.

First elected at a by-election in June 2009
caused by the death of Independent deputy
Tony Gregory, with whom she was associated
politically.

Co-opted briefly before by-election onto
Dublin City Council in 2009. Deeply involved in
community groups in East Wall area. Member
of Foreign Affairs Committee in 30th Dáil.
Member of the Technical Group of
Independent and United Left Alliance TDs in
the Dáil.

Mary Lou McDonald (SF)

Constituency Office
58 Faussagh Avenue, Cabra, Dublin 7; 139
North Strand Road, Dublin 3.
Contact Details
Constituency Office: (01) 868 3934;
(01) 727 7102. Dáil Office: (01) 618 3230.
Email: marylou.mcdonald@oireachtas.ie.
Website: www.maryloumcdonald.ie
Birth Place/Date
Dublin, 1 May 1969.
Marital Status
Married to Martin. One daughter, one son.
Education
TCD. University of Limerick. DCU. (BA in
English Language and Literature; MA in
European Law, Economics and Politics.)
Occupation
Full-time public representative.

Mary Lou McDonald is a new deputy.

Deputy Leader Sinn Féin and party
spokesperson on Public Expenditure and
Reform.

Previously MEP for Dublin from 2004–09,
when she lost her seat. Contested
unsuccessfully the general elections in 2002
(Dublin West) and 2007 (Dublin Central).

Before entering politics she was a consultant
for the Irish Productivity Centre, Researcher
for the Institute of European Affairs, and a
trainer in the trade union sponsored
Partnership Unit of the Educational and
Training Services Trust.

Dublin Central

Seats 4 Quota 6,923			Distribution of **Cooney, Hollywood, Hyland, Johnston** votes		Distribution of **Kearney, O'Loughlin, Steenson** votes	
COUNT		1		2		3
BRADY, Cyprian*	(FF)	1,637	(+2)	1,639	(+36)	1,675
BURKE, Christy	(Ind)	1,315	(+8)	1,323	(+70)	1,393
CLANCY, Aine	(Lab)	3,514	(+18)	3,532	(+264)	3,796
COONEY, Benny	(Ind)	25				
COSTELLO, Joe	(Lab)	6,273	(+16)	6,289	(+139)	6,428
DONOHOE, Paschal	(FG)	6,903	(+30)	6,933		
FITZPATRICK, Mary	(FF)	3,504	(+10)	3,514	(+92)	3,606
HOLLYWOOD, Thomas	(Ind)	65				
HYLAND, John Pluto	(Ind)	77				
JOHNSTON, Liam	(Ind)	48				
KEARNEY, Phil	(GP)	683	(+20)	703		
MCDONALD, Mary Lou	(SF)	4,526	(+10)	4,536	(+118)	4,654
O'SULLIVAN, Maureen*	(Ind)	4,139	(+32)	4,171	(+336)	4,507
O'LOUGHLIN, Paul	(CSP)	235	(+16)	251		
PERRY, Cieran	(Ind)	1,394	(+32)	1,426	(+106)	1,532
STEENSON, Malachy	(Ind)	274	(+11)	285		
NON-TRANSFERABLE				10		78

Distribution of **Burke** votes		Distribution of **Perry** votes		Distribution of **Brady** votes		Distribution of **Clancy** votes		Distribution of **O'Sullivan** surplus	
4		**5**		**6**		**7**		**8**	
(+50)	1,725	(+28)	1,753						
(+57)	3,853	(+125)	3,978	(+157)	4,135				
(+377)	6,805	(+310)	7,115						
(+22)	3,628	(+88)	3,716	(+1,105)	4,821	(+582)	5,403	(+340)	5,743
(+411)	5,065	(+357)	5,422	(+131)	5,553	(+656)	6,209	(+378)	6,587
(+323)	4,830	(+554)	5,384	(+202)	5,586	(+2,055)	7,641		
(+83)	1,615								
70		153		158		842		0	

Dublin Mid-West

Statistics

Seats	4
Electorate	64,880
Total Poll	43,193
Turnout	66.6%
Spoiled	471
Total Valid Poll	42,722
Quota	8,545
Candidates	14

Party Share of Vote

1st Preferences	Number	%	Gain/Loss
Fine Gael	13,214	30.93	18.93
Labour	13,138	30.75	19.84
Fianna Fáil	5,043	11.80	-21.20
Sinn Féin	5,060	11.84	2.57
United Left Alliance	3,093	7.24	7.24
Green Party	1,484	3.47	-7.36
Others	1,690	3.96	-7.54

	Quotas	Seats
Fine Gael	1.5	2
Labour	1.5	2
Fianna Fáil	0.6	–
Sinn Féin	0.6	–
United Left Alliance	0.4	–
Green Party	0.2	–
Others	0.2	–

FG gain 2, Lab 1; from FF, GP and Ind.

Joanna Tuffy (Lab)

Home Address
46A Esker Lawns, Lucan, Co. Dublin.
Constituency Office
Dispensary Lane, Lucan.
Contact Details
Constituency Office: (01) 621 8400.
Dáil Office: (01) 618 3822.
Email: joanna.tuffy@oireachtas.ie.
Website: www.joannatuffy.ie.
Twitter: @joannatuffytd.
Birth Place/Date
England, 9 March 1965.
Marital Status
Partner Philip. One daughter.
Education
St Joseph's College Lucan. TCD (BA English and History). DIT (Diploma in Legal Studies). Law Society (qualified as solicitor).
Occupation
Public representative.

First elected to the Dáil in 2007. Labour Party spokesperson on Environment and Heritage in the last Dáil.

Elected to the Seanad on the Administrative Panel in 2002 after unsuccessfully contesting the general election. Member, Joint Oireachtas Committee on Justice, Equality, Defence and Women's Rights, and Joint Committee on Education and Science 2002–07. Party spokesperson in the Seanad on: Education and Science; Justice, Equality, Law Reform and Defence.

Member, South Dublin County Council 1999–2003.

Frances Fitzgerald (FG)

Home Address
116 Georgian Village, Castleknock, Dublin 15.
Constituency Office
Laurel House, New Road, Clondalkin, Dublin 22.
Contact Details
Constituency Office: (01) 457 7712.
Dáil Office: (01) 635 4000.
E-mail: omc@health.gov.ie.
Website: www.omc.gov.ie.
Birth Place/Date
Croom, Co. Limerick, August 1950.
Marital Status
Married to Michael Fitzgerald. Three sons.
Education
Sion Hill, Blackrock, Co. Dublin. UCD (BSocSc). London School of Economics (MSc in Social Administration and Social Work).
Occupation
Government Minister.

Appointed Minister for Children and Youth Affairs on 9 March 2011.

She was first elected to the Dáil for Dublin South-East in 1992 but lost her seat in 2002. Elected to the Seanad on the Labour Panel in 2007 until her re-election to the Dáil in 2011. Leader of Fine Gael in the Seanad 2007–11. Previously Fine Gael front bench spokesperson for a number of portfolios.

Formerly Chairperson of the National Women's Council and Vice-President of the European Women's Lobby.

Robert Dowds (Lab)

Home Address
43 Castle Park, Clondalkin, Dublin 22.
Constituency Office
3 Main Street, Clondalkin, Dublin 22.
Contact Details
Office: (01) 618 3446. Mobile: (087) 652 0360.
Email: robert.dowds@oireachtas.ie.
Website: www.robertdowds.ie.
Facebook: Robert Dowds.
Twitter: @robert_dowdsTD.
Birth Place/Date
Dublin, 2 May 1953.
Marital Status
Married to Katherine. One son, one daughter.
Education
TCD (BA [Hons]). St Patrick's College,
Drumcondra (HDipEd).
Occupation
Public representative; primary school teacher.

Robert Dowds is a new deputy.

Elected to Dublin South County Council in
1999, topping the poll in the Clondalkin ward
in 2009. Mayor of South Dublin, 2004–05.

Taught at Scoil Mochua Clondalkin, a school
for young people with physical disabilities.
Previously principal of St John's National
School in Clondalkin.

Derek Keating (FG)

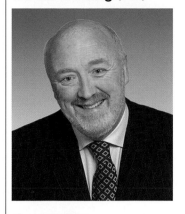

Home Address
66 Beech Park, Lucan, Co. Dublin.
Contact Details
Dáil Office: (01) 618 4014.
Mobile: (087) 285 7435.
Email: derek.keating@oireachtas.ie;
info@derekkeating.net.
Website: www.derekkeating.net.
Birth Place/Date
Ballyfermot, Dublin, May 1955.
Marital Status
Married to Áine. Two daughters.
Education
De La Salle primary and secondary schools,
Ballyfermot.
Occupation
Full-time public representative.

Derek Keating is a new deputy.

He has been a member of South Dublin
County Council since 1999, first elected as an
Independent until joining Fine Gael in 2008.
He has also been a member of Fianna Fáil and
the Progressive Democrats at different times.

Fine Gael Whip on the council from 2009 to
2011. Former Deputy Mayor of South Dublin
County Council.

Director of Pieta House, the suicide
prevention organisation.

Dublin Mid-West

		1	Distribution of **Smith** votes	**2**	Distribution of **McHale** votes	**3**	Distribution of **McGrath** votes	**4**
Seats 4 Quota 8,545								
COUNT								
CONNOLLY, Robert	(ULA)	622	(+2)	624	(+10)	634	(+3)	637
CURRAN, John*	(FF)	5,043	(+4)	5,047	(+21)	5,068	(+27)	5,095
DOWDS, Robert	(Lab)	5,643	(+2)	5,645	(+16)	5,661	(+34)	5,695
FINNEGAN, Mick	(WP)	694	(+6)	700	(+12)	712	(+10)	722
FITZGERALD, Frances	(FG)	7,281	(+4)	7,285	(+18)	7,303	(+20)	7,323
GOGARTY, Paul*	(GP)	1,484	(+6)	1,490	(+8)	1,498	(+11)	1,509
KEATING, Derek	(FG)	5,933	(+5)	5,938	(+7)	5,945	(+19)	5,964
KENNY, Gino	(ULA)	2,471	(+10)	2,481	(+32)	2,513	(+23)	2,536
MCGRATH, Colm	(Ind)	253	(+16)	269	(+50)	319		
MCHALE, Jim	(Ind)	255	(+9)	264				
Ó BROIN, Eoin	(SF)	5,060	(+6)	5,066	(+22)	5,088	(+29)	5,117
RYAN, Michael Anthony	(Ind)	375	(+22)	397	(+32)	429	(+85)	514
SMITH, Niall	(Ind)	113						
TUFFY, Joanna*	(Lab)	7,495	(+18)	7,513	(+20)	7,533	(+20)	7,553
NON-TRANSFERABLE				3		16		38

Distribution of **Ryan** votes		Distribution of **Connolly, Finnegan** votes		Distribution of **Gogarty, Kenny** votes		Distribution of **Curran** votes		Distribution of **Fitzgerald** surplus	
5		6		7		8		9	
(+12)	649								
(+35)	5,130	(+63)	5,193	(+320)	5,513				
(+39)	5,734	(+136)	5,870	(+649)	6,519	(+1,415)	7,934	(+178)	8,112
(+13)	735								
(+101)	7,424	(+69)	7,493	(+410)	7,903	(+1,310)	9,213		
(+25)	1,534	(+71)	1,605						
(+28)	5,992	(+80)	6,072	(+431)	6,503	(+741)	7,244	(+459)	7,703
(+61)	2,597	(+462)	3,059						
(+47)	5,164	(+235)	5,399	(+1,229)	6,628	(+492)	7,120	(+31)	7,151
(+80)	7,633	(+194)	7,827	(+1,121)	8,948				
	73		74		504		1,555		0

Dublin North

Statistics

Seats	4
Electorate	70,413
Total Poll	49,799
Turnout	70.7%
Spoiled	452
Total Valid Poll	49,347
Quota	9,870
Candidates	9

Party Share of Vote

1st Preferences Number		%	Gain/Loss
Fine Gael	15,488	31.39	17.35
Labour	13,014	26.37	16.76
Fianna Fáil	7,634	15.47	-26.63
Sinn Féin	0	0.00%	-2.66
United Left Alliance	7,513	15.22	15.22
Green Party	4,186	8.48	-8.17
Others	1,512	3.06	-9.33

	Quotas	Seats
Fine Gael	1.6	2
Labour	1.3	1
Fianna Fáil	0.8	–
Sinn Féin	0	–
United Left Alliance	0.8	1
Green Party	0.4	–
Others	0.2	–

FG gain 1, ULA gain 1, Lab gain 1; from FF, GP.

James Reilly (FG)

Home Address
Seafoam, South Shore Road, Rush, Co. Dublin.
Constituency Office
19 Bridge Street, Balbriggan, Co. Dublin.
Contact Details
Constituency Office: (01) 843 7014.
Dáil Office: (01) 618 3749.
Email: james.reilly@oireachtas.ie.
Birth Place/ Date
Dublin, 16 August 1955.
Marital Status
Married to Dorothy McEvoy. One daughter, four sons.
Education
St Conleth's and CUS, Dublin. Gormanston, Co. Meath. Royal College of Surgeons. Royal College of General Practitioners. Irish College of General Practitioners. Master of Medical Science at UCD.
Occupation
Government Minister; medical doctor.

Deputy Leader of Fine Gael since 2010, James Reilly was appointed Minister for Health on 9 March 2011.

First elected in 2007, he strongly supported Enda Kenny as Party Leader in 2010, replacing Kenny's rival, Richard Bruton, as Deputy Leader. Party spokesperson on Health from 2007. A former president of the Irish Medical Organisation; Chairman and President of the GP Committee of the IMO. Chairman of the GP Development Team and the IMO representative at the World Medical Association.

Former member, Eastern Health Board; chairman of its Community Care Committee and Psychiatric Hospitals and Mental Health Committee. Subsequently served on the Eastern Regional Health Authority and on the Northern Area Health Board. Former member of the Council of the Society for Autistic Children.

Brendan Ryan (Lab)

Home Address
Baltrasna, Skerries, Co. Dublin.
Contact Details
Constituency Office: (01) 849 0265.
Dáil Office: (01) 618 3421.
Email: brendan.ryan@oireachtas.ie;
bren@brendan-ryan.ie.
Website: www.brendan-ryan.ie.
Birth Place/Date
Portrane, Co. Dublin, 15 February 1953.
Marital Status
Married to Margie Monks. Three daughters.
Education
DIT. UCD. DCU. (Degree in Chemistry; Masters degrees in Food Science and Business Administration.)
Occupation
Full-time public representative. Formerly operations manager.

Brendan Ryan is a new deputy.

Elected to the Administrative Panel of the Seanad in 2007 after failing to win Dáil seat. Labour Party spokesperson on Education and Science, Transport, and Defence in Seanad. Member of the Joint Oireachtas Committee on Enterprise, Trade and Employment, and of the Joint Oireachtas Committee on Education and Science during last Dáil.

Brother of Seán Ryan, TD for Dublin North 1989–97 and 1998–2007; Senator 1997–98.

Clare Daly (SP)

Home Address
21 Elmood Drive, Swords, Co. Dublin.
Contact Details
Dáil Office: (01) 618 3390.
Mobile: (087) 241 5576.
Email: clare.daly@oireachtas.ie.
Website: www.claredaly.ie
Birth Place/Date
April 1968.
Marital Status
Married.
Education
DCU (Accounting and Finance).
Occupation
Public representative; airport worker.

Clare Daly is a new deputy.

She was elected to Fingal County Council in 1999 and re-elected again in 2004 and 2009. Trade union shop steward with SIPTU at Aer Lingus. Former president of Students' Union at NIHE/DCU.

Alan Farrell (FG)

Home Address
4 Drynam Drive, Drynam Hall, Kinsealy, Co. Dublin.
Constituency Office
Drynam Hall, Kettles Lane, Swords, Co. Dublin.
Contact Details
Office: (01) 618 4008.
Email: alan.farrell@oireachtas.ie.
Website: www.alanfarrell.ie.
Twitter: @alanfarrell.
Birth Place/Date
Dublin, 29 December 1977.
Marital Status
Married to Emma Doyle.
Education
Malahide Community School. Chanel College, Dublin. WIT.
Occupation
Public representative; estate agent.

Alan Farrell is a new deputy.

Elected to Fingal County Council at his first attempt in June 2004; Deputy Mayor 2005; Mayor 2007. Re-elected in 2009 in a newly amalgamated Howth/Malahide electoral area; tripling his first preference vote, he was returned to Fingal County Council.

Dublin North

		COUNT 1	Distribution of **Reilly** surplus 2		Distribution of **Harrold** votes 3	
DALY, Clare	(SP)	7,513	(+20)	7,533	(+342)	7,875
FARRELL, Alan	(FG)	5,310	(+165)	5,475	(+248)	5,723
HARROLD, Mark	(Ind)	1,512	(+6)	1,518		
KELLEHER, Tom	(Lab)	3,205	(+10)	3,215	(+152)	3,367
KENNEDY, Michael*	(FF)	3,519	(+12)	3,531	(+73)	3,604
O'BRIEN, Darragh*	(FF)	4,115	(+9)	4,124	(+125)	4,249
REILLY, Dr. James*	(FG)	10,178				
RYAN, Brendan	(Lab)	9,809	(+59)	9,868	(+190)	10,058
SARGENT, Trevor*	(GP)	4,186	(+27)	4,213	(+270)	4,483
NON-TRANSFERABLE				0		118

Seats 4
Quota 9,870

Distribution of **Kelleher** votes		Distribution of **Kennedy** votes		Distribution of **Sargent** votes		Distribution of **Daly** surplus	
4		**5**		**6**		**7**	
(+1,221)	9,096	(+369)	9,465	(+1,707)	11,172		
(+683)	6,406	(+263)	6,669	(+1,781)	8,450	(+709)	9,159
(+201)	3,805						
(+158)	4,407	(+2,479)	6,886	(+935)	7,821	(+246)	8,067
(+686)	5,169	(+441)	5,610				
418		253		1,187		347	

Dublin North-Central

Statistics

Seats	3
Electorate	52,992
Total Poll	39,187
Turnout	73.9%
Spoiled	413
Total Valid Poll	38,774
Quota	9,694
Candidates	9

Party Share of Vote

1st Preferences	Number	%	Gain/Loss
Fine Gael	14,644	37.77	12.22
Labour	8,731	22.52	15.24
Fianna Fáil	5,017	12.94	-31.08
Sinn Féin	2,140	5.52	1.74
United Left Alliance	1,424	3.67	3.67
Green Party	501	1.29	-3.90
Others	6,317	16.29	2.10

	Quotas	Seats
Fine Gael	1.5	1
Labour	0.9	1
Fianna Fáil	0.5	–
Sinn Féin	0.2	–
United Left Alliance	0.1	–
Green Party	0.1	–
Others	0.7	1

Lab gain 1 from FF.

Richard Bruton (FG)

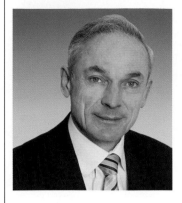

Home Address
210 Griffith Avenue, Drumcondra, Dublin 9.
Contact Details
Office: (01) 618 3103.
Email: richard.bruton@deti.ie.
Website: www.richardbruton.net. Facebook: richardbrutontd. Twitter: @richardbrutontd.
Birth Place/Date
Dublin, 15 March 1953.
Marital Status
Married to Susan Meehan. Two sons, two daughters.
Education
Belvedere College, Dublin. Clongowes Wood College, Co Kildare. UCD. Nuffield College, Oxford. BA, MA, MPhil (Oxon) Economics.
Occupation
Government Minister.

Richard Bruton TD was appointed Minister for Jobs, Enterprise and Innovation on 9 March 2011.

He was Minister for Enterprise and Employment 1994–97 and chaired the European Industrial Council during Ireland's presidency in 1996. Minister of State at the Department of Industry and Commerce 1986–87.

Twice ran for the leadership of Fine Gael, against Michael Noonan in 2002 and against Enda Kenny in 2010. Deputy Leader of Fine Gael in 2002.

First elected to the Dáil in 1982 and re-elected at all subsequent general elections. Held a large number of shadow cabinet positions, including spokesperson on Finance in the 30th Dáil until his challenge to Kenny's leadership. Previously spokesperson on: Education and Science; Employment; Economic Planning; and Public Sector Reform; as well as being Director of Policy.

Member of Meath County Council 1979–82 and Dublin City Council 1991–94 and 1999–2003.

He is a research economist by profession and brother of John Bruton, Taoiseach from 1994–97 and leader of Fine Gael 1990–2001.

Aodhán Ó Ríordáin (Lab)

Constituency Office
203 Philipsburgh Avenue, Marino, Dublin 3.
Contact Details
Dáil Office: (01) 618 3209.
Mobile: (086) 819 0336.
Email: aodhan.oriordain@oireachtas.ie.
Website: www.aodhanoriordain.blogspot.com.
Twitter: @aodhanoriordain.
Birth Place/Date
Dublin, 22 July 1976.
Marital Status
Married to Áine Kerr.
Education
Malahide Community School. UCD. Marino Institute of Education.
Occupation
Public representative. Formerly primary school principal.

Aodhán Ó Ríordáin is a new deputy; elected on his first attempt.

Principal of St Laurence O'Toole's Girls' N.S. in Sheriff Street, Dublin 1 until his election. Elected to Dublin City Council for the North Inner City ward in 2004 and re-elected in 2009 for the Clontarf ward.

Finian McGrath (Ind)

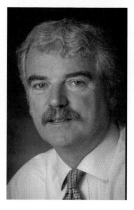

Home Address
342 Charlemont, Griffith Avenue, Dublin 9.
Constituency Office
Le Chéile Community Centre, Donnycarney,
Dublin 5.
Contact Details
Office: (01) 618 3031. Mobile: (087) 673 8041.
Email: finian.mgrath@oireachtas.ie.
Website: www.finianmcgrath.ie.
Birth Place/Date
Tuam, Co. Galway, 9 April 1953.
Marital Status
Widower. Two daughters.
Education
Tuam CBS. St Patrick's Training College,
Drumcondra, Dublin.
Occupation
Full-time public representative.

First elected as an independent in 2002; re-
elected in 2007. Initially supported the Fianna
Fáil/Green Party/Progressive Democrats
government in the 30th Dáil.

He campaigned as a member of the
Independent Health Alliance, calling for
improved health services in the 2002 election.
Contested the 1997 general election
unsuccessfully.

Member, Dublin City Council 1999–2003.
Board member of: Northside Centre for the
Unemployed, Coolock; Orthopaedic Hospital,
Clontarf.

Member, Irish National Teachers'
Organisation. Former primary school principal.

Dublin North-Central

Seats 3 Quota 9,694		COUNT 1	Distribution of **Clarke, Cooney** votes 2		Distribution of **Lyons** votes 3	
BRUTON, Richard*	(FG)	9,685	(+105)	9,790		
CLARKE, Paul	(Ind)	331				
COONEY, Donna	(GP)	501				
HAUGHEY, Sean*	(FF)	5,017	(+60)	5,077	(+51)	5,128
LYONS, John	(ULA)	1,424	(+163)	1,587		
MCCORMACK, Helen	(SF)	2,140	(+47)	2,187	(+415)	2,602
MCGRATH, Finian*	(Ind)	5,986	(+170)	6,156	(+545)	6,701
Ó'MUIRÍ, Naoise	(FG)	4,959	(+74)	5,033	(+65)	5,098
Ó RÍORDÁIN, Aodhán	(Lab)	8,731	(+180)	8,911	(+418)	9,329
NON-TRANSFERABLE			33		93	

Distribution of **McCormack** votes		Distribution of **Ó Ríordáin** surplus		Distribution of **Bruton** surplus		Distribution of **Haughey** votes	
4		5		6		7	
(+167)	5,295	(+43)	5,338	(+10)	5,348		
(+1,076)	7,777	(+342)	8,119	(+31)	8,150	(+2,875)	11,025
(+142)	5,240	(+113)	5,353	(+50)	5,403	(+996)	6,399
(+863)	10,192						
354		0		5		1,477	

Dublin North-East

Statistics

Seats	3
Electorate	58,542
Total Poll	42,287
Turnout	72.2%
Spoiled	448
Total Valid Poll	41,839
Quota	10,460
Candidates	11

Party Share of Vote

1st Preferences	Number	%	Gain/Loss
Fine Gael	12,332	29.47	6.53
Labour	14,371	34.35	19.19
Fianna Fáil	4,794	11.46	-28.23
Sinn Féin	5,032	12.03	-1.31
United Left Alliance	869	2.08	2.08
Green Party	792	1.89	-4.84
Others	3,649	8.72	8.72

	Quotas	Seats
Fine Gael	1.2	1
Labour	1.4	2
Fianna Fáil	0.5	–
Sinn Féin	0.5	–
United Left Alliance	0.1	–
Green Party	0.1	–
Others	0.3	–

Lab gain 1 from FF.

Terence Flanagan (FG)

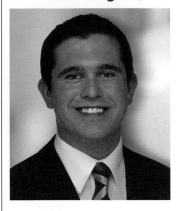

Home Address
74 Old Malahide Road, Dublin 5.
Contact Details
Office: (01) 618 3634. Mobile: (087) 995 2031.
Email: terence.flanagan@oireachtas.ie.
Birth Place/Date
Dublin, January 1975.
Marital Status
Single.
Education
St David's Boys' N.S., Kilmore Road, Dublin 5.
Chanel College, Malahide Road, Dublin 5.
Dublin Business School, Aungier Street,
Dublin 2.
Occupation
Public representative. Formerly accountant.

Terence Flanagan was first elected to the Dáil in 2007, on his first attempt.

He was re-elected in 2011 by topping the poll in the Dublin North-East constituency.

Co-opted to Dublin City Council in October 2003 to replace Deputy Richard Bruton, for whom he was a campaign worker for many years.

Percussion player with the Artane Senior Band, having started in the Artane Boys' Band.

Thomas P. Broughan (Lab)

Home Address
18 Thormanby Lawns, Howth, Dublin 13.
Contact Details
Constituency Office: (01) 847 7634.
Dáil Office: (01) 618 3557.
Email: thomas_p_broughan@oireachtas.ie.
Website: www.tommybroughan.com.
Twitter: @TommyBroughanTD.
Birth Place/Date
Clondalkin, Co. Dublin, August 1947.
Marital Status
Married to Carmel.
Education
Moyle Park College, Clondalkin. UCD (BA, HDipEd). London University (BSc [Econ]; MSc [Econ]).
Occupation
Full-time public representative. Formerly teacher.

First elected to the Dáil in 1992; re-elected in all subsequent general elections. Labour Party spokesperson on a variety of portfolios including: Enterprise, Trade and Employment (28th and 29th Dáileanna); Social Protection (28th Dáil); Communications, Marine and Natural Resources (Energy) (29th Dáil); and Transport (30th Dáil, up to July 2010).

Member of the Public Accounts Committee for eight years in the 27th and 30th Dáileanna (up to July 2010) and has worked on a wide range of other Dáil committees, including: Finance and the Public Service; Enterprise, Trade and Employment; Social and Family Affairs; Communications, Marine and Natural Resources (Energy); Transport; An Coiste Gaeilge; the Committee on Procedures and Privileges; and the Dáil Services Committee.

Labour's Deputy Whip in the 29th and 30th Dáileanna (from 2002). Elected to Dublin City Council in 1991 and 1999. Leader of the Labour Party and the Rainbow Alliance on Dublin City Council 1991–97 and 2001–03.

Sean Kenny (Lab)

Home Address
44 Woodbine Road, Raheny, Dublin 5.
Contact Details
Home: (01) 848 1806.
Email: info@seankenny.ie.
Website: www.seankenny.ie.
Birth Place/Date
Galway, 1 October 1942.
Marital Status
Married to Mairéad. Two children.
Education
Garbally College, Ballinasloe. TCD.
Occupation
Full-time public representative. Formerly
Executive Officer, CIE.

Sean Kenny was previously TD for Dublin
North-East in Dáil Éireann from 1992 to 1997,
where he acted as Chairperson of the Social
Affairs Committee and as a member of the
Forum for Peace and Reconciliation. Defeated
in the 1997 General Election.

First became involved in community activity in
Raheny in 1969 though participation in local
residents' associations and as a voluntary
worker and later Director with the Raheny and
District Credit Union.

Elected to Dublin City Council from 1979 until
2011, representing Raheny and later
Donaghamede electoral areas. Lord Mayor of
Dublin 1991–92, when he played a leading
role in Dublin's year as European City of
Culture, and the celebration of Trinity College
Dublin Quatercentenary. He received an
honorary degree from the college.

Dublin North-East

COUNT		1	Distribution of **Flanagan** surplus	2	Distribution of **Broughan** surplus	3	Distribution of **Eastwood, Sexton** votes	4
BLANEY, Eamonn	(Ind)	1,773	(+121)	1,894	(+19)	1,913	(+186)	2,099
BROUGHAN, Thomas P.*	(Lab)	10,006	(+732)	10,738				
EASTWOOD, Robert	(Ind)	242	(+22)	264	(+3)	267		
FLANAGAN, Terence*	(FG)	12,332						
GREENE, Brian	(ULA)	869	(+24)	893	(+4)	897	(+38)	935
GUERIN, Jimmy	(Ind)	1,283	(+136)	1,419	(+28)	1,447	(+125)	1,572
HEALY, David	(GP)	792	(+127)	919	(+15)	934	(+53)	987
KENNY, Sean	(Lab)	4,365	(+363)	4,728	(+157)	4,885	(+100)	4,985
O'TOOLE, Larry	(SF)	5,032	(+88)	5,120	(+23)	5,143	(+36)	5,179
POWER, Averil	(FF)	4,794	(+219)	5,013	(+23)	5,036	(+73)	5,109
SEXTON, Raymond	(Ind)	351	(+40)	391	(+6)	397		
NON-TRANSFERABLE				0		0		53

Distribution of **Greene** votes		Distribution of **Healy** votes		Distribution of **Guerin** votes		Distribution of **Blaney** votes		Distribution of **Power** votes	
	5		6		7		8		9
(+134)	2,233	(+168)	2,401	(+554)	2,955				
(+113)	1,685	(+114)	1,799						
(+62)	1,049								
(+231)	5,216	(+364)	5,580	(+420)	6,000	(+1,013)	7,013	(+2,356)	9,369
(+298)	5,477	(+77)	5,554	(+508)	6,062	(+508)	6,570	(+661)	7,231
(+25)	5,134	(+180)	5,314	(+265)	5,579	(+462)	6,041		
72		146		52		972		3,024	

Dublin North-West

Statistics

Seats	3
Electorate	49,269
Total Poll	33,262
Turnout	67.5%
Spoiled	451
Total Valid Poll	32,811
Quota	8,203
Candidates	12

Party Share of Vote

1st Preferences	Number	%	Gain/Loss
Fine Gael	5,496	16.75	6.79
Labour	14,158	43.15	22.85
Fianna Fáil	3,869	11.79	-37.05
Sinn Féin	7,115	21.68	5.95
United Left Alliance	677	2.06	2.06
Green Party	328	1.00	-1.76
Others	1,168	3.56	1.15

	Quotas	Seats
Fine Gael	0.7	–
Labour	1.7	2
Fianna Fáil	0.5	–
Sinn Féin	0.9	1
United Left Alliance	0.1	–
Green Party	0	–
Others	0.1	–

Lab gain 1, SF gain 1; from FF.

Róisín Shortall (Lab)

Home Address
12 Iveragh Road, Gaeltacht Park, Whitehall, Dublin 9.
Contact Details
Dáil Office: (01) 618 3593.
Email: roisin.shortall@oireachtas.ie.
Website: www.labour.ie/roisinshortall.
Birth Place/Date
Dublin, 25 April, 1954.
Marital Status
Married.
Education
Dominican College, Eccles Street, Dublin. UCD (BA in Economics and Politics). St Mary's College of Education, Marino, Dublin (BA NTDip Teacher of the Deaf).
Occupation
Minister of State.

Appointed Minister of State at the Department of Health, with responsibility for Primary Care, on 10 March 2011.

First elected to the Dáil in 1992; re-elected at every subsequent general election. Labour Party spokesperson on Social Protection 2007–11, and member of the Oireachtas Committee on Social Protection 2007–11. Member of the Public Accounts Committee 2007–11.

Previously Labour Party spokesperson on Transport, and on Education and Children. Member, Joint Oireachtas Committee on Transport 2003–07.

Member: Dublin City Council 1991–2003; Eastern Health Board 1991–2003 (Chairperson 1997). Board member: Ballymun Neighbourhood Council; Ballymun Local Drugs Task Force; Finglas Crime Task Force.

Dessie Ellis (SF)

Home Address
19 Dunsink Road, Finglas, Dublin 11.
Constituency Office
Unit 1, 50 Main Street, Finglas Village, Dublin 11.
Contact Details
Constituency Office: (01) 834 3390.
Mobile: (086) 854 1941.
Email: dessie.ellis@oireachtas.ie.
Website: www.dessieellis.ie.
Facebook: dessie.ellis.
Twitter: @cllrdessieellis.
Birth Place/Date
Finglas, Dublin, 1953.
Marital Status
Married.
Education
St Fergal's Boys' N.S., Finglas. Coláiste Eoin, Cappagh Road, Dublin 11. DIT.
Occupation
Full-time representative. Formerly business owner (TV repair).

Dessie Ellis is a new deputy.

Actively involved in community and republican politics all his adult life, he was elected to Dublin City Council in 1999 and unsuccessfully contested the general elections in 2002 and 2007.

Served a jail sentence in Portlaoise prison for possession of explosives and extradited to Britain in 1990 while on hunger strike on charges of causing explosions there. Acquitted by a jury in London in 1991.

John Lyons (Lab)

Home Address
Ballymun, Dublin.
Constituency Office
5 Main Street, Finglas, Dublin 11.
Contact Details
Dáil Office: (01) 618 3280.
Mobile: (087) 211 3154.
Email: john.lyons@oireachtas.ie.
Website: http://johnlyonstd.blogspot.com.
Birth Place/Date
Ballymun, Dublin, June 1977.
Marital Status
Single.
Education
Trinity Comprehensive, Ballymun. NUI
Maynooth (BA and HDip). TCD.
Occupation
Full-time public representative. Formerly
secondary teacher.

John Lyons is a new deputy.

Co-opted onto Dublin City Council in February
2008 and elected to the council in 2009.
Former teacher for students with special
needs in St Vincent's, Glasnevin.

Dublin North-West

		Distribution of **Shortall** surplus		Distribution of **Larkin** votes
Seats 3 Quota 8,203				
COUNT	1		2	3
BREEN, Gerry (FG)	2,988	(+95)	3,083	(+35) 3,118
CAREY, Pat* (FF)	3,869	(+65)	3,934	(+21) 3,955
DUNNE, John (WP)	345	(+10)	355	(+7) 362
ELLIS, Dessie (SF)	7,115	(+101)	7,216	(+13) 7,229
HOLOHAN, Ruairí (GP)	328	(+14)	342	(+6) 348
KEEGAN, Andrew (ULA)	677	(+20)	697	(+19) 716
LARKIN, Michael Pearse Francis(CSP)	173	(+2)	175	
LOFTUS, Michael J (Ind)	217	(+8)	225	(+20) 245
LYONS, John (Lab)	4,799	(+715)	5,514	(+11) 5,525
MOONEY, Sean (Ind)	433	(+11)	444	(+11) 455
SHORTALL, Róisín* (Lab)	9,359			
TORMEY, Dr. Bill (FG)	2,508	(+115)	2,623	(+13) 2,636
NON-TRANSFERABLE			0	19

Distribution of **Loftus** votes		Distribution of **Dunne, Holohan, Keegan, Mooney** votes		Distribution of **Tormey** votes		Distribution of **Carey** votes	
4		**5**		**6**		**7**	
(+14)	3,132	(+115)	3,247	(+1,663)	4,910	(+892)	5,802
(+11)	3,966	(+158)	4,124	(+226)	4,350		
(+9)	371						
(+14)	7,243	(+628)	7,871	(+248)	8,119	(+854)	8,973
(+10)	358						
(+33)	749						
(+37)	5,562	(+632)	6,194	(+474)	6,668	(+1,169)	7,837
(+84)	539						
(+12)	2,648	(+132)	2,780				
21		352		169		1,435	

Dublin South

Statistics

Seats	5
Electorate	102,387
Total Poll	73,105
Turnout	71.4%
Spoiled	459
Total Valid Poll	72,646
Quota	12,108
Candidates	16

Party Share of Vote

1st Preferences	Number	%	Gain/Loss
Fine Gael	26,404	36.35	9.09
Labour	13,059	17.98	7.55
Fianna Fáil	6,844	9.42	-31.91
Sinn Féin	1,915	2.64	-0.37
United Left Alliance	1,277	1.76	1.76
Green Party	4,929	6.78	-4.28
Others	18,218	25.08	24.79

	Quotas	Seats
Fine Gael	2.2	3
Labour	1.1	1
Fianna Fáil	0.6	–
Sinn Féin	0.2	–
United Left Alliance	0.1	–
Green Party	0.4	–
Others	1.5	1

Lab gain 1, Ind gains 1; from FF, GP.

Shane Ross (Ind)

Home Address
Blackberry Hill, Carrickmines, Dublin 18.
Constituency Office
Leinster House, Kildare Street, Dublin 2.
Contact Details
Dáil Office: (01) 618 3014.
Email: shane.ross@oireachtas.ie.
Website: www.shane-ross.ie.
Twitter: @Shane_RossTD.
Birth Place/Date
Dublin, 11 July 1949.
Marital Status
Married to Ruth Buchanan. Two children.
Education
St Stephen's School, Dundrum. Rugby School. University of Geneva. TCD.
Occupation
Independent TD; journalist; author. Formerly stockbroker.

Shane Ross is a new deputy.

He was a member of the Seanad, having won nine successive elections to represent the University of Dublin from 1981 until his election to the Dáil in March 2011. Topped the poll in South Dublin with almost 5,000 votes to spare.

Business Editor of the *Sunday Independent* and Journalist of the Year 2009 for his investigation into waste and extravagance at state agency FÁS. Author of two books on the end of the Celtic Tiger: *The Bankers: How the Banks Brought Ireland to its Knees* (Penguin Ireland, 2009); and, with Nick Webb, *Wasters* (Penguin Ireland, 2010).

Formerly: Executive Chairman of Dillon & Waldron stockbrokers; Director/Chairman of several investment funds, including the Barings New Russia and SVM Global funds; and Chairman of the Kleinwort European Privatisation Trust.

Son of John Ross, senator for University of Dublin 1961–65.

Alex White (Lab)

Home Address
30 Fortfield Road, Dublin 6W.
Constituency Office
1 Main Street, Rathfarnham, Dublin 14.
Contact Details
Dáil Office: (01) 618 3972.
Mobile: (087) 220 8533.
Email: alex.white@oireachtas.ie.
Website: www.alexwhite.ie.
Facebook: AlexWhiteTD.
Twitter: @AlexWhiteTD.
Birth Place/Date
Dublin, 3 December 1958.
Marital Status
Married to Mary Corcoran. Two children.
Education
Chanel College, Coolock. TCD (Economic and Social Studies). King's Inns, Dublin (Barrister-at-Law).
Occupation
Public representative and lawyer. Formerly TV producer.

Alex White is a new deputy.

Elected to the Seanad in 2007 after unsuccessfully standing for the Dáil. Leader of the Labour Party in the Seanad 2007–11 and party spokesperson on Children.

Current affairs producer with RTÉ for ten years; Producer of *The Gay Byrne Show* 1990–94. During his time with RTÉ, he was an active trade unionist and was Vice-President of the Public Sector region of SIPTU for four years.

Called to the Bar in 1987 and practised from 1994, specialising in employment and labour law. Became a Senior Counsel in October 2010. Lecturer on employment law and on media studies.

Elected to South Dublin County Council as a first-time candidate in June 2004 and was Deputy Mayor 2006–07.

Olivia Mitchell (FG)

Home Address
18 Ballawley Court, Dundrum, Dublin 16.
Constituency Office
Leinster House, Kildare Street, Dublin 2.
Contact Details
Dáil Office: (01) 618 3088.
Birth Place/Date
Birr, Co. Offaly, 31 July 1947.
Marital Status
Married to James Mitchell. Two sons, one daughter.
Education
Dominican Convent, Eccles Street, Dublin. TCD (BA, HDipEd).
Occupation
Full-time public representative. Formerly secondary school teacher.

A Fine Gael TD for Dublin South since 1997, Olivia Mitchell has served as party spokesperson in several portfolios: Dublin Traffic (1997–2001); Local Government and Housing (2001–02); Health (2002–04); Transport 2004–07; Arts, Sport and Tourism (2007–10). Lost her front bench position in 2011 after supporting challenge to Enda Kenny's leadership.

Received the highest vote of any female candidate in the country in the 2011 General Election.

Member of Oireachtas committees on: Health (2002–04); Transport (2004–07); Arts, Sport and Tourism (1997–2010); and Economic Regulatory Affairs (2010–11).

Member, Dublin County Council 1985–93 and of Dún Laoghaire–Rathdown County Council 1994–2003; Cathaoirleach, 1995–96.

Former member: Eastern Health Board; Dublin Regional Authority; Dublin Transport Office Steering Committee.

She was a member of the Fine Gael delegation to the Forum for Peace and Reconciliation. Former member, Co-ordinating Committee of the European Sustainable Cities and Towns Campaign.

Peter Mathews (FG)

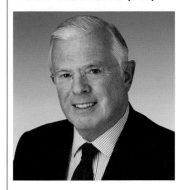

Home Address
64 The Rise, Mount Merrion, Co. Dublin.
Constituency Office
Leinster House, Kildare Street, Dublin 2.
Contact Details
Dáil Office: (01) 618 4443.
Mobile: (086) 109 1500.
Email: peter.mathews@oireachtas.ie.
Website: www.petermathewsfg.ie.
Birth Place/Date
Dublin, August 1951.
Marital Status
Married to Susan. Three sons, one daughter.
Education
Gonzaga College, Dublin. UCD (B.Comm; MBA).
Occupation
Public representative; chartered accountant; financial consultant.

Peter Mathews is a new deputy.

Elected at his first attempt, Peter Mathews is a financial and property consultant who was critical of the formation of the National Asset Management Agency (NAMA).

Alan Shatter (FG)

Home Address
57 Delbrook Manor, Ballinteer, Dublin 16.
Constituency Office
Department of Justice, 94 St Stephen's Green, Dublin 2.
Contact Details
Home: (01) 298 3045. Dáil Office: (01) 613 3911.
Email: alan.shatter@oireachtas.ie.
Website: www.alanshatter.com;
www.alanshatter.ie.
Birth Place/Date
Dublin, February 1951.
Marital Status
Married to Carol Danker. One son, one daughter.
Education
High School, Dublin. TCD. University of Amsterdam. Law School of the Incorporated Law Society.
Occupation
Government Minister; solicitor; author.

Alan Shatter was appointed Minister for Justice, Equality and Defence on 9 March 2011.

He was re-elected to the Dáil in 2007 after losing his seat in the 2002 election. He had previously been returned for Dublin South at every election since 1981.

He was Fine Gael spokesperson on: Justice, from 2010 to February 2011; Children, 2007–10; Justice, Law Reform and Defence, 2000–02; Equality and Law Reform, 1993–94; Justice, 1992–93; Labour, 1991; Environment, 1989–91; Law Reform, 1982, 1987–88.

Member: Dublin County Council 1979–93; South Dublin County Council 1994–99.

Director and former chairman of Free Legal Advice Centres (FLAC). Former Chairman of CARE (Campaign for Deprived Children). President, Irish Council Against Blood Sports, 1986–93.

Author of two books: *Shatter's Family Law in the Republic of Ireland* (4th edition, Butterworths, 1997) and *Laura* (1990, Poolbeg), a novel.

Dublin South

		Seats 5 Quota 12,108	COUNT	1	Distribution of **Ross** surplus		Distribution of **Dolan, Doyle, Hussein Hamed, Murphy, Whitehead, Zaidan** votes	

COUNT		1	2		3	
CORRIGAN, Maria	(FF)	6,844	(+324)	7,168	(+164)	7,332
CULHANE, Aidan	(Lab)	4,535	(+304)	4,839	(+101)	4,940
CURRY, Nicola	(ULA)	1,277	(+178)	1,455	(+209)	1,664
DOLAN, Gerard P	(Ind)	156	(+36)	192		
DOYLE, John Anthony	(Ind)	246	(+97)	343		
HUSSEIN HAMED, Buhidma	(Ind)	273	(+45)	318		
MATHEWS, Peter	(FG)	9,053	(+752)	9,805	(+182)	9,987
MITCHELL, Olivia*	(FG)	9,635	(+819)	10,454	(+123)	10,577
MURPHY, Jane	(CSP)	277	(+19)	296		
NIC CORMAIC, Sorcha	(SF)	1,915	(+150)	2,065	(+121)	2,186
ROSS, Shane	(Ind)	17,075				
RYAN, Eamon*	(GP)	4,929	(+560)	5,489	(+137)	5,626
SHATTER, Alan*	(FG)	7,716	(+783)	8,499	(+81)	8,580
WHITE, Alex	(Lab)	8,524	(+795)	9,319	(+148)	9,467
WHITEHEAD, Raymond Patrick	(Ind)	120	(+91)	211		
ZAIDAN, Éamonn	(Ind)	71	(+14)	85		
NON-TRANSFERABLE				0	179	

Distribution of **Curry** votes		Distribution of **Nic Cormaic** votes		Distribution of **Culhane** votes		Distribution of **White** surplus		Distribution of **Ryan** votes	
4		**5**		**6**		**7**		**8**	
(+68)	7,400	(+164)	7,564	(+198)	7,762	(+170)	7,932	(+1,231)	9,163
(+292)	5,232	(+459)	5,691						
(+60)	10,047	(+126)	10,173	(+321)	10,494	(+326)	10,820	(+1,250)	12,070
(+84)	10,661	(+102)	10,763	(+396)	11,159	(+468)	11,627	(+1,752)	13,379
(+431)	2,617								
(+172)	5,798	(+322)	6,120	(+416)	6,536	(+796)	7,332		
(+46)	8,626	(+112)	8,738	(+228)	8,966	(+335)	9,301	(+1,310)	10,611
(+280)	9,747	(+660)	10,407	(+3,796)	14,203				
231		672		336		0		1,789	

Dublin South-Central

Statistics

Seats	5
Electorate	80,203
Total Poll	51,744
Turnout	64.5%
Spoiled	817
Total Valid Poll	50,927
Quota	8,488
Candidates	18

Party Share of Vote

1st Preferences	Number	%	Gain/ Loss
Fine Gael	11,956	23.48	9.09
Labour	18,032	35.41	14.28
Fianna Fáil	4,837	9.50	-23.58
Sinn Féin	6,804	13.36	3.21
United Left Alliance	6,574	12.91	12.91
Green Party	1,015	1.99	-3.81
Others	1,709	3.36	-10.18

	Quotas	Seats
Fine Gael	1.4	1
Labour	2.1	2
Fianna Fáil	0.6	–
Sinn Féin	0.8	1
United Left Alliance	0.8	1
Green Party	0.1	–
Others	0.2	–

Lab gain 1, ULA gain 1; from FF.

Eric Byrne (Lab)

Home Address
32 Ashdale Road, Terenure, Dublin 6W.
Constituency Office
Leinster House, Kildare Street, Dublin 2.
Contact Details
Home: (01) 490 1305.
Office: (01) 618 3223. Mobile: (087) 254 8429.
Email: eric.byrne@oireachtas.ie;
ericbyrne@indigo.ie.
Website: www.ericbyrne.ie.
Facebook: EricByrne. Twitter: @EricByrneTD.
Birth Place/Date
Dublin, 21 April 1947.
Marital Status
Married to Prof. Ellen Hazelkorn. Two
daughters.
Education
Synge Street School, Dublin. Bolton Street
College of Technology.
Occupation
Public representative.

First elected to the Dáil for Democratic Left in
1989 but lost seat in the general election in
1992 by five votes after three recounts over
ten days. Re-elected in by-election June 1994
but lost the seat at general election in 1997.
Failed to win a seat in 2007 by sixty-nine
votes.

He has been a public representative since
1985, when he was first elected to Dublin City
Council; re-elected until he won a Dáil seat in
2011. Deputy Lord Mayor of Dublin in 2001.

Catherine Byrne (FG)

Home Address
30 Bulfin Road, Inchicore, Dublin 8.
Constituency Office
5A Tyrconnell Road, Inchicore, Dublin 8.
Contact Details
Office: (01) 473 5080.
Dáil Office: (01) 6183083.
Email: catherine.byrne@oireachtas.ie.
Website: www.catherinebyrne.finegael.ie.
Facebook: Catherine-Byrne-T.D.
Birth Place/Date
Bluebell, Dublin, 26 February 1956.
Marital Status
Married to Joseph. Four daughters, one son.
Education
Our Lady of the Wayside N. S., Bluebell,
Dublin 12. Holy Faith, The Coombe and
Clarendon Street, Dublin. Cathal Brugha
Catering College, Dublin. All Hallows (Lay
Ministry).
Occupation
Public representative.

First elected to the Dáil in 2007.

She was elected to Dublin City Council for the
South West Inner City ward on her first
attempt in 1999 and topped the poll in the
area in the 2004 local elections. Lord Mayor of
Dublin, 2005–06.

Former Chairperson of St Michael's
Community Centre. Member, Board of
Management of the Mercy Convent
Secondary School, Goldenbridge. Leader of St
Michael's Folk/Gospel Group for 15 years.
Played ladies' soccer at the highest level and
previously managed schoolboy soccer teams
in her locality. Completed a two-year Lay
Ministry course in All Hallows and also has a
City & Guilds Diploma in Catering.

Michael Conaghan (Lab)

Home Address
33 Lally Road, Ballyfermot, Dublin 10.
Constituency Office
Leinster House, Kildare Street, Dublin 2.
Contact Details
Home: (01) 626 9892. Dáil Office: (01) 618 4033.
Mobile: (086) 175 3747.
Email: michael.conaghan@oireachtas.ie.
Website: www.labour.ie/michaelconaghan.
Birth Place/Date
Donegal, September 1945.
Marital Status
Married. Two daughters.
Education
Ard Scoil na gCeithre Máistir. UCD (History and Politics). Manchester University.
Occupation
Full-time public representative. Formerly teacher.

Michael Conaghan is a new deputy.

Contested the February 1982 General Election for Democratic Socialist Party, the November 1982, 1987, 1989 and 1997 elections as an Independent. Joined the Labour Party in 1991; elected to Dublin City Council 1991, re-elected 2004 and 2009. Lord Mayor of Dublin, 2004.

Former Vice-Principal of Inchicore College of Further Education.

Joan Collins (PBPA)

Home Address
30 Ring Street, Inchicore, Dublin 8.
Constituency Office
Leinster House, Kildare Street, Dublin 2.
Contact Details
Dáil Office: (01) 618 3215.
Mobile: (086) 388 8151.
Email: joan.collins@peoplebeforeprofit.ie.
Website: www.joan-collins.org.
Birth Place/Date
Dublin, June 1961.
Marital Status
Lives with partner Dermot Connolly and his two children.
Education
St John of God Secondary School, Coolock, Dublin.
Occupation
Public representative. Formerly An Post clerk.

Joan Collins is a new deputy.

She was elected to Dublin City Council in 2004 and re-elected in 2009. She is a member of the Communications Workers' Union and of the United Left Alliance in the Dáil.

Aengus Ó Snodaigh (SF)

Home Address
12 Bóthar na Déise, Baile Fhormaid, Baile Átha Cliath 10.
Constituency Office
347 Ballyfermot Road, Dublin 10.
Contact Details
Constituency Office: (01) 625 9320;
Fax: (01) 620 3931.
Email: aosnodaigh@oireachtas.ie.
Website: www.aengusosnodaigh.ie.
Birth Place/Date
Dublin, 31 July 1964.
Marital Status
Married to Aisling Ó Dálaigh. Three children.
Education
Scoil Lorcain, Monkstown, Co. Dublin.
Coláiste Eoin, Booterstown, Co. Dublin.
UCD (BA, HDipEd).
Occupation
Full-time public representative. Formerly Bord na Gaeilge.

Aengus Ó Snodaigh was first elected in 2002. He is Sinn Féin Whip and party spokesperson on Social Protection.

Also Sinn Féin Whip in the last Dáil and party spokesperson on Justice and Equality, Culture, Gaeilge and Gaeltacht, International Affairs, and Defence.

He contested the constituency of Dublin South-East in the general election of 1987 and the by-election in Dublin South-Central in 1999.

Dublin South-Central

Seats 5
Quota 8,488

COUNT	1	Distribution of **Mooney** votes		Distribution of **Bennett** votes		Distribution of **Kelly** votes		Distribution of **King** votes		Distribution of **Connolly Farrell** votes	
	1	2		3		4		5		6	
BENNETT, Noel Francis (Ind)	128	(+)	128								
BRADLEY, Neville (Ind)	323	(+5)	328	(+36)	364	(+4)	368	(+23)	391	(+19)	410
BROPHY, Colm (FG)	3,376	(+1)	3,377	(+7)	3,384	(+3)	3,387	(+6)	3,393	(+3)	3,396
BYRNE, Catherine* (FG)	5,604	(+6)	5,610	(+4)	5,614	(+4)	5,618	(+8)	5,626	(+4)	5,630
BYRNE, Eric (Lab)	8,357	(+10)	8,367	(+13)	8,380	(+11)	8,391	(+10)	8,401	(+10)	8,411
CALLANAN, Colm (CSP)	239	(+)	239	(+2)	241	(+5)	246	(+1)	247	(+4)	251
COLLINS, Joan (PBPA)	6,574	(+11)	6,585	(+21)	6,606	(+24)	6,630	(+23)	6,653	(+38)	6,691
CONAGHAN, Michael (Lab)	5,492	(+5)	5,497	(+4)	5,501	(+4)	5,505	(+4)	5,509	(+28)	5,537
CONNOLLY FARRELL, Seán (Ind)	178	(+4)	182	(+8)	190	(+8)	198	(+19)	217		
KELLY, Gerry (Ind)	137	(+2)	139	(+4)	143						
KING, Paul (Ind)	146	(+10)	156	(+2)	158	(+18)	176				
MCGINLEY, Ruairí (FG)	2,976	(+4)	2,980	(+3)	2,983	(+)	2,983	(+8)	2,991	(+5)	2,996
MOONEY, Dominic (Ind)	102										
MULCAHY, Michael* (FF)	4,837	(+7)	4,844	(+1)	4,845	(+5)	4,850	(+15)	4,865	(+4)	4,869
Ó HALMHAIN, Oisín (GP)	1,015	(+)	1,015	(+4)	1,019	(+12)	1,031	(+7)	1,038	(+4)	1,042
O'NEILL, Peter (Ind)	456	(+9)	465	(+4)	469	(+10)	479	(+22)	501	(+38)	539
Ó SNODAIGH, Aengus* (SF)	6,804	(+15)	6,819	(+6)	6,825	(+13)	6,838	(+11)	6,849	(+25)	6,874
UPTON, Henry (Lab)	4,183	(+4)	4,187	(+5)	4,192	(+16)	4,208	(+10)	4,218	(+8)	4,226
NON-TRANSFERABLE		9		4		6		9		27	

Distribution of **Callanan** votes		Distribution of **Bradley, Ó hAlmhain, O'Neill** votes		Distribution of **McGinley** votes		Distribution of **Byrne** surplus		Distribution of **Upton** votes		Distribution of **Brophy** votes		Distribution of **Byrne** surplus	
7		**8**		**9**		**10**		**11**		**12**		**13**	
(+15)	425												
(+22)	3,418	(+119)	3,537	(+1,305)	4,842	(+5)	4,847	(+352)	5,199				
(+33)	5,663	(+252)	5,915	(+1,205)	7,120	(+22)	7,142	(+638)	7,780	(+4,087)	11,867		
(+5)	8,416	(+305)	8,721										
(+37)	6,728	(+344)	7,072	(+94)	7,166	(+28)	7,194	(+579)	7,773	(+205)	7,978	(+481)	8,459
(+7)	5,544	(+182)	5,726	(+93)	5,819	(+85)	5,904	(+2,290)	8,194	(+269)	8,463	(+1,395)	9,858
(+14)	3,010	(+118)	3,128										
(+63)	4,932	(+127)	5,059	(+127)	5,186	(+9)	5,195	(+270)	5,465	(+233)	5,698	(+463)	6,161
(+9)	1,051												
(+10)	549												
(+11)	6,885	(+156)	7,041	(+70)	7,111	(+12)	7,123	(+332)	7,455	(+114)	7,569	(+150)	7,719
(+5)	4,231	(+228)	4,459	(+216)	4,675	(+72)	4,747						
20		194		18		0		286		291		890	

Dublin South-East

Statistics

Seats	4
Electorate	58,217
Total Poll	35,246
Turnout	60.5%
Spoiled	327
Total Valid Poll	34,919
Quota	6,984
Candidates	16

Party Share of Vote

1st Preferences	Number	%	Gain/Loss
Fine Gael	12,402	35.52	16.87
Labour	8,857	25.36	8.71
Fianna Fáil	3,922	11.23	-17.49
Sinn Féin	1,272	3.64	-1.08
United Left Alliance	629	1.80	1.80
Green Party	2,370	6.79	-7.05
Others	5,467	15.66	11.40

	Quotas	Seats
Fine Gael	1.8	2
Labour	1.3	2
Fianna Fáil	0.6	–
Sinn Féin	0.2	–
United Left Alliance	0.1	–
Green Party	0.3	–
Others	0.8	–

FG gain 1, Lab gains 1; from FF, GP.

Ruairí Quinn (Lab)

Home Address
23 Strand Road, Sandymount, Dublin 4.
Contact Details
Dáil Office: (01) 618 3434.
Website: www.ruairiquinn.ie.
Birth Place/Date
Dublin, 2 April 1946.
Marital Status
Married to Liz Allman. One son. One son, one daughter from previous marriage.
Education
Blackrock College, Dublin. UCD (BArch). Athens Center of Ekistics, Greece (HCE).
Occupation
Government Minister.

Ruairí Quinn was appointed Minister for Education and Skills on 9 March 2011.

He was Leader of the Labour Party 1997–2002 and Deputy Leader 1989–97. He was Minister for Finance 1994–97; Minister for Enterprise and Employment 1993–94; Minister for Labour December 1983–87; Minister for the Public Service, February 1986–87; Minister of State at the Department of the Environment, with special responsibility for Urban Affairs and Housing, 1982–83.

He was first elected to the Dáil in Dublin South-East in 1977 but lost his seat in the 1981 General Election. He regained his seat in February 1982, having served as Senator, Industrial and Commercial Panel, August 1981–February 1982.

He was also a senator in 1976–77 when selected to fill a vacancy in the Taoiseach's nominees.

Treasurer and Member of the Presidency of the Party of European Socialists.

Member, Dublin City Council 1974–77 and 1991–93 (Leader, Labour group; Leader, Civic Alliance).

Lucinda Creighton (FG)

Home Address
75 Wilfield Road, Sandymount, Dublin 4.
Constituency Office
Leinster House, Kildare Street, Dublin 2.
Contact Details
Office: (01) 6194399.
Email: lucinda.creighton@taoiseach.gov.ie.
Website: www.lucindacreighton.ie.
Birth Place/Date
Mayo, 20 January 1980.
Marital Status
Married to Paul Bradford.
Education
Convent of Mercy, Claremorris, Co. Mayo. TCD (LLB). New York Bar. King's Inns, Dublin (Barrister-at-Law).
Occupation
Minister of State; TD; barrister.

Lucinda Creighton was appointed Minister of State for European Affairs on 10 March 2011.

First elected in 2007 when she took the seat of the then Progressive Democrats leader and Minister for Justice Michael McDowell and became the youngest member of the Dáil. Opposed Enda Kenny's leadership of Fine Gael in 2010.

Member of Fine Gael National Executive. Representative of Young Fine Gael and Fine Gael at European level. Vice-Chairperson of Fine Gael Taskforce charged with rejuvenating the party in Dublin in 2003.

Elected as the youngest member of Dublin City Council in 2004.

Eoghan Murphy FG

Home Address
Gallery Quay, Dublin 2.
Constituency Office
Ranelagh Triangle, Dublin 6.
Contact Details
Dáil Office: (01) 618 3324.
Mobile: (086) 086 3832.
Email: eoghan.murphy@oireachtas.ie.
Website: www.eoghanmurphy.ie.
Facebook: Eoghan Murphy.
Twitter: @MurphyEoghan.
Birth Place/Date
Dublin, April 1982.
Marital Status
Single.
Education
UCD (BA English & Philosophy). King's
College, London (MA International Relations).
Occupation
Full-time public representative.

Eoghan Murphy is a new deputy.

Joined Fine Gael in 2008 and elected to
Dublin City Council. Previously worked for
various organisations, including the United
Nations, in London, Geneva and Vienna on
international arms control, mostly in the area
of nuclear weapon disarmament. Left his job
as a speechwriter at the nuclear test-ban
treaty commission in Vienna to dedicate
himself full-time to politics in Ireland after
election to Dublin City Council.

Kevin Humphreys (Lab)

Home Address
O'Connell Gardens, Bath Avenue,
Sandymount, Dublin 4.
Contact Details
Dáil Office: (01) 618 3224.
Mobile: (087) 298 9103.
Email: kevin.humphreys@oireachtas.ie.
Website: www.kevinhumphreys.ie.
Facebook: cllrkevinhumphreys.
Twitter: @khumphreystd.
Birth Place/Date
Dublin, 4 February 1958.
Marital Status
Married to Catherine. Two children.
Education
Star of the Sea Sandymount N.S. Ringsend
Technical College.
Occupation
Public representative; production technician in
pharmaceutical industry.

Kevin Humphreys is a new deputy.

Member of Dublin City Council from South
East Inner City ward from 1999 until election
to the Dáil. Leader of the Labour Group on
Dublin City Council 2002–11. Former
Chairperson of City of Dublin VEC.

Dublin South-East

		COUNT	Distribution of **Coyle, Keigher, Mooney, Ó'Ceallaigh, Sheehy, Watson** votes		Distribution of **Flynn** votes		Distribution of **Mac Aodháin** votes	
Seats 4 Quota 6,984		**1**		**2**		**3**		**4**
ANDREWS, Chris*	(FF)	3,922	(+59)	3,981	(+78)	4,059	(+101)	4,160
COYLE, James	(Ind)	164						
CREIGHTON, Lucinda*	(FG)	6,619	(+75)	6,694	(+107)	6,801	(+54)	6,855
FLYNN, Mannix	(Ind)	1,248	(+155)	1,403				
GORMLEY, John*	(GP)	2,370	(+65)	2,435	(+112)	2,547	(+112)	2,659
HASKINS, Dylan	(Ind)	1,383	(+109)	1,492	(+262)	1,754	(+174)	1,928
HUMPHREYS, Kevin	(Lab)	3,450	(+118)	3,568	(+196)	3,764	(+295)	4,059
KEIGHER, John Dominic	(Ind)	27						
MAC AODHÁIN, Ruadhán	(SF)	1,272	(+133)	1,405	(+144)	1,549		
MOONEY, Annette	(ULA)	629						
MURPHY, Eoghan	(FG)	5,783	(+60)	5,843	(+48)	5,891	(+47)	5,938
Ó'CEALLAIGH, Peadar	(Ind)	18						
QUINN, Ruairí*	(Lab)	5,407	(+155)	5,562	(+238)	5,800	(+347)	6,147
SHEEHY, Hugh	(Ind)	195						
SOMMERVILLE, Paul	(Ind)	2,343	(+150)	2,493	(+128)	2,621	(+194)	2,815
WATSON, Noel	(Ind)	89						
NON-TRANSFERABLE				43		90		225

Distribution of **Haskins** votes	Distribution of **Gormley** votes	Distribution of **Quinn** surplus	Distribution of **Creighton** surplus	Distribution of **Sommerville** votes	Distribution of **Murphy** surplus
5	6	7	8	9	10
(+88) 4,248	(+250) 4,498	(+47) 4,545	(+49) 4,594	(+356) 4,950	(+243) 5,193
(+114) 6,969	(+459) 7,428				
(+249) 2,908					
(+235) 4,294	(+380) 4,674	(+345) 5,019	(+38) 5,057	(+837) 5,894	(+527) 6,421
(+198) 6,136	(+398) 6,534	(+102) 6,636	(+279) 6,915	(+1,441) 8,356	
(+453) 6,600	(+955) 7,555				
(+381) 3,196	(+261) 3,457	(+77) 3,534	(+32) 3,566		
210	205	0	46	932	602

Dublin South-West

Statistics

Seats	4
Electorate	70,613
Total Poll	47,475
Turnout	67.2%
Spoiled	511
Total Valid Poll	46,964
Quota	9,393
Candidates	10

Party Share of Vote

1st Preferences	Number	%	Gain/Loss
Fine Gael	13,044	27.77	7.74
Labour	17,032	36.27	16.28
Fianna Fáil	5,059	10.77	-28.49
Sinn Féin	8,064	17.17	5.01
United Left Alliance	2,462	5.24	5.24
Green Party	480	1.02	-2.69
Others	823	1.75	-3.08

	Quotas	Seats
Fine Gael	1.4	1
Labour	1.8	2
Fianna Fáil	0.5	–
Sinn Féin	0.9	1
United Left Alliance	0.3	–
Green Party	0.1	–
Others	0.1	–

Lab gains 1, SF gains 1; from FF.

Pat Rabbitte (Lab)

Home Address
56 Monastery Drive, Clondalkin, Dublin 22.
Constituency Office
29–31 Adelaide Road, Dublin 2.
Contact Details
Home: (01) 459 3191. Constituency Office: (01) 678 2011. Dáil Office: (01) 618 3772.
Email: pat.rabbitte@oireachtas.ie; minister.rabbitte@dcenr.gov.ie.
Birth Place/Date
Claremorris, Co. Mayo, 18 May 1949.
Marital Status
Married to Derry McDermott. Three daughters.
Education
St Colman's College, Claremorris, Co. Mayo. NUI Galway (BA, HDipEd, LLB).
Occupation
Government Minister.

Minister for Communications, Energy and Natural Resources, appointed 9 March 2011. Previously leader of the Labour Party from October 2002 to August 2007 and Labour's spokesperson on Justice in the last Dáil.

First elected to the Dáil in 1989 for the Workers' Party. During the 26th Dáil, six of the party's TDs formed the Democratic Left Party. During the 28th Dáil in 1999, DL merged with Labour. Rabbitte was re-elected in Dublin South-West as a Labour deputy in 2002.

Minister of State to the Government and at the Department of Enterprise and Employment, with special responsibility for Commerce, Science and Technology and Consumer Affairs, 1994–97.

Member, Dublin County Council 1985–95 and last chairperson before it became three separate administrative counties. Elected to South Dublin County Council 1999.

Member, Irish Transport and General Workers' Union (now SIPTU). Formerly National Secretary. President, UCG Students' Union 1970–71. President, Union of Students in Ireland 1972–74.

Brian Hayes (FG)

Home Address
48 Dunmore Park, Kingswood Heights, Tallaght, Dublin 24.
Contact Details
Home: (01) 462 6545.
Dáil Office: (01) 618 3567.
Email: brian.hayes@oireachtas.ie.
Website: www.brianhayes.ie.
Birth Place/Date
Dublin, 23 August 1969.
Marital Status
Married to Genevieve. Two sons, one daughter.
Education
St Joseph's College, Garbally Park, Ballinsloe, Co. Galway. NUI Maynooth (BA). TCD (HDipEd).
Occupation
Full-time public representative. Formerly secondary teacher.

Brian Hayes was appointed Minister of State at the Department of Finance, with responsibility for the Office of Public Works and Public Sector Reform, on 10 March 2011.

First elected to the Dáil in 1997 but lost his seat in 2002 and regained it in 2007. Taoiseach's nominee to the Seanad 1995–97 and elected to Seanad's Cultural and Educational Panel 2002. Fine Gael leader in the Seanad, 2002–07.

Member of Fine Gael front bench from 2003 and spokesperson on several portfolios, including Education and Science (2007–10). Lost front bench position in 2010 after supporting Richard Bruton against Enda Kenny for party leadership. Former National Youth and Education Officer with Fine Gael.

Member, South Dublin County Council 1995–2003. Member, Irish Council for European Movement.

Seán Crowe (SF)

Home Address
16 Raheen Green, Tallaght, Dublin 24.
Constituency Office
Leinster House, Kildare Street, Dublin 2.
Contact Details
Dáil Office: (01) 618 3719.
Mobile: (086) 386 4303.
Email: sean.crowe@oireachtas.ie.
Website: www.seancrowe.ie.
Birth Place/Date
Dublin, 7 March 1957.
Marital Status
Married to Pamela Kane.
Education
Dundrum Technical School, Dundrum, Dublin.
Occupation
Full-time public representative.

Sinn Féin spokesperson on Education and Skills, Seán Crowe was first elected to the Dáil in 2002 but lost his seat in the 2007 General Election. Contested the general elections in 1989, 1992 and 1997 without success, along with the 1999 European Parliament elections.

Elected to South Dublin County Council in 1999, he was co-opted back onto the council in 2008 and re-elected in 2009.

Eamonn Maloney (Lab)

Home Address
84 St Maelruan's Park, Tallaght, Dublin 24.
Constituency Office
Leinster House, Kildare Street, Dublin 2.
Contact Details
Dáil Office: (01) 618 3588.
Email: eamonn.maloney@oireachtas.ie.
Website: www.labour.ie/eamonnmaloney.
Birth Place/Date
Letterkenny, Co. Donegal, 1953.
Marital Status
Married to Vivienne. Three children.
Education
Christian Brothers' N.S. Vocational Educational School, Letterkenny.
Occupation
Full-time public representative.

Eamonn Maloney is a new deputy.

Elected to South Dublin County Council in 1999 and re-elected in 2004 and 2009. Mayor of the council in 2006 and again in 2010. Chairman of the campaign to have Tallaght granted city status.

Founder of Ireland's first aluminium can recycling company as a co-op in 1988 and worker/director until it closed in 2009. Author of a local history book, *Tallaght – A Place with History*, first published in 2010.

Dublin South-West

		COUNT 1	Distribution of **Rabbitte** surplus	COUNT 2	Distribution of **Hayes** surplus	COUNT 3
CROWE, Seán	(SF)	8,064	(+365)	8,429	(+86)	8,515
DUFFY, Francis Noel	(GP)	480	(+31)	511	(+10)	521
HAYES, Brian*	(FG)	9,366	(+514)	9,880		
KEANE, Cáit	(FG)	3,678	(+145)	3,823	(+122)	3,945
KELLY, Ray	(Ind)	823	(+47)	870	(+13)	883
LENIHAN, Conor*	(FF)	2,341	(+52)	2,393	(+21)	2,414
MALONEY, Eamonn	(Lab)	4,165	(+2,043)	6,208	(+155)	6,363
MURPHY, Mick	(ULA)	2,462	(+162)	2,624	(+38)	2,662
O'CONNOR, Charlie*	(FF)	2,718	(+115)	2,833	(+31)	2,864
RABBITTE, Pat*	(Lab)	12,867				
NON-TRANSFERABLE				0		11

Distribution of **Duffy, Kelly** votes		Distribution of **Lenihan** votes		Distribution of **Murphy** votes		Distribution of **Crowe** surplus		Distribution of **O'Connor** votes	
4		**5**		**6**		**7**		**8**	
(+257)	8,772	(+139)	8,911	(+1,278)	10,189				
(+210)	4,155	(+560)	4,715	(+187)	4,902	(+149)	5,051	(+1,082)	6,133
(+74)	2,488								
(+340)	6,703	(+166)	6,869	(+914)	7,783	(+543)	8,326	(+1,331)	9,657
(+258)	2,920	(+55)	2,975						
(+84)	2,948	(+1,415)	4,363	(+160)	4,523	(+77)	4,600		
181		153		436		27		2,187	

Dublin West

Statistics

Seats	4
Electorate	62,348
Total Poll	42,799
Turnout	68.6%
Spoiled	327
Total Valid Poll	42,472
Quota	8,495
Candidates	10

Party Share of Vote

1st Preferences	Number	%	Gain/Loss
Fine Gael	11,549	27.19	6.80
Labour	12,313	28.99	11.93
Fianna Fáil	7,044	16.59	-20.86
Sinn Féin	2,597	6.11	1.33
United Left Alliance	8,084	19.03	19.03
Green Party	605	1.42	-2.36
Others	280	0.66	-14.25

	Quotas	Seats
Fine Gael	1.4	1
Labour	1.4	1
Fianna Fáil	0.8	1
Sinn Féin	0.3	–
United Left Alliance	1	1
Green Party	0.1	–
Others	0	–

ULA gain 1 seat. Constituency has 1 extra seat since 2007.

St Margaret's
Mulhuddart
Corduff
Barberstown
Blanchardstown
Clonsilla
Carpenterstown
Castleknock

Joan Burton (Lab)

Home Address
81 Old Cabra Road, Dublin 7.
Constituency Office
Leinster House, Kildare Street, Dublin 2.
Contact Details
Dáil Office: (01) 618 4006.
Email: joan.burton@oireachtas.ie.
Website: http://www.joanburton.ie. Facebook:
Joan-Burton. Twitter: @joan_burton.
Birth Place/Date
Dublin, 1 February 1949.
Marital Status
Married to Pat Carroll. One daughter.
Education
Sisters of Charity, Stanhope Street, Dublin.
UCD (BComm). Fellow of Institute of
Chartered Accountants.
Occupation
Government Minister.

Appointed Minister for Social Protection on
9 March 2011.

Joan Burton is Deputy Leader of the Labour
Party and had been its Finance spokesperson
for some six years in previous Dáileanna. She
was the first candidate to be elected in the
2011 General Election, topping the poll in
Dublin West.

First elected to the Dáil in 1992 but lost her
seat in 1997 and regained it in 2002. Minister
of State at the Department of Social Welfare
1992–94; Minister of State at the Department
of Foreign Affairs, with responsibility for
Overseas Development, and at the
Department of Justice 1995–97.

She was an unsuccessful candidate for the
leadership of the Labour Party in 2002.

Member, Dublin County Council 1991–99;
Fingal County Council 1999–2003; Leader of
the Labour Party group.

Chair of Steering Committee of
Blanchardstown Women's Refuge. Board
member of Centre for Independent Living,
campaigning for transport rights of wheelchair
users.

Leo Varadkar (FG)

Home Address
30 Rosehaven, Carpenterstown Road,
Castleknock, Dublin 15.
Constituency Office
37A Main Street, Ongar, Dublin 15.
Contact Details
Constituency Office: (01) 640 3133.
Dáil Office: (01) 604 1062.
Email: leo.varadkar@oireachtas.ie;
minister@dttas.ie.
Website: www.leovaradkar.ie.
Birth Place/Date
Dublin, 18 January 1979.
Marital Status
Single.
Education
St Francis Xavier N. S., Coolmine, Dublin 15.
The King's Hospital, Palmerstown, Dublin 20.
TCD (BA; MB; BCh; BAO; post-graduate GP
training programme attached to TCD).
Occupation
Government Minister; medical doctor.

Leo Varadkar was appointed Minister for
Transport, Tourism and Sport on 9 March
2011. He was first elected in 2007 and was
Fine Gael spokesperson on Enterprise, Trade
and Employment 2007–10 and on
Communications, Energy and Natural
Resources 2010–11.

He was co-opted to Fingal County Council in
November 2003 and was elected in his own
right in June 2004 in the Castleknock electoral
area with the highest first preference vote in
the country. Leas-Chathaoirleach 2004. Area
Chairperson for Dublin 15 in 2006–7. Member,
transport and housing strategic policy
committees. Member of the Institute of
European Affairs and the European
Movement.

Joe Higgins (SP)

Home Address
155 Briarwood Close, Mulhuddart, Dublin 15.
Constituency Office
Leinster House, Kildare Street, Dublin 2.
Contact Details
Constituency Office: (01) 820 1753.
Dáil Office: (01) 618 3370.
Email: joe.higgins@oireachtas.ie.
Website: www.joehiggins.eu.
Twitter: @joehigginsTD.
Birth Place/Date
Dingle, Co. Kerry, 1 May 1949.
Education
Christian Brothers' School, Dingle. UCD (BA;
HDipEd).
Occupation
Full-time public representative. Formerly
secondary school teacher.

Joe Higgins was first elected to the Dáil in
1997, was re-elected in 2002 and defeated in
2007. Elected to the European Parliament in
2009 and stepped down when re-elected to
the Dáil in 2011. He contested the 1992
General Election in Dublin West and a by-
election in the constituency in 1996 as a
Militant Labour candidate. One of the
founders of the Socialist Party in 1996, after
earlier expulsion from Labour Party, and
became its first TD.

Elected to Dublin County Council in 1991 and
a member of Fingal County Council until 2003.
Leader of the United Left Alliance in the Dáil.

Brian Lenihan (FF)

Home Address
Longwood, Somerton Road, Strawberry Beds,
Dublin 20.
Birth Place/Date
Dublin, 21 May 1959.
Marital Status
Married to Patricia Ryan. One son, one daughter.
Education
Belvedere College, Dublin. TCD (BA;
Foundation Scholar). Cambridge University
(LLB). King's Inns.
Occupation
Public representative; Senior Counsel.

Brian Lenihan died on 10 June 2011 from
pancreatic cancer diagnosed in late 2009.
Deputy Leader of Fianna Fáil and party
spokesperson on Finance at the time of his
death. Minister for Finance from May 2008 to
March 2011; and Minister for Justice, Equality
and Law Reform from June 2007 to May 2008.

Previously Minister of State at: the
Departments of Health and Children; the
Department of Justice, Equality and Law
Reform; and the Department of Education and
Science from 2002–07.

First elected to the Dáil in April 1996 in the by-
election caused by the death of his father
Brian: former Tánaiste; Minister in various
portfolios; Dáil deputy for Roscommon–
Leitrim 1961–73; and for Dublin West
1977–95.

Brother of Conor Lenihan: Minister of State
2004–11; and Dáil deputy for Dublin South-
West 1997–2011. Nephew of Mary O'Rourke:
TD for Longford–Westmeath 2007–11 and
1982–2002; and holder of various ministerial
posts. Grandson of Patrick Lenihan, Dáil
deputy 1965–70.

Dublin West

Seats 4 Quota 8,495		1	Distribution of **Burton** surplus	2	Distribution of **Esebamen, McGuinness, O'Gorman** votes	3	Distribution of **Donnelly** votes	4	Distribution of **Dennison** votes	5
COUNT		1		2		3		4		5
BURTON, Joan*	(Lab)	9,627								
DENNISON, Kieran	(FG)	3,190	(+58)	3,248	(+192)	3,440	(+253)	3,693		
DONNELLY, Paul	(SF)	2,597	(+49)	2,646	(+103)	2,749				
ESEBAMEN, Clement	(Ind)	280	(+8)	288						
HIGGINS, Joe	(SP)	8,084	(+220)	8,304	(+299)	8,603				
LENIHAN, Brian*	(FF)	6,421	(+73)	6,494	(+556)	7,050	(+273)	7,323	(+966)	8,289
MCGUINNESS, David	(FF)	623	(+8)	631						
NULTY, Patrick	(Lab)	2,686	(+500)	3,186	(+264)	3,450	(+1,251)	4,701	(+1,628)	6,329
O'GORMAN, Roderic	(GP)	605	(+20)	625						
VARADKAR, Leo*	(FG)	8,359	(+196)	8,555						
NON-TRANSFERABLE				0		130		972		1,099

Eamon Ryan and Trevor Sargent at the launch of the Green Party's Election 2011 Campaign at the Sugar Club in Dublin.
Photograph: Bryan O'Brien.

Dún Laoghaire

Statistics

Seats	4
Electorate	80,115
Total Poll	57,157
Turnout	71.3%
Spoiled	481
Total Valid Poll	56,676
Quota	11,336
Candidates	14

Party Share of Vote

1st Preferences	Number	%	Gain/Loss
Fine Gael	19,591	34.57	11.01
Labour	17,217	30.38	14.38
Fianna Fáil	8,632	15.23	-19.64
Sinn Féin	0	0.00	-2.20
United Left Alliance	6,206	10.95	10.95
Green Party	2,156	3.80	-3.92
Others	2,874	5.07	-3.84

	Quotas	Seats
Fine Gael	1.7	2
Labour	1.5	1
Fianna Fáil	0.8	–
Sinn Féin	0	–
United Left Alliance	0.5	1
Green Party	0.2	–
Others	0.3	–

Constituency has 1 less seat since 2007.

Eamon Gilmore (Lab)

Home Address
1 Corbawn Close, Shankill, Co. Dublin.
Contact Details
Constituency Office: (01) 408 2018.
Email: eamon.gilmore@oireachtas.ie.
Website: www.labour.ie/eamongilmore.
Facebook: EamonGilmore.
Birth Place/Date
Caltra, Co. Galway, 24 April 1955.
Marital Status
Married to Carol Hanney. Two sons, one daughter.
Education
Caltra N.S. St Joseph's College, Ballinasloe. NUI Galway (BA Psychology).
Occupation
Tánaiste and Government Minister; Leader of the Labour Party.

Eamon Gilmore was appointed Tánaiste and Minister for Foreign Affairs and Trade on 9 March 2011. Leader of the Labour Party since September 2007 when he was elected without a contest, replacing Pat Rabbitte following that year's general election.

First elected to the Dáil in 1989 as a Workers' Party deputy, having contested the general elections in November 1982 and 1987; re-elected at all subsequent general elections. He was among the six Workers' Party TDs who formed Democratic Left during the 26th Dáil. Minister of State at the Department of the Marine during the 'Rainbow Coalition' of Fine Gael, Labour and DL 1994–97. Subsequently helped negotiate the merger of DL and the Labour Party in 1999.

Labour Party spokesperson on the Environment, Marine, Agriculture and Public Enterprise 1997–2002; spokesperson on Environment, Housing and Local Government 2002–07.

Member, Dublin County Council and Dún Laoghaire Borough Corporation 1985–95. Member, Dún Laoghaire–Rathdown County Council 1999–2004.

President, UCG Students' Union 1974–75; President, Union of Students in Ireland 1976–78.

Sean Barrett (FG)

Home Address
Avondale, Ballinclea Road, Killiney, Co. Dublin.
Constituency Office
6 Rogan's Court, Patrick Street, Dún Laoghaire.
Contact Details
Dáil Office: (01) 618 3895. Office: (01) 284 5333.
Birth Place/Date
Dublin, 9 August 1944.
Marital Status
Married to Sheila Hyde. Two sons, three daughters.
Education
CBC Monkstown, Co. Dublin. Presentation College, Glasthule. College of Commerce, Rathmines.
Occupation
Ceann Comhairle. Formerly insurance broker.

Sean Barrett was elected Ceann Comhairle of the 31st Dáil unopposed on 9 March 2011. First elected to the Dáil in 1981 and at every subsequent election until he retired at the 2002 General Election and was asked to run again in 2007.

He was Minister for Defence and Minister for the Marine 1995–97. Minister of State at the Department of the Taoiseach, and Government Chief Whip 1994–95. Minister of State at the Department of the Taoiseach, Minister of State at the Department of Education, and Leader of the House 1986–87. Government Chief Whip and Minister of State at the Department of the Taoiseach and Department of Defence 1982–86.

Fine Gael Chief Whip 1997–2002. Front bench spokesperson on: Defence and Marine 1993–94; Environment 1994; Industry and Commerce 1989–91; Justice 1987–89. Chairman Joint Oireachtas Committee on Climate Change & Energy Security 2007–10. Spokesperson on Foreign Affairs 2010–11.

Member, Dublin County Council 1974–82 (Chairman 1981–82). Member, Board of Management, Cabinteely School from 1975 and Chairman 1977 and 1980.

Mary Mitchell O'Connor (FG)

Home Address
31 Maple Manor, Cabinteely, Dublin 18.
Contact Details
Dáil Office: (01) 618 3302.
Mobile: (086) 818 6725. Email:
mary.mitchelloconnor@oireachtas.ie. Website:
www.marymitchelloconnor.com.
Birth Place/Date
Milltown Co. Galway, 10 June 1959.
Marital Status
Divorced. Two sons.
Education
Carysfort College. NUI (Bachelor of
Education). NUI Maynooth (Masters in
Education and School Leadership). The
European Coaching Institute (Diploma in
Life Coaching).
Occupation
Public representative. Formerly primary school
teacher.

Mary Mitchell O'Connor is a new deputy.

Formerly Principal of Harold Primary School in
Glasthule, Co. Dublin, she was elected to Dún
Laoghaire–Rathdown County Council as a
member of the Progressive Democrats in
2004. Joined Fine Gael in 2007 and re-elected
to the council for the party in 2009.

Richard Boyd Barrett (PBPA)

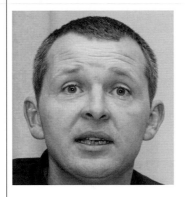

Home Address
Brigadoon, Station Road, Glenageary, Co.
Dublin.
Contact Details
Office: (01) 618 3449. Mobile: (087) 632 9511.
Website: www.richardboydbarrett.ie
Facebook: Richard Boyd Barrett.
Twitter: @RBoydBarrett.
Birth Place/Date
London, November 1967.
Marital Status
Single. One son. One stepson.
Education
Johnstown N.S. St Michael's College,
Ailesbury Road. UCD (BA; MA in English
Literature).
Occupation
Full-time public representative.

Richard Boyd Barrett is a new deputy.

He is a member of the Trotskyist Socialist
Workers' Party. He was an unsuccessful
candidate in the 2004 local elections but was
elected to Dún Laoghaire–Rathdown County
Council in 2009, topping the poll in the Dún
Laoghaire ward.

He was also unsuccessful in his first attempt
to be elected to the Dáil for Dún Laoghaire in
2007 as a candidate for the People Before
Profit Alliance but was elected in 2011 as part
of the United Left Alliance.

Prominent in the Irish Anti-War Movement he
opposed the Iraq War and the war in
Afghanistan. He supported the campaign of
the Rossport Five against the Shell gas
pipeline and voiced opposition to the bail out
of the Irish banks.

Dún Laoghaire

Seats 4
Quota 11,336

		1	Distribution of **Gilmore** surplus	2	Distribution of **Deegan** votes	3	Distribution of **Crawford** votes	4	Distribution of **Fitzgerald** votes	5
COUNT		1		2		3		4		5
ANDREWS, Barry*	(FF)	3,542	(+3)	3,545	(+9)	3,554	(+15)	3,569	(+25)	3,594
BACIK, Ivana	(Lab)	5,749	(+77)	5,826	(+31)	5,857	(+47)	5,904	(+12)	5,916
BARRETT, Sean*	(FG)	10,504	(+12)	10,516	(+22)	10,538	(+35)	10,573	(+93)	10,666
BOYD BARRETT, Richard	(PBPA)	6,206	(+22)	6,228	(+43)	6,271	(+61)	6,332	(+52)	6,384
BOYHAN, Victor	(Ind)	834	(+1)	835	(+16)	851	(+61)	912	(+29)	941
CRAWFORD, Mick	(Ind)	394	(+)	394	(+44)	438				
CUFFE, Ciaran*	(GP)	2,156	(+2)	2,158	(+29)	2,187	(+35)	2,222	(+12)	2,234
DEEGAN, Mike	(Ind)	311	(+)	311						
FITZGERALD, Daire	(CSP)	434	(+)	434	(+7)	441	(+9)	450		
GILMORE, Eamon*	(Lab)	11,468								
HANAFIN, Mary*	(FF)	5,090	(+6)	5,096	(+11)	5,107	(+23)	5,130	(+87)	5,217
HAUGHTON, Carl J	(Ind)	456	(+1)	457	(+43)	500	(+63)	563	(+31)	594
MITCHELL O'CONNOR, Mary	(FG)	9,087	(+7)	9,094	(+26)	9,120	(+43)	9,163	(+76)	9,239
PATTON, Trevor Frederick	(Ind)	445	(+1)	446	(+21)	467	(+33)	500	(+15)	515
NON-TRANSFERABLE				0		9		13		18

Distribution of Boyhan, Haughton, Patton votes		Distribution of Cuffe votes		Distribution of Andrews votes		Distribution of Barrett surplus		Distribution of Bacik votes		Distribution of Mitchell-O'Connor surplus	
6		**7**		**8**		**9**		**10**		**11**	
(+119)	3,713	(+173)	3,886								
(+284)	6,200	(+753)	6,953	(+307)	7,260	(+46)	7,306				
(+247)	10,913	(+361)	11,274	(+449)	11,723						
(+411)	6,795	(+337)	7,132	(+281)	7,413	(+40)	7,453	(+2,461)	9,914	(+880)	10,794
(+195)	2,429										
(+175)	5,392	(+214)	5,606	(+2,268)	7,874	(+139)	8,013	(+876)	8,889	(+531)	9,420
(+329)	9,568	(+430)	9,998	(+311)	10,309	(+142)	10,451	(+2,554)	13,005		
290		161		270		20		1,415		258	

Galway East

Statistics

Seats	4
Electorate	83,651
Total Poll	59,836
Turnout	71.5%
Spoiled	560
Total Valid Poll	59,276
Quota	11,856
Candidates	13

Party Share of Vote

1st Preferences	Number	%	Gain/Loss
Fine Gael	25,409	42.87	3.74
Labour	7,831	13.21	10.08
Fianna Fáil	10,694	18.04	-21.64
Sinn Féin	3,635	6.13	2.92
United Left Alliance	0	0.00	0.00
Green Party	402	0.68	-1.21
Others	11,305	19.07	12.06

	Quotas	Seats
Fine Gael	2.1	2
Labour	0.7	1
Fianna Fáil	0.9	1
Sinn Féin	0.3	–
United Left Alliance	0	–
Green Party	0	–
Others	1	–

Lab gain 1 from FF.

Michael P. Kitt (FF)

Home Address
Castleblakeney, Ballinasloe, Co. Galway.
Constituency Office
Castleblakeney, Ballinasloe.
Contact Details
Constituency Office: (090) 967 8147.
Dáil Office: (01) 618 3473. Mobile: (087) 254 4345. Email: michael.kitt@oireachtas.ie.
Website: www.michaelkitt.com.
Birth Place/Date
Tuam, Co. Galway, 17 May 1950.
Marital Status
Married to Catherine Mannion. Three sons, one daughter.
Education
St Jarlath's College, Tuam. NUI Galway. St Patrick's Training College, Drumcondra, Dublin. UCD (BA, HDipEd).
Occupation
Public representative. Formerly primary school teacher.

Appointed Leas-Cheann Comhairle of the Dáil in March 2011, he was Minister of State at the Department of Foreign Affairs with special responsibility for Overseas Development, June 2007–May 2008; and at the Department of the Environment, Heritage and Local Government, May 2008–April 2009.

First elected at a by-election caused by the death of his father in 1975. Defeated in 1977 but won back his seat in 1981 after a spell in the Seanad. Lost his seat again in 2002 but regained it in 2007. Taoiseach's nominee to the Seanad 2002–07.

Minister of State at the Department of the Taoiseach 1991–92. Chairman of Education and Science Committee in the 28th Dáil, 1997–2002.

Member, Galway County Council 1975-91.

Son of Michael F. Kitt, Dáil deputy for Galway East constituencies 1948–51 and 1957–75. Brother of Tom Kitt: Dublin South TD 1987–2011 and Minister of State at various departments 1992–94 and 1997–2008. Their sister, Áine Brady, was TD for Kildare North 2007–11 and Minister of State for Older People and Health Promotion 2009–11.

Paul Connaughton Jnr (FG)

Home Address
Ballinlass, Mountbellew, Ballinasloe, Co. Galway.
Contact Details
Dáil Office: (01) 618 4373.
Mobile: (087) 235 4682.
Email: paul.connaighton@oireachtas.ie;
connaughtonpaul1@hotmail.com.
Website: www.paulconnaughton.ie.
Birth Place/Date
Galway, January 1982.
Marital Status
Married to Edel Burke.
Education
Holy Rosary College, Mountbellew. Mountbellew Agricultural College. GMIT. NUI Galway (HDip in Marketing).
Occupation
Public representative.

Paul Connaughton Jnr is a new deputy.

He succeeds his father, also Paul, who was: TD for Galway East 1981–2011; Minister of State at the Department of Agriculture with special responsibility for Land Structure and Development 1982–87; and Senator 1977–81.

Elected to Galway County Council 2009. Formerly youth worker with Foróige.

Ciarán Cannon (FG)

Home Address
Carrabane, Athenry, Co. Galway.
Constituency Office
King Street, Loughrea, Co. Galway.
Contact Details
Constituency Office: (091) 880 790.
Mobile: (087) 228 3377.
Email: ciaran.cannon@oireachtas.ie.
Website: www.ciarancannon.ie.
Birth Place/Date
Kiltulla, Co. Galway, 19 September 1965.
Marital Status
Married to Niamh. One son.
Education
Presentation College Athenry. Institute of
Public Administration.
Occupation
Public representative.

Ciarán Cannon is a new deputy.

He was appointed Minister of State for
Training and Skills on 10 March 2011. As a
member of the Progressive Democrats he
was appointed to the Seanad in 2007 as a
Taoiseach's nominee. Became Leader of the
party in 2008, but left to join Fine Gael before
the PD party dissolved itself in November
2009.

Elected to Galway County Council for
Loughrea area as a PD member in 2004 and
was an unsuccessful candidate in the 2007
General Election.

Colm Keaveney (Lab)

Home Address
Kilcreevanty, Tuam, Co. Galway.
Constituency Office
Kilcreevanty, Tuam, Co. Galway.
Contact Details
Dáil Office: (01) 618 3821.
Mobile: (087) 677 6812.
Email: colm.keaveney@oireachtas.ie.
Website: www.colmkeaveney.ie.
Birth Place/Date
Dunmore, Co. Galway, January 1971.
Marital Status
Married to Deirdre. Three children.
Education
St Jarlath's College, Tuam. Letterkenny IT.
Smurfit Business School, UCD.
Occupation
Public representative and SIPTU regional
organiser.

Colm Keaveney is a new deputy.

Contested the 2007 General Election
unsuccessfully in this constituency. Elected to
Galway County Council 2004 and re-elected in
2009. Former president of Union of Students
in Ireland 1995–96.

Galway East

Seats 4
Quota 11,856

COUNT		1	Distribution of **Kennedy, O'Donnell** votes		Distribution of **Connelly** votes		Distribution of **Dolan** votes	
				2		3		4
BRODERICK, Tim	(Ind)	5,137	(+105)	5,242	(+1,036)	6,278	(+238)	6,516
CANNEY, Seán	(Ind)	5,567	(+78)	5,645	(+295)	5,940	(+187)	6,127
CANNON, Ciarán	(FG)	6,927	(+134)	7,061	(+207)	7,268	(+297)	7,565
CONNAUGHTON Jnr, Paul	(FG)	7,255	(+55)	7,310	(+247)	7,557	(+245)	7,802
CONNELLY, Dermot	(SF)	3,635	(+88)	3,723				
DOLAN, Michael F	(FF)	4,109	(+46)	4,155	(+135)	4,290		
HIGGINS, Lorraine	(Lab)	3,577	(+236)	3,813	(+610)	4,423	(+228)	4,651
KEAVENEY, Colm	(Lab)	4,254	(+90)	4,344	(+349)	4,693	(+92)	4,785
KENNEDY, Ciaran	(GP)	402						
KITT, Michael P.*	(FF)	6,585	(+47)	6,632	(+228)	6,860	(+2,666)	9,526
MCCLEARN, Jimmy	(FG)	5,395	(+45)	5,440	(+194)	5,634	(+144)	5,778
MCHUGH, Tom	(FG)	5,832	(+36)	5,868	(+82)	5,950	(+84)	6,034
O'DONNELL, Emer	(Ind)	601						
NON-TRANSFERABLE				43		340		109

Distribution of **Higgins** votes		Distribution of **McClearn** votes		Distribution of **Canney** votes		Distribution of **Broderick** votes		Distribution of **Kitt** surplus	
5		**6**		**7**		**8**		**9**	
(+330)	6,846	(+795)	7,641	(+724)	8,365				
(+214)	6,341	(+90)	6,431						
(+560)	8,125	(+1,837)	9,962	(+317)	10,279	(+1,582)	11,861		
(+289)	8,091	(+1,733)	9,824	(+1,053)	10,877	(+1,733)	12,610		
(+2,451)	7,236	(+233)	7,469	(+1,167)	8,636	(+1,170)	9,806	(+320)	10,126
(+267)	9,793	(+430)	10,223	(+892)	11,115	(+1,735)	12,850		
(+209)	5,987								
(+91)	6,125	(+611)	6,736	(+1,635)	8,371	(+294)	8,665	(+183)	8,848
240		258		643		1,851		491	

Galway West

Statistics

Seats	5
Electorate	88,840
Total Poll	61,268
Turnout	69.0%
Spoiled	643
Total Valid Poll	60,625
Quota	10,105
Candidates	17

Party Share of Vote

1st Preferences Number		%	Gain/Loss
Fine Gael	18,627	30.72	10.33
Labour	7,489	12.35	1.30
Fianna Fáil	12,703	20.95	-16.20
Sinn Féin	3,808	6.28	3.32
United Left Alliance	0	0.00	0.00
Green Party	1,120	1.85	-3.64
Others	16,878	27.84	20.97

	Quotas	Seats
Fine Gael	1.8	2
Labour	0.7	1
Fianna Fáil	1.3	1
Sinn Féin	0.4	–
United Left Alliance	0	–
Green Party	0.1	–
Others	1.7	1

FG gain 1 from FF.

Éamon Ó Cuív (FF)

Home Address
Corr na Móna, Co. na Gaillimhe.
Constituency Office
Teach Kirwan, Sráid Thobar an Iarla, Gaillimh.
Contact Details
Home: (094) 954 8021. Constituency Office:
(091) 562 846. Dáil Office: (01) 618 4231.
Email: eamon.ocuiv@oireachtas.ie;
info@eamonocuiv.ie. Website:
www.eamonocuiv.ie.
Birth Place/Date
Dublin, 1 June 1950.
Marital Status
Married to Áine Ní Choincheannain. Three
sons, one daughter.
Education
Oatlands College, Mount Merrion, Dublin.
UCD (BSc).
Occupation
Public representative. Deputy leader of
Fianna Fáil and party spokesperson on
Communications, Energy and Natural
Resources.

First elected in 1992, he was Minister for
Community, Rural and Gaeltacht Affairs
2002–10 and Minister for Social Protection
March 2010 to March 2011.

Minister of State at the Department of
Agriculture, Food and Rural Development
2001–02; at the Department of Arts, Heritage,
Gaeltacht and the Islands 1997–2001. Senator,
Cultural and Educational Panel, 1989–92.
Member, Galway County Council 1991–97.

Grandson of Éamon de Valera: President
1959–73; Taoiseach 1937–48, 1951–54, 1957–59;
President of Executive Council, Irish Free State,
1932–37; President First Dáil 1919–21; President
Second Dáil 1921 to January 1922.

Nephew of Major Vivion de Valera, TD for Dublin
North City and Central City constituencies 1945–81.

Cousin of Síle de Valera: MEP 1979–84; Dáil
deputy for Clare 1987–2007 and for Dublin Mid-
County 1977–81; Minister of State at the
Department of Education and Science 2002–06;
Minister for Arts, Culture and the Gaeltacht
1997–2002.

Derek Nolan (Lab)

Home Address
Riverside, Galway.
Constituency Office
Bóthar na Long, New Docks, Galway.
Contact Details
Constituency Office: (091) 561 006.
Mobile: (086) 377 7624.
Email: derek.nolan@oireachtas.ie.
Website: www.dereknolan.com.
Facebook: dereknolan.galway.
Twitter: @dereknolanTD.
Birth Place/Date
Galway, October 1982.
Marital Status
Unmarried.
Education
Mervue Boys' School. St Mary's College. NUI
Galway (Bachelor of Corporate Law, LLB.)
Occupation
Public representative.

Derek Nolan is a new TD.

Member of the Public Accounts Committee
and the Investigations, Oversight and
Petitions Committee.

Worked in several multinational companies in
Ireland and in Germany prior to being elected
to Galway City Council in 2009 for the Galway
City East ward. Chairperson of Galway City's
Housing Strategic Policy Committee and was
a member of the Corporate Policy Group.

Brian Walsh (FG)

Home Address
Drum East, Bushy Park, Galway.
Constituency Office
Leinster House, Kildare Street, Dublin 2.
Contact Details
Dáil Office: (01) 618 4236.
Mobile: (086) 833 3054.
Email: brian.walsh@oireachtas.ie;
brianwalsh100@eircom.net.
Website: www.brianwalshcampaign.ie.
Birth Place/Date
Galway, September 1972.
Marital Status
Married to Fiona Flatley. One daughter.
Education
St Michael's Mervue. St Joseph's, Galway.
GMIT.
Occupation
Public representative; financial management
business owner.

Brian Walsh is a new deputy.

Elected to Galway City Council in 2004 and re-elected in 2009. Mayor of Galway 2005 06.
Former Students' Union President in GMIT
and worked in financial services before setting
up his own financial management company in
1999.

Noel Grealish (Ind)

Home Address
Carnmore, Oranmore, Co. Galway.
Constituency Office
Unit 14, Briarhill Business Park, Briarhill,
Galway.
Contact Details
Office: (091) 764807. Mobile: (086) 850 9466.
Email: noel.grealish@oireachtas.ie.
Website: www.noelgrealish.com.
Facebook: noelgrealishtd.
Birth Place/Date
Galway, 16 December 1965.
Marital Status
Single.
Education
Carnmore N.S. St Mary's College, Galway.
Occupation
Full-time public representative.

First elected to the Dáil in 2002 for the
Progressive Democrats, succeeding the
party's founder member, Bobby Molloy. He
was one of the two PD deputies to survive
the 2007 election but became an Independent
when the party disbanded in 2009.

PD spokesperson on Rural Planning in 29th
Dáil. Member, Oireachtas Committee for the
Environment and Local Government;
Oireachtas Committee for Members'
Interests and Procedures and Privileges.
Chairman, PD Parliamentary Party 2004.

Member, Galway County Council 1999–2003.

Seán Kyne (FG)

Home Address
Clydagh, Moycullen, Co. Galway.
Contact Details
Dáil Office: (01) 618 4426.
Mobile: (087) 613 7372.
Email: sean.kyne@oireachtas.ie;
kynesean@eircom.net.
Website: www.seankyne.ie.
Birth Place/Date
Galway, May 1975.
Marital Status
Single.
Education
St Mary's College, Galway. NUI Galway.
UCD (Masters in Agricultural Science).
Occupation
Public representative.

Seán Kyne is a new deputy.

Won the last Galway West seat by 17 votes
after two re-counts; the last Dáil seat to be
filled in the 2011 General Election. Elected to
Galway County Council in 2004 and re-elected
in 2009. Contested the 2007 General Election
and Seanad election without success.

Galway West

Seats 5
Quota 10,105

COUNT	1	Distribution of **Cubbard, Holmes, King** votes — 2		Distribution of **Ó Brolcháin** votes — 3		Distribution of **Walsh** votes — 4		Distribution of **Crowe** votes — 5		Distribution of **Welby** votes — 6	
CONNOLLY, Catherine (Ind)	4,766	(+207)	4,973	(+241)	5,214	(+285)	5,499	(+104)	5,603	(+285)	5,888
CROWE, Michael (FF)	1,814	(+41)	1,855	(+15)	1,870	(+25)	1,895				
CUBBARD, Mike (Ind)	853										
FAHEY, Frank* (FF)	3,448	(+26)	3,474	(+15)	3,489	(+37)	3,526	(+307)	3,833	(+184)	4,017
GREALISH, Noel* (Ind)	6,229	(+117)	6,346	(+50)	6,396	(+193)	6,589	(+221)	6,810	(+306)	7,116
HEALY-EAMES, Fidelma (FG)	5,046	(+34)	5,080	(+93)	5,173	(+117)	5,290	(+57)	5,347	(+140)	5,487
HOLMES, Uinseann Eoin (Ind)	186										
KING, Thomas Gerard (Ind)	65										
KYNE, Seán (FG)	4,550	(+31)	4,581	(+49)	4,630	(+74)	4,704	(+25)	4,729	(+1,012)	5,741
NAUGHTON, Hildergarde (FG)	3,606	(+49)	3,655	(+90)	3,745	(+113)	3,858	(+50)	3,908	(+85)	3,993
NOLAN, Derek (Lab)	7,489	(+183)	7,672	(+334)	8,006	(+260)	8,266	(+197)	8,463	(+240)	8,703
Ó BROLCHÁIN, Niall (GP)	1,120	(+33)	1,153								
Ó CLOCHARTAIGH, Trevor (SF)	3,808	(+119)	3,927	(+72)	3,999	(+97)	4,096	(+45)	4,141	(+266)	4,407
Ó CUÍV, Éamon* (FF)	7,441	(+45)	7,486	(+61)	7,547	(+102)	7,649	(+549)	8,198	(+729)	8,927
WALSH, Brian (FG)	5,425	(+48)	5,473	(+42)	5,515	(+129)	5,644	(+225)	5,869	(+95)	5,964
WALSH, Eamon (Ind)	1,481	(+100)	1,581	(+43)	1,624						
WELBY, Thomas J (Ind)	3,298	(+27)	3,325	(+20)	3,345	(+139)	3,484	(+20)	3,504		
NON-TRANSFERABLE			44		28		53		95		162

Distribution of **Naughton** votes		Distribution of **Fahey** votes		Distribution of **Ó Cuív** surplus		Distribution of **Ó Clochartaigh** votes		Distribution of **Nolan** surplus		Distribution of **Healy-Eames** votes		Distribution of **Walsh** surplus	
7		**8**		**9**		**10**		**11**		**12**		**13**	
(+260)	6,148	(+242)	6,390	(+161)	6,551	(+1,656)	8,207	(+168)	8,375	(+708)	9,083	(+12)	9,095
(+45)	4,062												
(+208)	7,324	(+592)	7,916	(+396)	8,312	(+370)	8,682	(+54)	8,736	(+1,075)	9,811	(+18)	9,829
(+1,055)	6,542	(+170)	6,712	(+89)	6,801	(+189)	6,990	(+30)	7,020				
(+729)	6,470	(+151)	6,621	(+84)	6,705	(+324)	7,029	(+45)	7,074	(+1,946)	9,020	(+92)	9,112
(+416)	9,119	(+189)	9,308	(+107)	9,415	(+1,016)	10,431						
(+40)	4,447	(+141)	4,588	(+95)	4,683								
(+108)	9,035	(+2,103)	11,138										
(+1,044)	7,008	(+234)	7,242	(+101)	7,343	(+148)	7,491	(+29)	7,520	(+2,707)	10,227		
88		240		0		980		0		584		0	

Kerry North–Limerick West

Statistics

Seats	3
Electorate	63,614
Total Poll	46,027
Turnout	72.4%
Spoiled	413
Total Valid Poll	45,614
Quota	11,404
Candidates	11

Party Share of Vote

1st Preferences	Number	%	Gain/Loss
Fine Gael	18,599	40.77	*
Labour	9,159	20.08	
Fianna Fáil	5,230	11.47	
Sinn Féin	9,282	20.35	
United Left Alliance	0	0.00	
Green Party	239	0.52	
Others	3,105	6.81	

* New constituency; gain/loss not comparable with last election.

	Quotas	Seats
Fine Gael	1.6	1
Labour	0.8	1
Fianna Fáil	0.5	–
Sinn Féin	0.8	1
United Left Alliance	0	–
Green Party	0	–
Others	0.3	–

Jimmy Deenihan (FG)

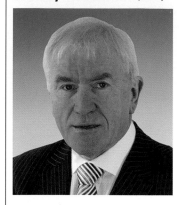

Home Address
Finuge, Lixnaw, Co. Kerry.
Contact Details
Home: (068) 40235/40154.
Office: (01) 631 3806.
Mobile: (087) 811 3661.
Birth Place/Date
Listowel, Co. Kerry, 11 September 1952.
Marital Status
Married to Mary Dowling.
Education
Dromclough N.S. St Michael's College, Listowel. National College of Physical Education, Limerick (BEd).
Occupation
Government Minister. Formerly teacher.

Jimmy Deenihan was appointed Minister for Arts, Heritage and the Gaeltacht on 9 March 2011.

First elected in 1987, he was Minister of State at the Department of Agriculture, Food and Forestry, with special responsibility for Rural Development, the LEADER programme and monitoring the activities of An Bord Bia and the food industry 1994–97.

Senator, Taoiseach's nominee, 1982–87. Spokesperson on: the Office of Public Works, 1997–2002; Defence, from September 2007; Arts, Sport and Tourism in the 29th Dáil and from July 2010.

Member: Kerry County Council 1985–94; Kerry County Vocational Educational Committee; Library Committee 1985–94.

Member, Gaelic Athletic Association. He won All-Ireland football medals in 1975, 1978, 1979, 1980 and 1981 and was captain of the 1981 team. He also won four National League medals and five Railway Cup medals. GAA All-Star Award 1981.

Martin Ferris (SF)

Home Address
18 Casement View, Ardfert, Co. Kerry.
Constituency Office
2 Moyderwell, Tralee, Co. Kerry; Market Street, Listowel, Co. Kerry.
Contact Details
Constituency Office: (066) 712 9545; Fax: (066) 712 9572 (Tralee); (068) 24949 (Listowel).
Birth Place/Date
Tralee, 28 March 1952.
Marital Status
Married to Marie Hoare. Three sons, three daughters, four grandchildren.
Education
Barrow N. S., Ardfert. Tralee CBS (The Green).
Occupation
Full-time public representative. Formerly fisherman.

Martin Ferris is Sinn Féin spokesperson on Communications, Energy and Natural Resources.

He was first elected in 2002 and was re-elected in 2007 and 2011. He was an unsuccessful candidate in the general election of 1997.

He first became a member of the Sinn Féin Ard Comhairle in 1983. He was arrested on board the *Marita Ann* in 1984 attempting to import arms for the IRA. Imprisoned in Portlaoise Prison 1984–94 for possession of explosive substances for unlawful purpose and for possession of firearms and ammunition with intent to endanger life. Also served prison sentences in 1970s and spent forty-seven days on hunger strike in Portlaoise Prison in 1976. Member, Sinn Féin negotiating team for Good Friday Agreement 1998. Member, Sinn Féin delegation to Leeds Castle talks 2004 and St Andrew's talks 2006.

Member of Kerry County Council 1999–2003. Member, Joint Community Policing Committee in Tralee.

Arthur Spring (Lab)

Home Address
1 Brook Lodge, Oak View, Tralee, Co. Kerry.
Contact Details
Office: (066) 712 5337.
Dáil Office: (01) 618 3471.
Mobile: (087) 097 7260.
Facebook: arthurspring. Twitter: @springaj.
Birth Place/Date
Tralee, 5 July 1976.
Marital Status
Married to Fiona.
Education
Tralee CBS. Cistercian College, Roscrea. DIT.
Jonkoping International Business School,
Sweden.
Occupation
Public representative; businessman; owner of
juice bar in Tralee.

Arthur Spring is a new deputy.

He won back the Dáil seat held in North Kerry
by his uncle Dick Spring 1981–2002 and by his
grandfather Dan Spring 1943–81.

Elected to Kerry County Council and Tralee
Town Council in 2009.

Nephew of Dick Spring: Tánaiste 1982–87 and
1993–97; Minister for Environment 1982–83;
Minister for Energy 1983–87; Minister for
Foreign Affairs 1993–97; Minister of State,
Department of Justice 1981–82. Leader of
Labour Party 1982–1997. TD for Kerry North
1981–2002.

Grandson of Dan Spring, TD for Kerry North
1943–81; Parliamentary Secretary to Minister
for Local Government 1956–57.

Kerry North–Limerick West

Seats 3
Quota 11,404

COUNT		1	Distribution of **Deenihan** surplus	2	Distribution of **Donovan, McKenna** votes	3
DEENIHAN, Jimmy*	(FG)	12,304				
DONOVAN, Tom	(GP)	239	(+8)	247		
FERRIS, Martin*	(SF)	9,282	(+158)	9,440	(+49)	9,489
FITZGIBBON, Mary	(Ind)	706	(+16)	722	(+43)	765
LOCKE, Sam	(Ind)	486	(+6)	492	(+6)	498
MCELLISTRIM, Thomas*	(FF)	5,230	(+45)	5,275	(+31)	5,306
MCKENNA, John	(Ind)	101	(+2)	103		
O'BRIEN, Bridget	(Ind)	1,455	(+22)	1,477	(+44)	1,521
REIDY, Michael	(Ind)	357	(+5)	362	(+11)	373
SHEAHAN, John	(FG)	6,295	(+382)	6,677	(+49)	6,726
SPRING, Arthur	(Lab)	9,159	(+256)	9,415	(+99)	9,514
NON-TRANSFERABLE				0		18

Distribution of **Reidy** votes		Distribution of **Fitzgibbon, Locke** votes		Distribution of **O'Brien** votes		Distribution of **McEllistrim** votes	
4		**5**		**6**		**7**	
(+51)	9,540	(+244)	9,784	(+380)	10,164	(+1,252)	11,416
(+84)	849						
(+21)	519						
(+23)	5,329	(+122)	5,451	(+227)	5,678		
(+56)	1,577	(+373)	1,950				
(+55)	6,781	(+111)	6,892	(+250)	7,142	(+902)	8,044
(+57)	9,571	(+376)	9,947	(+738)	10,685	(+1,560)	12,245
26		142		355		1,964	

Kerry South

Statistics

Seats	3
Electorate	59,629
Total Poll	44,679
Turnout	74.9%
Spoiled	299
Total Valid Poll	44,380
Quota	11,096
Candidates	10

Party Share of Vote

1st Preferences	Number	%	Gain/Loss
Fine Gael	14,482	32.63	7.54
Labour	4,926	11.10	-2.38
Fianna Fáil	5,917	13.33	-27.32
Sinn Féin	0	0.00	-3.52
United Left Alliance	0	0.00	0.00
Green Party	401	0.90	-0.99
Others	18,654	42.03	26.68

	Quotas	Seats
Fine Gael	1.3	1
Labour	0.4	–
Fianna Fáil	0.5	–
Sinn Féin	0	–
United Left Alliance	0	–
Green Party	0	–
Others	1.7	2

Ind gains 1 from FF.

Brendan Griffin (FG)

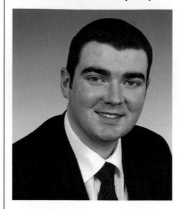

Home Address
Keel, Castlemaine, Co. Kerry.
Contact Details
Dáil Office: (01) 618 4480.
Mobile: (087) 652 8841.
Website: www.brendangriffin.ie.
Facebook: Brendan Griffin.
Twitter: @cllrbgriffin.
Birth Place/Date
Cork, March 1982.
Marital Status
Married to Róisín.
Education
Castledrum N.S. Intermediate School Killorglin. NUI Galway (BA).
Occupation
Full-time public representative. Formerly publican.

Brendan Griffin is a new deputy.

Topped the poll to win seat at first attempt. Promised to accept only half a TD salary if elected.

Elected to Kerry County Council in 2009.

Tom Fleming (Ind)

Home Address
Scartaglin Village, Co. Kerry.
Contact Details
Dáil Office: (01) 618 3354.
Mobile: (087) 781 4781.
Email: tomfleming@gmail.com.
Website: www.tomflemingelection.com
Birth Place/Date
Kerry, February 1951.
Marital Status
Married to Lena. Three daughters.
Education
Scartaglin N.S. St Patrick's College, Castleisland, Co. Kerry.
Occupation
Public representative; publican.

Tom Fleming is a new deputy.

Elected to Kerry County Council for Fianna Fáil in 1985 and at every subsequent local election. Unsuccessful Dáil candidate for Fianna Fáil in 2002 and 2007. Left the party shortly before the 2011 General Election to stand as an Independent.

Michael Healy-Rae (Ind)

Home Address
Sandymount, Kilgarvan, Co. Kerry.
Contact Details
Constituency Office: (064) 663 2467.
Mobile: (087) 246 1678.
Email: michael.healy-rae@oireachtas.ie;
michaelhealyraekilgarvan@gmail.com.
Birth Place/Date
Kerry, 9 January 1967.
Marital Status
Married to Eileen. Five children.
Education
Kilgarvan N.S. Kenmare Vocational School.
Pallaskenry Agricultural College.
Occupation
Full-time public representative.

Michael Healy-Rae is a new deputy. Succeeds his father Jackie Healy-Rea, TD for Kerry South 1997–2010, for whom he worked as a parliamentary assistant and ran his successful election campaigns.

Elected to Kerry County Council 1999 for Killorglin area and re-elected in 2004 and 2009 when he headed poll in his ward. Mayor of Kerry 2002–03 and 2007–08. Chairman of the Strategic Policy Committee on the Environment for five years. Brother Danny also elected to Kerry County Council after taking over their father's seat there in 2003.

Kerry South

Seats 3
Quota 11,096

COUNT	1	Distribution of **Behal, Comerford, Finn** votes		Distribution of **Moloney** votes		Distribution of **O'Donoghue** votes		Distribution of **Gleeson** votes		Distribution of **Griffin** surplus	
	1		**2**		**3**		**4**		**5**		**6**
BEHAL, Richard (Ind)	348										
COMERFORD, Oonagh (GP)	401										
FINN, Dermot (Ind)	281										
FLEMING, Tom (Ind)	6,416	(+132)	6,548	(+809)	7,357	(+1,389)	8,746	(+1,643)	10,389	(+308)	10,697
GLEESON, Michael (Ind)	4,939	(+283)	5,222	(+1,156)	6,378	(+659)	7,037				
GRIFFIN, Brendan (FG)	8,808	(+135)	8,943	(+1,071)	10,014	(+851)	10,865	(+1,771)	12,636		
HEALY-RAE, Michael (Ind)	6,670	(+119)	6,789	(+623)	7,412	(+1,734)	9,146	(+983)	10,129	(+197)	10,326
MOLONEY, Marie (Lab)	4,926	(+206)	5,132								
O'DONOGHUE, John* (FF)	5,917	(+43)	5,960	(+240)	6,200						
SHEAHAN, Tom* (FG)	5,674	(+62)	5,736	(+841)	6,577	(+749)	7,326	(+1,342)	8,668	(+741)	9,409
NON-TRANSFERABLE			50		392		818		1,298		294

Mick Wallace (left) and Joe Higgins arrive for a meeting at Leinster House. Photograph: Bryan O'Brien.

Kildare North

Statistics

Seats	4
Electorate	77,959
Total Poll	51,610
Turnout	66.2%
Spoiled	388
Total Valid Poll	51,222
Quota	10,245
Candidates	12

Party Share of Vote

1st Preferences	Number	%	Gain/Loss
Fine Gael	17,050	33.29	12.07
Labour	14,979	29.24	11.80
Fianna Fáil	7,436	14.52	-24.98
Sinn Féin	2,896	5.65	3.21
United Left Alliance	0	0.00	0.00
Green Party	905	1.77	-3.13
Others	7,956	15.53	3.21

	Quotas	Seats
Fine Gael	1.7	2
Labour	1.5	1
Fianna Fáil	0.7	–
Sinn Féin	0.3	–
United Left Alliance	0	–
Green Party	0.1	–
Others	0.8	1

FG gain 1, Ind gains 1; from FF.

Bernard Durkan (FG)

Home Address
Timard, Maynooth, Co. Kildare.
Contact Details
Home: (01) 628 6063; (01) 628 5215.
Mobile: (086) 255 3370.
Birth Place/Date
Killasser, Swinford, Co. Mayo, 26 March 1945.
Marital Status
Married to Hilary Spence. Two sons.
Education
St John's N.S., Carramore, Co. Mayo.
Occupation
Full-time public representative. Formerly agricultural contractor.

Bernard Durkan was first elected to the Dáil in 1981, lost his seat in February 1982 and regained it in November 1982. He has since been re-elected in all successive general elections.

Minister of State at the Department of Social Welfare, with special responsibility for Information and Customer Services and the Integration of the Tax and Social Welfare Codes, 1994–97. Spokesperson on Overseas Development Assistance and Human Rights in 28th Dáil. Spokesperson on: Health 1994; the Office of the Tánaiste and the National Development Plan 1993–94; the Insurance Industry 1991–92; Trade and Marketing 1989–91; on Food Industry 1987–89. Assistant Whip 1986–87.

Member, Kildare County Council 1976–94 (Chairperson 1986–87). He has served on the Eastern Regional Development Organisation and various Dáil committees including Public Accounts and Foreign Affairs.

Emmet Stagg (Lab)

Home Address
736 Lodge Park, Straffan, Co. Kildare.
Contact Details
Home: (01) 627 2149. Dáil Office: (01) 618 3797.
Email: emmet.stagg@oireachtas.ie.
Web: www.labour.ie/emmetstagg.
Birth Place/Date
Mayo, October 1944.
Marital Status
Married to Mary Morris. One son, one daughter.
Education
Ballinrobe CBS. College of Technology, Kevin Street, Dublin. Member, Institute of Medical Laboratory Sciences.
Occupation
Full-time public representative. Formerly medical laboratory technologist.

First elected to the Dáil in 1987 and re-elected in all subsequent elections.

Appointed the Labour Party's Chief Whip in September 2002. He was Minister of State at the Department of the Environment, with special responsibility for Housing and Urban Renewal, 1993–94; Minister of State at the Department of Transport, Energy and Communications, with special responsibility for Nuclear Safety, Renewable Energy, Gas and Oil Industry, Air Safety, Road Haulage and Bus Regulation, 1994–97.

Labour Party spokesperson on: Public Enterprise 1997-2002; Social Welfare 1989–92; Agriculture 1987–89. Vice-Chairman of the Labour Party 1987–89.

Member: Kildare County Council 1978–93 and 1999–2003 (Chairperson, 1981–82); Kildare County Vocational Education Committee 1985–93; Eastern Health Board 1978–85; Kildare County Library Committee 1975–89.

Member, SIPTU.

Member, Gaelic Athletic Association and President of Celbridge Soccer Club. President, Maynooth Soccer Club.

Catherine Murphy (Ind)

Home Address
46 Leixlip Park, Leixlip, Co. Kildare.
Constituency Office
4 The Post House, Leixlip Shopping Mall,
Main Street, Leixlip, Co. Kildare.
Contact Details
Constituency Office: (01) 615 6625.
Dáil Office: (01) 618 3099.
Email: catherine.murphy@oireachtas.ie.
Website: www.catherinemurphy.ie.
Twitter: @MurphyCatherine.
Birth Place/Date
Dublin, 1 September 1953.
Marital Status
Married to Derek Murphy. One son, one
daughter.
Education
Dominican Convent Ballyfermot. College of
Commerce Rathmines. IPA/NCC Higher
Diploma in Computer Studies.
Occupation
Public representative.

Catherine Murphy was first elected to the Dáil
at a by-election in March 2005 to replace
Fianna Fáil TD Charlie McCreevy but lost the
seat in the 2007 General Election.

First elected to Leixlip Town Commissioners
in 1988, and in 1991 to Kildare County Council
for the Workers' Party. Joined Democratic
Left when it split from the Workers' Party and
ran unsuccessfully in the 1992 and 1997
general elections. Re-elected to Kildare
County Council in 1999 for Labour Party after
merge with DL. Re-elected as an Independent
in 2004 and 2009 after absence while a TD.

Anthony Lawlor (FG)

Home Address
14 Riverlawns, Kill, Co. Kildare.
Constituency Office
56 South Main Street, Naas, Co. Kildare.
Contact Details
Constituency Office: (045) 888 488.
Email: anthony.lawlor@oireachtas.ie.
Website: www.anthonylawlor.ie.
Birth Place/Date
Dublin, 13 June 1959.
Marital Status
Married to Margaret.
Education
Naas CBS. Newbridge College. UCD (Bachelor
of Agricultural Science). NUI Maynooth
(HDipEd).
Occupation
Farmer. Formerly teacher.

Anthony Lawlor is a new deputy.

He was co-opted to Kildare County Council in
1998 following the death of his mother Patsey
Lawlor and re-elected the following year as an
Independent. Did not seek re-election in 2004
and subsequently joined Fine Gael and was
elected to the council for the party in 2009.

Kildare North

Seats 4 Quota 10,245		Distribution of **Beirne, Doyle Higgins, Fitzgerald, Murphy** votes		Distribution of **Durkan** surplus and **Fitzpatrick** votes		Distribution of **Kelly** votes		Distribution of **McGinley** votes	
COUNT	1		2		3		4		5
BEIRNE, Michael (Ind)	422								
BRADY, Aine* (FF)	4,777	(+133)	4,910	(+1,717)	6,627	(+194)	6,821	(+467)	7,288
DOYLE HIGGINS, Eric (Ind)	423								
DURKAN, Bernard* (FG)	10,168	(+252)	10,420						
FITZGERALD, Shane (GP)	905								
FITZ PATRICK, Michael* (FF)	2,659	(+55)	2,714						
KELLY, Martin (SF)	2,896	(+147)	3,043	(+68)	3,111				
LAWLOR, Anthony (FG)	6,882	(+192)	7,074	(+209)	7,283	(+384)	7,667	(+1,421)	9,088
MCGINLEY, John (Lab)	5,261	(+228)	5,489	(+101)	5,590	(+859)	6,449		
MURPHY, Bart (Ind)	200								
MURPHY, Catherine (Ind)	6,911	(+563)	7,474	(+222)	7,696	(+1,020)	8,716	(+2,923)	11,639
STAGG, Emmet* (Lab)	9,718	(+258)	9,976	(+288)	10,264				
NON-TRANSFERABLE			122		109		654		1,638

Gerry Adams launches the Sinn Féin Manifesto for the General Election. Photograph: Alan Betson.

Kildare South

Statistics

Seats	3
Electorate	58,867
Total Poll	38,623
Turnout	65.6%
Spoiled	353
Total Valid Poll	38,270
Quota	9,568
Candidates	8

Party Share of Vote

1st Preferences	Number	%	Gain/Loss
Fine Gael	12,755	33.33	16.16
Labour	10,645	27.82	7.14
Fianna Fáil	8,307	21.71	-28.66
Sinn Féin	2,308	6.03	6.03
United Left Alliance	0	0.00	0.00
Green Party	523	1.37	-4.81
Others	3,732	9.75	8.52

	Quotas	Seats
Fine Gael	1.3	1
Labour	1.1	1
Fianna Fáil	0.9	1
Sinn Féin	0.2	–
United Left Alliance	0	–
Green Party	0.1	–
Others	0.4	–

FG gain 1 from FF.

Martin Heydon (FG)

Home Address
Blackrath, Colbinstown, Co. Kildare.
Contact Details
Home: (045) 487 624.
Email: martin.heydon@oireachtas.ie.
Website: www.martinheydon.com.
Facebook: martinheydonfg.
Twitter: @martinheydonfg.
Birth Place/Date
Dublin, 9 August 1978.
Marital Status
Single.
Education
Crookstown N.S. Cross & Passion College,
Kilcullen, Co. Kildare. Kildalton Agricultural
College, Piltown, Co. Kilkenny.
Occupation
Public representative; farmer.

Martin Heydon is a new deputy.

Elected at his first attempt in 2011, topping
the poll. Member of Kildare County Council for
Athy electoral area since 2009 and acted as
Fine Gael whip on the council.

Jack Wall (Lab)

Home Address
Castlemitchell, Athy, Co. Kildare.
Constituency Office
15 Leinster Street, Athy.
Contact Details
Home: (059) 863 1495.
Constituency Office: (059) 863 2874;
Fax: (059) 863 3157. Mobile: (087) 257 0275.
Birth Place/Date
Castledermot, Co. Kildare, 1 July 1945.
Marital Status
Married to Ann Byrne. Two sons, two
daughters.
Education
Castledermot Vocational School. Kevin Street
College of Technology, Dublin.
Occupation
Full-time public representative. Formerly
electrician.

First elected to the Dáil in 1997; re-elected in
all subsequent elections.

Party spokesperson on: Community and Rural
Affairs; Arts, Sport and Tourism; Agriculture;
Defence; and Social Protection. Member,
Joint Oireachtas Committee on Arts, Sport
and Tourism.

Senator (Taoiseach's nominee) 1993–97.
Spokesperson in the Seanad on Social
Welfare.

Member, Kildare County Council 1999–2002.
Member, Athy Urban District Council
1994–2002 (Chairperson 1996).

Chairperson, Kildare GAA County Board
1989–1999. Director, Athy Credit Union.

Seán Ó Fearghaíl (FF)

Home Address
Fennor House, Kildare.
Constituency Office
4 Offaly Street, Athy, Co. Kildare.
Contact Details
Home: (045) 522 966. Office: (059) 863 4805.
Mobile: (087) 236 7155.
Website: www.seanofearghail.ie.
Facebook: Sean O Fearghail.
Twitter: @SOFearghail.
Birth Place/Date
Dublin, 17 April 1960.
Marital Status
Married to Mary Clare Meaney. One son,
three daughters.
Education
De La Salle N.S., Kildare. St Joseph's
Academy, Kildare.
Occupation
Public representative; farmer.

Seán Ó Fearghaíl is Fianna Fáil spokesperson
on Foreign Affairs and Trade and party Chief
Whip.

He was first elected to the Dáil in 2002,
having contested the previous four general
elections in 1987, 1989, 1992 and 1997.

In the last Dáil he was a member of: the Joint
Oireachtas Committee on Justice, Equality,
Defence and Women's Rights; Committee on
Procedure and Privileges; and the sub-
committee on the Barron Report into the
murder of Seamus Ludlow. He was convenor
of the Joint Oireachtas Committee on
Agriculture and Food. He was a senator on
the Agricultural Panel 1997–2002.

Member, Kildare County Council 1985–2003.
Director and/or chairperson of a number of
voluntary housing associations in the
constituency.

Kildare South

		COUNT	Distribution of **Heydon** surplus		Distribution of **Wall** surplus	
Seats 3 Quota 9,568		**1**		**2**		**3**
CUMMINS, Vivian	(GP)	523	(+421)	944	(+101)	1,045
HEYDON, Martin	(FG)	12,755				
KENNEDY, Paddy	(Ind)	2,806	(+1,019)	3,825	(+256)	4,081
Ó FEARGHAÍL, Seán*	(FF)	4,514	(+447)	4,961	(+136)	5,097
POWER, Seán*	(FF)	3,793	(+514)	4,307	(+138)	4,445
REID, Clifford T.	(Ind)	926	(+484)	1,410	(+234)	1,644
TURNER, Jason	(SF)	2,308	(+302)	2,610	(+212)	2,822
WALL, Jack*	(Lab)	10,645				
NON-TRANSFERABLE			0		0	

Distribution of **Cummins** votes		Distribution of **Reid** votes		Distribution of **Turner** votes		Distribution of **Power** votes	
4		5		6		7	
(+306)	4,387	(+769)	5,156	(+1,685)	6,841	(+869)	7,710
(+80)	5,177	(+138)	5,315	(+237)	5,552	(+3,155)	8,707
(+97)	4,542	(+108)	4,650	(+238)	4,888		
(+229)	1,873						
(+82)	2,904	(+349)	3,253				
251		509		1,093		864	

Laois–Offaly

Statistics

Seats	5
Electorate	108,142
Total Poll	75,213
Turnout	69.6%
Spoiled	1,055
Total Valid Poll	74,158
Quota	12,360
Candidates	21

Party Share of Vote

1st Preferences Number		%	Gain/Loss
Fine Gael	25,032	33.75	6.39
Labour	5,802	7.82	5.44
Fianna Fáil	19,860	26.78	-29.60
Sinn Féin	8,032	10.83	5.72
United Left Alliance	561	0.76	0.76
Green Party	306	0.41	-0.73
Others	14,565	19.64	17.93

	Quotas	Seats
Fine Gael	2	2
Labour	0.5	–
Fianna Fáil	1.6	2
Sinn Féin	0.6	1
United Left Alliance	0	–
Green Party	0	–
Others	1.2	–

SF gain 1 from FF.

Charles Flanagan (FG)

Home Address
Glenlahan, Portlaoise, Co. Laois.
Office
Lismard Court, Portloaise, Co. Laois.
Contact Details
Home: (057) 866 0707. Office: (057) 862 0232;
Fax: (057) 862 159. Mobile: (087) 257 8450.
Birth Place/Date
Dublin, November 1956.
Marital Status
Married to Mary McCormack. Two daughters.
Education
Coláiste na Rinne, Waterford. Knockbeg
College, Carlow. UCD. Law School of the
Incorporated Law Society.
Occupation
Public representative; solicitor.

Charles Flanagan is Chairman of the Fine Gael
parliamentary party. First elected in 1987 but
lost his seat in 2002 and was re-elected in
2007.

Member of FG front bench 1997 –2002 and
2007–2010. Chief Whip (1997–2001) under
John Bruton's leadership. Spokesperson on
Enterprise, Trade and Employment under
Michael Noonan's leadership and on Justice
under Enda Kenny's leadership from 2007
until he supported the leadership heave of
2010.

Previously FG spokesperson on: Criminal Law
Reform and Northern Ireland 1997–2002;
Health 1993–94; Transport and Tourism
1992–93; Law Reform 1988–90. FG Chief
Whip 1990–92; Assistant Whip 1987–88.
Member Laois County Council 1984–2004.

Son of Oliver J. Flanagan: TD for Laois–Offaly
1943–87; Minister for Defence 1976–77;
Parliamentary Secretary to the Minister for
Local Government 1975–76 and to Minister
for Agriculture and Fisheries 1954-57.

Marcella Corcoran Kennedy (FG)

Home Address
Oakley Park, Clareen, Birr, Co. Offaly.
Constituency Office
5 The Courtyard, Emmet Street, Birr,
Co. Offaly.
Contact Details
Constituency Office: (057) 912 5825.
Mobile: (087) 633 0039.
Email:
marcella.corcorankennedy@oireachtas.ie.
Website: www.corcorankennedy.ie.
Birth Place/Date
London, 7 January 1963.
Marital Status
Married to Seamus Kennedy. One son, one
daughter.
Education
St Joseph of Cluny and St Saran's Secondary
School, Ferbane, Co. Offaly. Roscrea
Community College.
Occupation
Full-time public representative.

Marcella Corcoran Kennedy is a new deputy.

She was elected to Offaly County Council to
represent the Ferbane electoral area in 1999.
Re-elected in 2004 when she became
Whip/Secretary of Fine Gael councillors'
group. Served on the Midlands Regional
Authority from 2002–09, chairing it in 2006.
Unsuccessful in the 2009 local elections due
to boundary revision.

Represented Fine Gael councillors on the
party's national executive from 2004–09.

Barry Cowen (FF)

Home Address
Lahinch, Clara, Co. Offaly.
Constituency Office
Grand Canal House, William Street, Tullamore, Co. Offaly.
Contact Details
Office: (057) 932 1976.
Dáil Office: (01) 618 3662.
Birth Place/Date
Dublin, August 1967.
Marital status
Married to Mary. Two sons, two daughters.
Education
Cistercian College, Roscrea, Co. Tipperary.
Occupation
Public representative; auctioneer; valuer.

Barry Cowen is a new deputy. He is Fianna Fáil spokesperson on Social Protection. He was first elected to Offaly County Council in 1999 and re-elected in 2004 and 2009.

Brother of Brian Cowen: Taoiseach 2008–11; leader of Fianna Fáil 2008 to January 2011; Tánaiste 2007–08; Minister for: Finance 2004–08, Foreign Affairs 2000–04, Health 1997–2000, Energy 1993–94, Labour 1992–93; TD for Laois–Offaly 1984–2011.

Son of Bernard Cowen: TD for Laois–Offaly 1969–73 and 1977–84; Senator on Agricultural Panel 1973–77; Minister of State at the Department of Agriculture 1982.

Brian Stanley (SF)

Home Address
40 Clonrooske Abbey, Portlaoise.
Contact Details
Home: (057) 866 2851.
Dáil Office: (01) 618 3987.
Birth Place/Date
January 1958.
Marital status
Married to Caroline. One son, one daughter.
Education
Mountrath Vocational School. Waterford Institute of Technology.
Occupation
Public representative.

Brian Stanley is a new deputy.

Sinn Féin spokesperson on Environment, Community and Local Government.

He was elected to Portlaoise Town Council in 1999 and to Laois County Council in 2004 and 2009.

Seán Fleming (FF)

Home Address
Silveracre, Castletown, Portlaoise, Co. Laois.
Contact Details
Home: (057) 873 2692.
Dáil Office: (01) 618 3472.
Birth Place/Date
The Swan, Co. Laois, 1 February 1958.
Marital status
Married to Mary O'Gorman. One son.
Education
Salesian College, Ballinakill. UCD (BComm). Fellow of the Institute of Chartered Accountants.
Occupation
Full-time public representative. Formerly accountant and Financial Director of Fianna Fáil at national level.

Seán Fleming is Fianna Fáil spokesperson on Public Expenditure and Public Sector Reform. He was first elected to the Dáil in 1997. He was chairperson of the Oireachtas Committee on Finance and a member of the Public Accounts Committee in the 29th Dáil.

Member, Laois County Council 1999–2003.

Seats 5 Quota 12,360		Distribution of **Boland, Cox** votes		Distribution of **Fettes** votes		Distribution of **Fanning** votes		Distribution of **Dumpleton** votes		Distribution of **Adebari, Bracken, Fitzpatrick, McDonnell** votes	
COUNT	1		2		3		4		5		6
ADEBARI, Rotimi (Ind)	628	(+6)	634	(+28)	662	(+13)	675	(+16)	691		
BOLAND, John (Ind)	119										
BRACKEN, John (Ind)	625	(+31)	656	(+9)	665	(+9)	674	(+21)	695		
CORCORAN KENNEDY, Marcella (FG)	5,817	(+21)	5,838	(+33)	5,871	(+48)	5,919	(+59)	5,978	(+185)	6,163
COWEN, Barry (FF)	8,257	(+24)	8,281	(+4)	8,285	(+17)	8,302	(+30)	8,332	(+165)	8,497
COX, Michael (Ind)	60										
DUMPLETON, Liam (Ind)	382	(+11)	393	(+6)	399	(+37)	436				
FANNING, James (Ind)	335	(+8)	343	(+9)	352						
FETTES, Christopher (GP)	306	(+2)	308								
FITZPATRICK, Eddie (Ind)	2,544	(+9)	2,553	(+12)	2,565	(+21)	2,586	(+33)	2,619	(+157)	2,776
FITZPATRICK, Ray (ULA)	561	(+1)	562	(+22)	584	(+10)	594	(+10)	604		
FLANAGAN, Charles* (FG)	10,427	(+5)	10,432	(+16)	10,448	(+21)	10,469	(+22)	10,491	(+169)	10,660
FLEMING, Seán* (FF)	6,024	(+2)	6,026	(+10)	6,036	(+7)	6,043	(+7)	6,050	(+51)	6,101
FOLEY, John (Ind)	4,465	(+4)	4,469	(+9)	4,478	(+22)	4,500	(+24)	4,524	(+406)	4,930
LEAHY, John (Ind)	4,882	(+17)	4,899	(+9)	4,908	(+52)	4,960	(+72)	5,032	(+227)	5,259
MCDONNELL, Fergus (Ind)	525	(+1)	526	(+1)	527	(+6)	533	(+9)	542		
MOLONEY, John* (FF)	5,579	(+9)	5,588	(+9)	5,597	(+10)	5,607	(+9)	5,616	(+54)	5,670
MORAN, John (FG)	4,306	(+1)	4,307	(+11)	4,318	(+8)	4,326	(+2)	4,328	(+45)	4,373
QUINN, Liam (FG)	4,482	(+4)	4,486	(+13)	4,499	(+17)	4,516	(+10)	4,526	(+93)	4,619
STANLEY, Brian (SF)	8,032	(+10)	8,042	(+16)	8,058	(+21)	8,079	(+53)	8,132	(+461)	8,593
WHELAN, John (Lab)	5,802	(+3)	5,805	(+85)	5,890	(+22)	5,912	(+39)	5,951	(+304)	6,255
NON-TRANSFERABLE			10		6		11		20		215

Distribution of **Fitzpatrick** votes		Distribution of **Moran** votes		Distribution of **Flanagan** surplus		Distribution of **Leahy** votes		Distribution of **Quinn** votes		Distribution of **Moloney** votes		Distribution of **Foley** votes	
7		**8**		**9**		**10**		**11**		**12**		**13**	
(+126)	6,289	(+306)	6,595	(+394)	6,989	(+1,302)	8,291	(+3,546)	11,837	(+269)	12,106	(+1,022)	13,128
(+139)	8,636	(+11)	8,647	(+4)	8,651	(+763)	9,414	(+242)	9,656	(+998)	10,654	(+1,206)	11,860
(+347)	11,007	(+2,508)	13,515										
(+105)	6,206	(+363)	6,569	(+116)	6,685	(+153)	6,838	(+129)	6,967	(+3,226)	10,193	(+658)	10,851
(+560)	5,490	(+16)	5,506	(+7)	5,513	(+817)	6,330	(+901)	7,231	(+290)	7,521		
(+179)	5,438	(+11)	5,449	(+3)	5,452								
(+319)	5,989	(+104)	6,093	(+23)	6,116	(+177)	6,293	(+106)	6,399				
(+64)	4,437												
(+165)	4,784	(+564)	5,348	(+449)	5,797	(+478)	6,275						
(+326)	8,919	(+193)	9,112	(+58)	9,170	(+623)	9,793	(+269)	10,062	(+645)	10,707	(+1,068)	11,775
(+234)	6,489	(+275)	6,764	(+101)	6,865	(+423)	7,288	(+526)	7,814	(+394)	8,208	(+818)	9,026
212		86		0		716		556		577		2,749	

Limerick City

Statistics

Seats	4
Electorate	64,909
Total Poll	43,617
Turnout	67.2%
Spoiled	429
Total Valid Poll	43,188
Quota	8,638
Candidates	13

Party Share of Vote

1st Preferences	Number	%	Gain/Loss
Fine Gael	18,696	43.29	*
Labour	8,764	20.29	
Fianna Fáil	9,259	21.44	
Sinn Féin	3,711	8.59	
United Left Alliance	721	1.67	
Green Party	490	1.13	
Others	1,547	3.58	

*New constituency; gain/loss not comparable with last election.

	Quotas	Seats
Fine Gael	2.2	2
Labour	1	1
Fianna Fáil	1.1	1
Sinn Féin	0.4	–
United Left Alliance	0.1	–
Green Party	0.1	–
Others	0.2	–

Michael Noonan (FG)

Home Address
18 Gouldavoher Estate, Father Russell Road, Limerick.
Contact Details
Home: (061) 229 350. Mobile: (087) 647 8111. Email: michael.noonan@oireachtas.ie
Birth Place/Date
Limerick, 22 May 1943.
Marital Status
Married to Florence Knightly. Three sons, two daughters.
Education
St Patrick's Secondary School, Glin, Co. Limerick. St Patrick's Teachers' Training College, Drumcondra, Dublin. UCD (BA, HDipEd).
Occupation
Government Minister.

Michael Noonan was appointed Minister for Finance on 9 March 2011. He was elected leader of Fine Gael in February 2001, succeeding John Bruton, but resigned after the 2002 General Election in which the party fared badly.

He was Chairman of the Public Accounts Committee 2004–07. First elected to the Dáil in 1981 and re-elected at all subsequent general elections. He was: Minister for Justice 1982–86; Minister for Industry and Commerce 1986–87; Minister for Energy, January–March 1987.

He was party spokesperson on Finance 1987–93 and Minister for Health 1994–97. He was again party spokesperson on Finance 1997–2001.

Member, Limerick County Council 1974–82 and 1991–94.

Kieran O'Donnell (FG)

Home Address
8 Milltown Manor, Monaleen, Castletroy, Limerick.
Constituency Office
27 William Street, Limerick.
Contact Details
Home: (061) 330 652. Office: (061) 204 040; Fax: (061) 204 057. Mobile: (086) 843 0202.
Birth Place/Date
Limerick, 8 May 1963.
Marital Status
Married to Phil FitzGerald. Two sons, two daughters.
Education
Ard Scoil Mhuire, Bruff, Co. Limerick. University of Limerick (BBS [Honours]). Fellow of the Institute of Chartered Accountants in Ireland (FCA).
Occupation
Full-time public representative. Formerly chartered accountant.

Kieran O'Donnell was elected to the Dáil at his first attempt in 2007 and took the second seat in the new constituency of Limerick City in 2011.

He was elected to Limerick County Council representing the Castleconnell electoral area in June, 2004. Member, Mid-West Regional Authority and Limerick Market Trustees, Planning and Transport Strategic Policy Committees of Limerick County Council, June 2004 to May 2007.

An active local community worker, he has served as Chairperson of the Castleconnell Electoral Area and Community and Voluntary Forum (2001–03) and is involved in various local community and sports organisations. He has a special interest in the disabled and has campaigned on their behalf.

He is a nephew of Tom O'Donnell: TD for Limerick East 1961–87; Minister for the Gaeltacht 1973–77; and MEP for Munster 1979–89.

Willie O'Dea (FF)

Home Address
Milltown, Kilteely, Co. Limerick.
Constituency Office
2 Glenview Gardens, Farranshore, Limerick.
Contact Details
Office: (061) 454 488. Dáil Office:
(01) 618 4259. Mobile: (087) 919 3666.
Website: www.willieodea.ie.
Facebook: WillieO'Dea.
Twitter: @willieodeaLIVE.
Birth Place/Date
Limerick, November 1952.
Marital Status
Married to Geraldine Kennedy.
Education
Patrician Brothers, Ballyfin, Co. Laois. UCD.
King's Inns, Dublin. Institute of Certified
Accountants (BCL, LLM, BL, Certified
Accountant).
Occupation
Public representative. Formerly barrister and
lecturer.

Fianna Fáil spokesperson on Enterprise, Jobs
and Innovation.

First elected in February 1982, he was
Minister for Defence September 2004 to
February 2010. Chairman of Government Task
Force on Emergency Planning and of All-Party
1916 Centenary Commemoration Committee.

Minister of State at: the Department of
Justice, Equality and Law Reform, with
responsibility for Equality Issues including
Disability Issues, 2002–04; the Department of
Education, Science and Technology, with
special responsibility for Adult Education,
Youth Affairs and School Transport,
1997–2002; the Departments of Justice and
Health, 1993–94; the Department of Justice,
February 1992 to January 1993.

Jan O'Sullivan (Lab)

Home Address
7 Lanahone Avenue, Corbally, Limerick.
Constituency Office
Mechanics' Institute, Hartstonge Street,
Limerick
Contact Details
Constituency Office: (061) 31236.
Mobile: (087) 243 0299.
Email: jan.osullivan@oireachtas.ie.
Website: www.labour.ie/janosullivan.
Facebook: JanOSullivanTD.
Twitter: @JanOSullivanTD.
Birth Place/Date
Limerick, 6 December 1950.
Marital Status
Married to Dr Paul O'Sullivan. One son, one
daughter.
Education
Villiers School, Limerick. TCD.
Occupation
Minister of State. Formerly pre-school
teacher.

Jan O'Sullivan was appointed Minister of
State for Trade and Development on 10
March 2011.

First elected to the Dáil in 1998 in a by-
election caused by the death of Jim Kemmy.
Labour Party spokesperson on Health from
September 2007 to March 2011. Previously:
spokesperson on Education and Science;
Vice-Chairperson of Oireachtas Committee on
Education and Science; Member, All-Party
Committee on the Constitution in last Dáil.
Previously Member, Oireachtas Committee
on Justice, Equality, Defence and Women's
Rights.

Elected to the Seanad in 1993 and was leader
of the Labour group there 1993–97. Member
of Forum for Peace and Reconciliation and the
National Economic and Social Forum.

Member, Democratic Socialist Party until it
merged with the Labour Party.

Limerick City

Seats 4 Quota 8,638		COUNT	1	Distribution of **Noonan** surplus		Distribution of **Larkin, O'Donoghue, Riordan** votes	
			1		**2**		**3**
CAHILL, Sheila	(GP)		490	(+30)	520	(+22)	542
KIELY, Kevin Anthony	(Ind)		1,129	(+71)	1,200	(+70)	1,270
LARKIN, Matt	(Ind)		59	(+3)	62		
LEDDIN, Joe	(Lab)		2,411	(+217)	2,628	(+17)	2,645
NOONAN, Michael*	(FG)		13,291				
O'DEA, Willie*	(FF)		6,956	(+413)	7,369	(+34)	7,403
O'DONNELL, Kieran*	(FG)		5,405	(+2,901)	8,306	(+108)	8,414
O'DONOGHUE, Conor	(CSP)		186	(+11)	197		
O'SULLIVAN, Jan*	(Lab)		6,353	(+769)	7,122	(+39)	7,161
POWER, Peter*	(FF)		2,303	(+96)	2,399	(+30)	2,429
PRENDIVILLE, Cian	(ULA)		721	(+19)	740	(+29)	769
QUINLIVAN, Maurice	(SF)		3,711	(+118)	3,829	(+48)	3,877
RIORDAN, Denis	(Ind)		173	(+5)	178		
NON-TRANSFERABLE					0		40

Distribution of **Cahill** votes		Distribution of **Kiely, Prendiville** votes		Distribution of **Power** votes		Distribution of **O'Dea** surplus	
4		5		6		7	
(+36)	1,306						
(+67)	2,712	(+214)	2,926	(+158)	3,084	(+207)	3,291
(+29)	7,432	(+336)	7,768	(+1,656)	9,424		
(+131)	8,545	(+229)	8,774				
(+153)	7,314	(+414)	7,728	(+351)	8,079	(+441)	8,520
(+37)	2,466	(+67)	2,533				
(+30)	799						
(+17)	3,894	(+624)	4,518	(+116)	4,634	(+124)	4,758
42		221		252		14	

Limerick

Statistics

Seats	3
Electorate	65,083
Total Poll	45,512
Turnout	69.9%
Spoiled	471
Total Valid Poll	45,041
Quota	11,261
Candidates	10

Party Share of Vote

1st Preferences	Number	%	Gain/Loss
Fine Gael	21,925	48.68	*
Labour	7,910	17.56	
Fianna Fáil	9,361	20.78	
Sinn Féin	0	0.00	
United Left Alliance	0	0.00	
Green Party	354	0.79	
Others	5,491	12.19	

*New constituency; gain/loss not comparable with last election.

	Quotas	Seats
Fine Gael	1.9	2
Labour	0.7	1
Fianna Fáil	0.8	–
Sinn Féin	0	–
United Left Alliance	0	–
Green Party	0	–
Others	0.5	–

Dan Neville (FG)

Home Address
Kiltannan, Croagh, Co. Limerick.
Constituency Office
Main Street, Rathkeale, Co. Limerick.
Contact Details
Home/Constituency Office: (061) 396 351;
Fax: (061) 396 351. Mobile: (086) 243 5536.
Website: www.danneville.ie.
Birth Place/Date
Croagh, 12 December 1946.
Marital Status
Married to Goretti O'Callaghan. Two sons,
two daughters.
Education
Adare CBS. University of Limerick, School of
Management Studies. UCC (Industrial
Engineering, Personnel Management, Social
Science).
Occupation
Full-time public representative. Formerly
personnel manager.

Dan Neville was Fine Gael's deputy
spokesperson on Health with special
responsibility for Children and Mental Health
in the last Dáil. He was also Fine Gael
Assistant Whip.

He was a member of the Oireachtas
Committee on Health and Children and of the
Dáil Committee on Procedure and Privileges
in the 29th Dáil.

He was first elected to the Dáil in 1997 when
Fine Gael took two seats in Limerick West for
the first time, defeating his running mate
Michael Finucane by only one vote. Dan Neville
was a candidate in the general elections of
1987 and 1992. He was a Senator, Labour
Panel, 1989–97; Deputy Leader of Fine Gael in
the Seanad and spokesperson on Justice and
Law Reform 1992–97.

Member, Limerick County Council 1985–2003.

President of the Irish Association of
Suicidology and a director of the Irish Palatine
Association.

Patrick O'Donovan (FG)

Home Address
Churchtown Road, Newcastle West,
Co. Limerick.
Constituency Office
24 Maiden Street, Newcastle West,
Co. Limerick; Main Street, Cappamore,
Co. Limerick.
Contact Details
Constituency Office: (069) 77998.
Dáil Office: (01) 618 3610.
Mobile: (087) 907 6267.
Email: patrick.odonovan@oireachtas.ie.
Website: www.patrickodonovan.ie.
Twitter: @podonovan.
Birth Place/Date
Limerick, 21 March 1977.
Marital Status
Single.
Education
Scoil Iósaf, Newcastle West. Courtenay
School, Newcastle West. Scoil Mhuire agus
Íde, Newcastle West. UCC (BSc. Chemistry).
Mary Immaculate College, Limerick (Graduate
Diploma in Primary Education).
Occupation
Public representative; primary teacher.
Formerly industrial chemist; environmental,
health and safety officer.

Patrick O'Donovan is a new deputy.

Member of Limerick County Council 2003–11
during which he was: leader of the Fine Gael
Group; Chairperson of the Environment and
Emergency Services Strategic Policy
Committee; Member, Board of West Limerick
Resources; Member, Co. Limerick Joint
Policing Committee.

Former member of the Fine Gael National
Executive and President of Young Fine Gael.

Niall Collins (FF)

Home Address
Red House Hill, Patrickswell, Co. Limerick.
Contact Details
Home: (061) 300 149. Dáil Office:
(01) 618 4277. Mobile: (086) 835 5219.
Email: niall.collins@oireachtas.ie.
Website: www.niallcollinstd.ie.
Birth Place/Date
Limerick, 30 March, 1973.
Marital status
Married to Eimear O'Connor. One son,
one daughter.
Education
St Munchin's College, Limerick. Limerick
Institute of Technology.
Occupation
Public representative; accountant. Formerly
lecturer at Limerick Institute of Technology,
and Shannon Regional Fisheries Board
employee.

Niall Collins is Fianna Fáil spokesperson on
Environment, Community and Local
Government.

He was elected to Limerick County Council in
June 2004 at his first attempt, receiving 1,600
first preference votes and was elected to the
Dáil at his first attempt in 2007. Elected to
Limerick County Council 2004 for Bruff/Adare
area.

He is a grandson of Jimmy Collins, TD for
Limerick West from 1948 to 1967. Nephew
of Gerard Collins: TD for Limerick West
1967–97; Cabinet Minister 1970–73,
1977–81, 1982, 1987–92; and MEP
1994–2004. He is also a nephew of Michael
Collins, TD for Limerick West 1997–2007.

Seats 3 Quota 11,261		COUNT 1	Distribution of **Cremin, O'Doherty, Sherlock, Wall** votes		Distribution of **O'Donnell** votes		Distribution of **Dillon** votes	
			2		3		4	
COLLINS, Niall*	(FF)	9,361	(+127)	9,488	(+265)	9,753	(+1,056)	10,809
CREMIN, Con	(Ind)	430						
DILLON, John	(Ind)	4,395	(+372)	4,767	(+308)	5,075		
HEFFERNAN, James	(Lab)	7,910	(+326)	8,236	(+657)	8,893	(+1,211)	10,104
NEVILLE, Dan*	(FG)	9,176	(+171)	9,347	(+1,344)	10,691	(+1,037)	11,728
O'DONOVAN, Patrick	(FG)	8,597	(+196)	8,793	(+1,558)	10,351	(+965)	11,316
O'DOHERTY, Patrick	(Ind)	247						
O'DONNELL, William	(FG)	4,152	(+70)	4,222				
SHERLOCK, Seamus	(Ind)	419						
WALL, Stephen	(GP)	354						
NON-TRANSFERABLE			188		90		806	

Longford–Westmeath

Statistics

Seats	4
Electorate	85,918
Total Poll	58,186
Turnout	67.7%
Spoiled	661
Total Valid Poll	57,525
Quota	11,506
Candidates	15

Party Share of Vote

1st Preferences	Number	%	Gain/Loss
Fine Gael	21,887	38.05	7.10
Labour	15,366	26.71	9.06
Fianna Fáil	11,197	19.46	-21.69
Sinn Féin	4,339	7.54	3.65
United Left Alliance	0	0.00	0.00
Green Party	309	0.54	-1.21
Others	4,427	7.70	7.28

	Quotas	Seats
Fine Gael	1.9	2
Labour	1.3	1
Fianna Fáil	1	1
Sinn Féin	0.4	–
United Left Alliance	0	–
Green Party	0	–
Others	0.4	–

FG gain 1 from FF.

Willie Penrose (Lab)

Home Address
Ballintue, Ballynacargy, Co. Westmeath.
Constituency Office
Convent Lane, Bishopgate Street, Mullingar, Co. Westmeath.
Contact Details
Home: (044) 73264. Constituency Office: (044) 43966. Mobile: (087) 824 1933. Email: ministerofstate@environ.ie.
Birth Place/Date
Mullingar, August 1956.
Marital status
Married to Anne Fitzsimons. Three daughters.
Education
St Mary's CBS, Mullingar. Multyfarnham Agricultural College, Co. Westmeath. UCD (BAgrSc; MAgrSc [Economics]). King's Inns, Dublin (Diploma in Legal Studies, Barrister-at-Law).
Occupation
Public representative; barrister.

Minister of State at the Department of the Environment and Local Government, with special responsibility for Housing and Planning. A 'Super Junior' Minister with seat at cabinet.

Willie Penrose was first elected to the Dáil in 1992. He was Labour Party spokesperson on Social and Family Affairs in the 29th Dáil and for the Environment and Local Government in 2002. Chairman of the Joint Oireachtas Committee on Social and Family Affairs 2002–07. He was spokesperson on Agriculture 1997–2002.

Member, Westmeath County Council 1984–2003 and the Council's Planning and Environmental Committee, Agricultural Committee and Coiste Gaeilge.

Member: Ballynacargy GAA Club; Cullion Hurling Club; GAA County Board Committee on Cusack Park, Mullingar Development; Royal Canal Development Group. Director: Ballynacargy Community Childcare Ltd; Westmeath County Childcare Committee Ltd.

James Bannon (FG)

Home Address
Newtown House, Legan, Co. Longford.
Constituency Office
Richmond Street, Longford.
Contact Details
Constituency Office: (043) 333 6185. Dáil Office: (01) 618 4226. Mobile: (087) 203 1816. Email: james.bannon@oireachtas.ie. Website: www.jamesbannon.finegael.org. Facebook: jamesbannon TD. Twitter: @James Bannon TD.
Birth Place/Date
Legan, 26 March 1953.
Marital Status
Single.
Education
Secondary School, Ballymahon, Co. Longford.
Occupation
Public representative; farmer; auctioneer.

First elected to the Dáil in 2007. Party deputy spokesperson on the Environment, with responsibility for Heritage 2007–10. Deputy spokesperson on the Environment 2010–11.

Member of the Seanad Industrial and Commercial Panel 2002–07, where he was Fine Gael spokesperson on the Environment and Local Government.

Member of Longford County Council 1985–2003. Formerly chairman of the council 1991–92. Former general secretary of LAMA, the Local Authorities Members Association.

Nicky McFadden (FG)

Home Address
9 Arcadia Crescent, Athlone, Co. Westmeath.
Constituency Office
Irishtown, Athlone.
Contact Details
Constituency Office: (090) 647 8004. Dáil Office: (01) 618 3938. Mobile: (087) 677 1267. Email: nicky.mcfadden@oireachtas.ie. Website: www.nickymcfadden.ie. Facebook: Nicky-McFadden.
Birth Place/Date
Athlone, December 1962.
Marital Status
Divorced. One daughter, one son.
Education
St Joseph's College, Summerhill, Athlone. Athlone Institute of Technology (Diploma in Legal Studies).
Occupation
Full-time public representative. Formerly medical secretary; ESB employee.

Nicky McFadden is a new deputy. She was a member of the Seanad from 2007 to 2011, elected to the Administrative Panel after standing unsuccessfully for the Dáil in the 2007 General Election.

Fine Gael spokesperson on Social Protection in the Seanad. Member of Athlone Town Council from 1999 and co-opted to Westmeath County Council on her father Brendan McFadden's retirement in 2003.

Robert Troy (FF)

Home Address
Main Street, Ballynacargy, Co. Westmeath.
Constituency Office
Domnic Street, Mullingar, Co. Westmeath.
Contact Details
Office: (044) 933 0769.
Dáil Office: (01) 618 3059. Mobile: (087) 797 9890. E-mail: roberttroy2004@eircom.net.
Birth Place/Date
Ballynacargy, January 1982.
Marital Status
Single.
Education
Emper N.S. St Finian's College, Mullingar. Studying for BESS at TCD, 2011.
Occupation
Full-time public representative. Formerly postmaster.

Robert Troy is a new deputy.

He is Fianna Fáil spokesperson on Arts and Heritage.

Elected to Westmeath County Council 2004 and 2009.

Longford–Westmeath

Seats 4
Quota 11,506

		Distribution of Boland, Cooney, D'Arcy, Jackson, Kinahan votes		Distribution of O'Rourke votes
COUNT	1		2	3
BANNON, James* (FG)	9,129	(+49)	9,178	(+114) 9,292
BOLAND, John (Ind)	330			
BURKE, Peter (FG)	6,629	(+88)	6,717	(+90) 6,807
COONEY, Benny (Ind)	130			
D'ARCY, David (Ind)	159			
HOGAN, Paul (SF)	4,339	(+125)	4,464	(+183) 4,647
JACKSON, Donal (Ind)	101			
KELLY, Peter* (FF)	3,876	(+28)	3,904	(+481) 4,385
KINAHAN, Siobhan (GP)	309			
MCFADDEN, Nicky (FG)	6,129	(+111)	6,240	(+386) 6,626
MORAN, Kevin (Boxer) (Ind)	3,707	(+192)	3,899	(+434) 4,333
O'ROURKE, Mary* (FF)	3,046	(+55)	3,101	
PENROSE, Willie* (Lab)	11,406	(+154)	11,560	
SEXTON, Mae (Lab)	3,960	(+86)	4,046	(+129) 4,175
TROY, Robert (FF)	4,275	(+48)	4,323	(+1,130) 5,453
NON-TRANSFERABLE		93		154

Distribution of **Sexton** votes		Distribution of **Moran** votes		Distribution of **Kelly** votes		Distribution of **Bannon** surplus		Distribution of **Hogan** votes	
4		**5**		**6**		**7**		**8**	
(+1,596)	10,888	(+129)	11,017	(+1,423)	12,440				
(+169)	6,976	(+171)	7,147	(+60)	7,207	(+110)	7,317	(+780)	8,097
(+519)	5,166	(+897)	6,063	(+277)	6,340	(+147)	6,487		
(+591)	4,976	(+185)	5,161						
(+363)	6,989	(+1,917)	8,906	(+165)	9,071	(+174)	9,245	(+1,419)	10,664
(+226)	4,559								
(+171)	5,624	(+329)	5,953	(+2,537)	8,490	(+267)	8,757	(+644)	9,401
540		931		699		236		3,644	

Louth

Statistics

Seats	5
Electorate	99,530
Total Poll	70,190
Turnout	70.5%
Spoiled	871
Total Valid Poll	69,319
Quota	13,864
Candidates	16

Party Share of Vote

1st Preferences	Number	%	Gain/Loss
Fine Gael	21,825	31.48	2.11
Labour	13,264	19.13	14.16
Fianna Fáil	10,858	15.66	-26.47
Sinn Féin	15,072	21.74	6.70
United Left Alliance	0	0.00	0.00
Green Party	3,244	4.68	-2.90
Others	5,056	7.29	6.40

	Quotas	Seats
Fine Gael	1.6	2
Labour	1	1
Fianna Fáil	0.8	1*
Sinn Féin	1.1	1
United Left Alliance	0	–
Green Party	0.2	–
Others	0.4	–

*The 5th seat was filled by Séamus Kirk (FF) Ceann Comhairle, who was returned automatically.

FG gain 1, Lab gain 1; FF lose 1.
Constituency has 1 extra seat since 2007.

Séamus Kirk (FF)

Home Address
Rathiddy, Knockbridge, Co. Louth.
Contact Details
Home: (042) 933 1032. Dáil Office: (01) 618 3362.
Birth Place/Date
Drumkeith, Co. Louth, 26 April 1945.
Marital Status
Married to Mary McGeough. Three sons, one daughter.
Education
Dundalk CBS.
Occupation
Full-time public representative; farmer.

Séamus Kirk is party spokesperson on Horticulture and Rural Affairs.

He was Ceann Comhairle in the 30th Dáil and returned automatically to the 31st Dáil. Chairman of the Fianna Fáil Parliamentary Party from 2002 until October 2009, when he was appointed Ceann Comhairle on the resignation of John O'Donoghue. First elected to the Dáil in November 1982. Minister of State at the Department of Agriculture and Food, with special responsibility for Horticulture, March 1987 to February 1992.

During the 28th Dáil he was Chairman of the European Affairs Committee, a member of the All-Party Committee on the Constitution and the Oireachtas Committee on Local Government.

Member: Forum for Peace and Reconciliation 1994–96; British–Irish Inter-Parliamentary Body.

Member: Louth County Council 1974–85; Louth County Health Committee 1974–85; Louth County Committee of Agriculture 1974–85; East Border Region Committee 1974–85.

Member of the GAA since 1958. Member, Tidy Towns Committee.

Gerry Adams (SF)

Home Address
Baile Mhic Eileiod, Ravensdale, Co. Louth.
Constituency Office
7 Williamsons Place, Dundalk; 46 Magdalene Street, Drogheda.
Contact Details
Constituency Office: (042) 932 8859 (Dundalk); (041) 987 3823 (Drogheda). Email: gerry.adams@oireachtas.ie. Website: www.sinnfein.ie; www.unitingireland.ie. Facebook: Sinn-Fein_President-Gerry-Adams. Website: leargas.blogspot.com.
Birth Place/Date
Belfast, 6 October 1948.
Marital Status
Married to Collette McArdle. Three children.
Education
St Finian's Primary School, Belfast. St Mary's Grammar School, Belfast.
Occupation
Public representative.

Gerry Adams is a new deputy.

President of Sinn Féin since 1983 and played a leading role in initiating and seeing through the peace process in Northern Ireland.

Elected MP for West Belfast in the UK General Election in 1983 but never took his seat in the House of Commons. Lost the seat in 1992 to SDLP; regained it in 1997, until 2011 when he resigned to run for the Dáil. Member of the Northern Ireland Assembly, June 1998 to December 2010, when he resigned to contest the Dáil election in Louth.

Involved in the civil rights movement in the North and sided with the Provisionals in the republican movement split in 1969/70. Interned in March 1972; released three months later to take part in secret talks with Northern Ireland Secretary William Whitelaw. Re-interned 1973–1976. Instrumental in ending the Sinn Féin abstentionist policy in the South.

Author of numerous books of memoir, short stories and political writings.

Fergus O'Dowd (FG)

Home Address
24 St Mary's Villas, Drogheda, Co. Louth.
Constituency Office
10 Boyne Shopping Centre, Drogheda.
Contact Details
Home: (041) 983 3392. Office: (041) 984 2275.
Mobile: (087) 235 2920.
Birth Place/Date
Thurles, Co. Tipperary, September 1948.
Marital Status
Married to Margaret Thornton. Three sons.
Education
Drogheda CBS. Diploma in General and Rural
Science.
Occupation
Full-time public representative. Formerly
teacher.

Minister of State at the Department of the
Environment and also at the Department of
Communications.

Fergus O'Dowd was first elected in 2002. He
was Fine Gael front bench spokesperson on
the Environment, Heritage and Local
Government from 2004 and previously
spokesperson on Community, Rural and
Gaeltacht Affairs in the 29th Dáil.

He was a Senator on the Administrative Panel
from 1997 to 2002.

Member: Louth County Council 1979–2003;
Drogheda Corporation 1974–2003. Served
three terms as Mayor (1977–78, 1981–82,
1994–95). Member, North Eastern Health
Board. Founding Chairman of the Droichead
Arts Centre, Drogheda. Campaigned for
closure of Sellafield nuclear re-processing
plant and against a local incinerator.

Gerald Nash (Lab)

Home Address
115 Newfield, Drogheda, Co. Louth.
Contact Details
Dáil Office: (01) 618 3576.
Mobile: (087) 271 6816.
Website: www.geraldnash.com.
Birth Place/Date
Drogheda, December 1975.
Marital status
Unmarried.
Education
St Joseph's CBS, Drogheda. UCD.
Occupation
Full-time public representative. Formerly
assistant to MEP, Nessa Childers; prior to
that, PR consultant in voluntary sector.

Gerald Nash is a new deputy.

He was an unsuccessful Dáil candidate in the
general election of 2007. Elected to Drogheda
Corporation 1999. Co-opted to Louth County
Council 2002. Elected to Louth County
Council 2004 and 2009 and re-elected to
Drogheda Corporation. Mayor of Drogheda
2004–2005.

Peter Fitzpatrick (FG)

Home Address
18 Belfrey Gardens, Dundalk, Co. Louth.
Constituency Office
2 The Courthouse Square, Dundalk.
Contact Details
Office: (042) 933 0100.
Dáil Office: (01) 618 3563.
Mobile: (086) 251 2577.
Website: www.peterfitzpatrick@finegael.ie.
Birth Place/Date
Dundalk, May 1962.
Marital status
Married. One son, two daughters.
Education
De La Salle, Dundalk. O'Fiaich College,
Dundalk.
Occupation
Public representative; businessman.

Peter Fitzpatrick is a new deputy.

He is manager of the Louth football team that
lost the controversial 2010 Leinster Senior
Football final to Meath.

He had no previous political experience before
contesting the 2011 General Election.

Louth

Seats 5 **Quota 13,864**		Distribution of **Adams** surplus		Distribution of **Glynn** surplus		Distribution of **O'Dowd** surplus		Distribution of **Bradley** votes		Distribution of **Crilly, Martin** votes	
COUNT		**1**	**2**		**3**		**4**		**5**		**6**
ADAMS, Gerry	(SF)	15,072									
BRADLEY, David	(Ind)	174	(+37)	211	(+4)	215	(+)	215			
BREATHNACH, Declan	(FF)	5,177	(+68)	5,245	(+)	5,245	(+2)	5,247	(+16)	5,263	(+22)	5,285
CARROLL, James	(FF)	5,681	(+68)	5,749	(+2)	5,751	(+8)	5,759	(+15)	5,774	(+18)	5,792
CLARE, Thomas	(Ind)	2,233	(+85)	2,318	(+6)	2,324	(+4)	2,328	(+62)	2,390	(+66)	2,456
CRILLY, Gerry	(Ind)	222	(+30)	252	(+2)	254	(+)	254	(+13)	267		
DEAREY, Mark	(GP)	3,244	(+114)	3,358	(+4)	3,362	(+4)	3,366	(+8)	3,374	(+47)	3,421
FITZPATRICK, Peter	(FG)	7,845	(+153)	7,998	(+4)	8,002	(+50)	8,052	(+17)	8,069	(+61)	8,130
GLYNN, Robert	(Ind)	61	(+4)	65							
GODFREY, Frank	(Ind)	649	(+65)	714	(+13)	727	(+4)	731	(+23)	754	(+27)	781
MARTIN, Luke	(Ind)	224	(+65)	289	(+4)	293	(+)	293	(+7)	300		
MATTHEWS, Fred	(Ind)	957	(+47)	1,004	(+9)	1,013	(+2)	1,015	(+9)	1,024	(+65)	1,089
MORAN, Mary	(Lab)	4,546	(+192)	4,738	(+4)	4,742	(+5)	4,747	(+1)	4,748	(+60)	4,808
NASH, Gerald	(Lab)	8,718	(+224)	8,942	(+6)	8,948	(+36)	8,984	(+14)	8,998	(+39)	9,037
O'DOWD, Fergus*	(FG)	13,980									
WILSON, Robin	(Ind)	536	(+56)	592	(+5)	597	(+1)	598	(+12)	610	(+82)	692
NON-TRANSFERABLE			0		2		0		18		80

Distribution of **Wilson** votes		Distribution of **Godfrey, Matthews** votes		Distribution of **Clare** votes		Distribution of **Dearey** votes		Distribution of **Breathnach** votes		Distribution of **Moran** votes		Distribution of **Nash** surplus	
7		**8**		**9**		**10**		**11**		**12**		**13**	
(+12)	5,297	(+76)	5,373	(+230)	5,603	(+398)	6,001						
(+11)	5,803	(+184)	5,987	(+494)	6,481	(+288)	6,769	(+3,942)	10,711	(+474)	11,185	(+203)	11,388
(+113)	2,569	(+455)	3,024										
(+85)	3,506	(+166)	3,672	(+267)	3,939								
(+47)	8,177	(+298)	8,475	(+507)	8,982	(+948)	9,930	(+696)	10,626	(+1,144)	11,770	(+553)	12,323
(+48)	829												
(+118)	1,207												
(+100)	4,908	(+216)	5,124	(+312)	5,436	(+994)	6,430	(+544)	6,974				
(+61)	9,098	(+306)	9,404	(+417)	9,821	(+659)	10,480	(+178)	10,658	(+3,962)	14,620		
97		335		797		652		641		1,394		0	

Mayo

Statistics

Seats	5
Electorate	101,160
Total Poll	74,795
Turnout	73.9%
Spoiled	641
Total Valid Poll	74,154
Quota	12,360
Candidates	15

Party Share of Vote

1st Preferences	Number	%	Gain/ Loss
Fine Gael	48,170	64.96	10.91
Labour	3,644	4.91	3.75
Fianna Fáil	11,920	16.07	-8.48
Sinn Féin	4,802	6.48	1.40
United Left Alliance	0	0.00	0.00
Green Party	266	0.36	-0.46
Others	5,352	7.22	-7.11

	Quotas	Seats
Fine Gael	3.9	4
Labour	0.3	–
Fianna Fáil	1	1
Sinn Féin	0.4	–
United Left Alliance	0	–
Green Party	0	–
Others	0.4	–

FG gain 1 from FF.

Enda Kenny (FG)

Home Address
Hawthorn Avenue, Lightfort, Castlebar, Co. Mayo.
Constituency Office
Tucker Street, Castlebar.
Contact Details
Office: (094) 902 5600; Fax: (094) 902 6554. Email: taoiseach@taoiseach.ie. Website: www.gov.ie; www.merrionstreet.ie; www.finegael.ie.
Birth Place/Date
Castlebar, 24 April 1951.
Marital Status
Married to Fionnuala O'Kelly. Two sons, one daughter.
Education
St Gerald's Secondary School, Castlebar. St Patrick's Training College, Drumcondra, Dublin. NUI Galway.
Occupation
Taoiseach and Leader of Fine Gael. Formerly national school teacher.

Elected Taoiseach on 9 March 2011. Longest-serving TD in the Dáil. Elected Leader of Fine Gael in June 2002 following the resignation of Michael Noonan. Defeated by Noonan in the contest for the leadership in January 2001.

Minister for Tourism and Trade 1994–97; Minister of State at the Department of Education, and at the Department of Labour, February 1986 to March 1987. First elected to the Dáil at a by-election in November 1975 caused by his father's death.

Party spokesperson on Arts, Heritage, Gaeltacht and the Islands 1997–2002. Fine Gael Chief Whip 1992–94 and spokesperson on Regional Development 1994. Spokesperson on: the Gaeltacht 1987–88 and in 1982; Western Development 1982; Youth Affairs and Sport 1977–80. Member, Mayo County Council 1975–95.

Son of Henry Kenny, TD for Mayo South 1954–69 and for Mayo West 1969–75, and Parliamentary Secretary to the Minister for Finance 1973–75.

Michael Ring (FG)

Home Address
Westport, Co. Mayo.
Constituency Office
Quay Street, Westport.
Contact Details
Constituency Office: (098) 27012. Email: michael.ring@oireachtas.ie. Website: www.michaelringtd.com.
Birth Place/Date
Westport, 24 December 1953.
Marital Status
Married to Ann Fitzgerald. One son, two daughters.
Education
Westport Vocational School
Occupation
Full-time public representative.

Michael Ring was appointed Minister of State at the Department of Transport, Tourism and Sport, with responsibility for Tourism and Sport, on 10 March 2011.

First elected to the Dáil in a by-election in June 1994 in the old Mayo West constituency following the resignation of Pádraig Flynn (FF) to become an EU Commissioner. Fine Gael spokesperson on: Social Protection 2010–11; Social and Family Affairs 2002–04; and Agriculture – Livestock, Breeding and Horticulture 1997–2000. Deputy spokesperson on Health 2000–02.

Member of Joint Committee on Health and Children in 28th Dáil. Member British–Irish Inter-Parliamentary Body.

Member: Mayo County Council 1991–2003; Westport Urban District Council 1979–2003 (Chairman 1982–83 and 1988–89).

Michelle Mulherin (FG)

Home Address
47 Moy Heights, Ballina, Co. Mayo.
Contact Details
Constituency Office: (096) 77596.
Mobile: (087) 931 7406.
Email: fgballina@hotmail.com.
Twitter: @mulherinfg.
Birth Place/Date
Castlebar, January 1972.
Marital status
Single.
Education
St Mary's Convent of Mercy, Ballina. UCD.
Law Society of Ireland.
Occupation
Public representative; solicitor.

Michelle Mulherin is a new deputy.

Elected to: Ballina Town Council in 1999;
Mayo County Council 2004 and 2009. Mayor
of Ballina 2008–09.

John O'Mahony (FG)

Home Address
'Tower House', Charlestown Road,
Ballaghaderreen, Co. Mayo.
Constituency Office
D'Alton Street, Claremorris, Co. Mayo.
Contact Details
Office: (094) 937 3560. Dáil Office: (01) 618
3706; Fax: (01) 618 4595. Mobile: (086) 833
8017. Website: www.johnomahony.ie.
Facebook: john.omahonytd. Twitter:
@omahonytd.
Birth Place/Date
Kilmovee, Co. Mayo, 8 June 1953.
Marital Status
Married to Gerardine Towey. Five daughters.
Education
Magheraboy N.S. St Nathy's College,
Ballaghaderreen. St Patrick's College
Maynooth (BA). NUI Galway (HDipEd).
Occupation
Public representative. Formerly secondary
school teacher.

John O'Mahony was first elected to the Dáil
in 2007, at his first attempt.

Winner of two All-Ireland medals as a Mayo
player, minor (1971) and under-21 (1974).
Winner of six All-Ireland titles and fifteen
Connacht titles as team manager with Mayo,
Galway, Leitrim, St Nathy's and St Bridget's.

A teacher in St Nathy's College,
Ballaghaderreen, Co. Mayo from 1974
to 2006.

Dara Calleary (FF)

Home Address
8 Quignalecka, Sligo Road, Ballina, Co. Mayo.
Constituency Office
19 Pearse Street, Ballina.
Contact Details
Constituency Office: (096) 77613.
Dáil Office: (01) 618 3331.
Email: dara.calleary@oireachtas.ie.
Website: www.daracalleary.ie.
Facebook: daracallearytd.
Twitter: @daracallearytd.
Birth Place/Date
Mayo, 10 May 1973.
Marital Status
Single.
Education
St Oliver Plunkett N.S., Ballina. St Muredach's
College, Ballina. TCD (BA [Hons] in Business
and Politics).
Occupation
Full-time public representative.

Dara Calleary was appointed Fianna Fáil
spokesperson on Justice, Equality & Defence
in April 2011.

Minister of State at the Department of
Enterprise, Trade and Employment, April 2009
to March 2011; Minister of State at the
Department of An Taoiseach and at the
Department of Finance, with responsibility for
Public Service Reform, from 2010 to March
2011.

First elected to the Dáil in 2007. Joint
Honorary Secretary of Fianna Fáil. Chairman of
Ógra Fianna Fáil 2008–09.

Son of Seán Calleary: TD for East Mayo
1973–92; Minister of State at the Department
of the Public Service 1979–81; Minister of
State at the Department of Industry and
Commerce 1982; and Minister of State at the
Department of Foreign Affairs 1987–92.

Grandson of P.A. Calleary, TD for North Mayo
1952–69.

Mayo

Seats 5 Quota 12,360		COUNT	Distribution of **Kenny** surplus		Distribution of **Ring** surplus	
		1		**2**		**3**
CALLEARY, Dara*	(FF)	8,577	(+168)	8,745	(+30)	8,775
CAREY, John Andrew	(GP)	266	(+14)	280	(+2)	282
CHAMBERS, Lisa	(FF)	3,343	(+121)	3,464	(+27)	3,491
CLARKE, Loretta	(Ind)	218	(+8)	226	(+2)	228
CONWAY WALSH, Rose	(SF)	2,660	(+92)	2,752	(+61)	2,813
COWLEY, Dr Jerry	(Lab)	3,644	(+311)	3,955	(+82)	4,037
DALY, Martin Joseph	(Ind)	893	(+26)	919	(+7)	926
FORKIN, Sean	(Ind)	29	(+2)	31	(+)	31
KENNY, Enda*	(FG)	17,472				
KILCOYNE, Michael	(Ind)	3,996	(+645)	4,641	(+74)	4,715
MCDONNELL, Dermot	(Ind)	216	(+21)	237	(+1)	238
MULHERIN, Michelle	(FG)	8,851	(+1,963)	10,814	(+296)	11,110
O'MAHONY, John*	(FG)	8,667	(+1,623)	10,290	(+221)	10,511
RING, Michael*	(FG)	13,180				
RUANE, Thérèse	(SF)	2,142	(+118)	2,260	(+17)	2,277
NON-TRANSFERABLE				0		0

Distribution of Carey, Clarke, Daly, Forkin, McDonnell votes		Distribution of Ruane votes		Distribution of Chambers votes		Distribution of Conway Walsh votes		Distribution of Cowley votes	
4		**5**		**6**		**7**		**8**	
(+194)	8,969	(+94)	9,063	(+2,539)	11,602	(+620)	12,222	(+775)	12,997
(+61)	3,552	(+67)	3,619						
(+126)	2,939	(+1,428)	4,367	(+160)	4,527				
(+257)	4,294	(+235)	4,529	(+185)	4,714	(+1,185)	5,899		
(+232)	4,947	(+181)	5,128	(+334)	5,462	(+675)	6,137	(+1,242)	7,379
(+324)	11,434	(+143)	11,577	(+95)	11,672	(+490)	12,162	(+1,141)	13,303
(+177)	10,688	(+176)	10,290	(+221)	10,511	(+177)	10,688	(+176)	12,111
(+161)	2,438								
	173		114		166		1,221		1,970

Meath East

Statistics

Seats	3
Electorate	64,873
Total Poll	43,098
Turnout	66.4%
Spoiled	346
Total Valid Poll	42,752
Quota	10,689
Candidates	9

Party Share of Vote

1st Preferences	Number	%	Gain/ Loss
Fine Gael	17,471	40.87	14.99
Labour	8,994	21.04	9.10
Fianna Fáil	8,384	19.61	-23.95
Sinn Féin	3,795	8.88	4.94
United Left Alliance	0	0.00	0.00
Green Party	461	1.08	-2.01
Others	3,647	8.53	-0.83

	Quotas	Seats
Fine Gael	1.6	2
Labour	0.8	1
Fianna Fáil	0.8	–
Sinn Féin	0.4	–
United Left Alliance	0	–
Green Party	0	–
Others	0.3	–

FG gain 1, Lab gain 1; from FF.

Dominic Hannigan (Lab)

Home Address
Dunshaughlin, Co. Meath.
Contact Details
Constituency Office: (01) 835 3871.
Dáil Office: (01) 618 4007.
Mobile: (087) 641 8960.
Website: www.domnichannigan.com.
Birth Place/Date
Drogheda, 1 July 1965.
Marital Status
Single.
Education
Cushenstown N.S., Kilmoon, Co. Meath. St Mary's CBS, Drogheda. UCD (Engineering degree). City University London (MA in Transport). University of London (MA in Finance).
Occupation
Full-time public representative. Formerly engineer with Camden Council, London.

Dominic Hannigan is a new deputy.

He was an unsuccessful candidate for the Dáil in the Meath by-election of 2005 and the general election of 2007 but was elected to the Seanad on the Industrial and Commercial Panel in 2007.

He was elected to Meath County Council as an Independent in 2004.

Regina Doherty (FG)

Home Address
2 Glebe Park, Rathoath, Co. Meath.
Contact Details
Dáil Office: (01) 618 3573.
Mobile: (087) 268 0182.
Website: www.reginadoherty.com.
Twitter: @reginado.
Birth Place/Date
Dublin, January 1971.
Marital Status
Married to Declan Doherty. Two sons, two daughters.
Education
St Mary's Holy Faith, Glasnevin. College of Marketing and Design, Dublin.
Occupation
Full-time public representative. Formerly worked in sales.

Regina Doherty is a new deputy.

She was an unsuccessful candidate in the 2007 General Election. A primary concern of hers is the impact of the recession on people who are unable to repay their mortgages.

Shane McEntee (FG)

Home Address
Castletown, Kilpatrick, Navan, Co. Meath.
Constituency Offices
Copper Beech, Duleek, Co. Meath;
Main Street, Nobber, Co. Meath.
Contact Details
Constituency Offices: Duleek: (041) 988 2727;
Fax: (041) 988 2477. Nobber: (046) 905 2653;
Fax: (046) 905 2561.
Birth Place and Date
Nobber, 19 December 1956.
Marital Status
Married to Kathleen Corbally. Three children.
Education
St Finian's College, Mullingar.
Occupation
Minister of State; publican. Formerly farmer
and agricultural sales representative.

Shane McEntee was appointed Minister of
State at the Department of Agriculture, with
special responsibilities for Food, Food Safety
and Horticulture, on 10 March 2011.

First elected at a by-election in 2005 to
replace former Taoiseach and Fine Gael leader
John Bruton on his appointment as EU
Ambassador to the United States. Re-elected
in 2007 and deputy spokesperson for
Department of Transport, with special
responsibility for Road Safety, until October
2010. Deputy spokesperson for Agriculture,
with special responsibility for Food and
Fisheries, October 2010 to March 2011.

Involved in numerous voluntary organisations,
particularly the GAA. Has trained many
football teams over the last twenty years,
including Meath minors.

Seats 3
Quota 10,689

COUNT	1	Distribution of **Keogan, Ó Buachalla** votes	2	Distribution of **Killian** votes	3	Distribution of **Bonner, Gallagher** votes	4
BONNER, Joe (Ind)	2,479	(+387)	2,866	(+208)	3,074		
BYRNE, Thomas* (FF)	5,715	(+177)	5,892	(+1,462)	7,354	(+819)	8,173
DOHERTY, Regina (FG)	8,677	(+181)	8,858	(+447)	9,305	(+1,142)	10,447
GALLAGHER, Michael (SF)	3,795	(+163)	3,958	(+67)	4,025		
HANNIGAN, Dominic (Lab)	8,994	(+389)	9,383	(+286)	9,669	(+2,713)	12,382
KEOGAN, Sharon (Ind)	1,168						
KILLIAN, Nick (FF)	2,669	(+50)	2,719				
MCENTEE, Shane* (FG)	8,794	(+200)	8,994	(+148)	9,142	(+1,001)	10,143
Ó BUACHALLA, Seán (GP)	461						
NON-TRANSFERABLE			82		101		1,424

Meath West

Statistics

Seats	3
Electorate	62,776
Total Poll	40,591
Turnout	64.7%
Spoiled	413
Total Valid Poll	40,178
Quota	10,045
Candidates	13

Party Share of Vote

1st Preferences	Number	%	Gain/Loss
Fine Gael	18,450	45.92	16.89
Labour	5,432	13.52	9.48
Fianna Fáil	7,285	18.13	-33.45
Sinn Féin	6,989	17.40	6.11
United Left Alliance	0	0.00	0.00
Green Party	479	1.19	-1.31
Others	1,543	3.84	2.28

	Quotas	Seats
Fine Gael	1.8	2
Labour	0.5	–
Fianna Fáil	0.7	–
Sinn Féin	0.7	1
United Left Alliance	0	–
Green Party	0	–
Others	0.2	–

FG gain 1, SF gain 1; from FF.

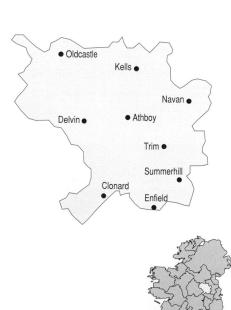

Damien English (FG)

Home Address
40 Watergate Street, Navan, Co. Meath.
Constituency Office
16 Bridge Street, Navan.
Contact Details
Office: (046) 907 1667; Fax: (046) 907 2225.
Mobile: (086) 814 3495.
Website: www.damienenglish.ie.
Birth Place/Date
Drogheda, Co. Louth, 21 February 1978.
Marital Status
Married to Laura Kenny. One son.
Education
Kells Community School. Chartered Institute of Management Accountants.
Occupation
Full-time public representative.

Damien English was first elected to the Dáil in 2002, the youngest TD returned at that election. He was Fine Gael's deputy spokesperson on Justice and Community Affairs, with special responsibility for Drugs, Alcohol and Crime Prevention, in the last Dáil. He was previously deputy spokesperson on Arts, Sports and Tourism.

He was elected Secretary to the Fine Gael Parliamentary Party in September 2002.

He was a member of Meath County Council from 1999 to 2003. Member: Meath County Development Board; Navan Shamrock Festival Board.

Peadar Tóibín (SF)

Home Address
123 An Coillearnach, Navan, Co. Meath.
Contact Details
Dáil Office: (01) 618 3518.
Mobile: (087) 270 7985.
Email: peadartoibin@gmail.com.
Website: www.peadartoibin.ie.
Twitter: Toibin1.
Birth Place/Date
Co. Louth, June 1974.
Marital Status
Married.
Education
UCD (BA; Smurfit School of Business). NUI Maynooth (certificate in Training and Further Education).
Occupation
Full-time public representative. Formerly self-employed management consultant.

Peadar Tóibín is a new deputy.

Sinn Féin spokesperson on Enterprise, Jobs, Innovation and the Gaeltacht.

Elected to Navan Town Council, June 2009. Deputy Mayor of Navan, 2010.

Ray Butler (FG)

Home Address
7 Swift Court, Trim, Co. Meath.
Constituency Office
1 St Martin's House, Finnegan's Way, Trim,
Co. Meath.
Contact Details
Constituency Office: (046) 948 6717.
Mobile: (087) 259 6680.
Email: ray.butler@oireachtas.ie.
Website: www.raybutler.finegael.ie.
Twitter: @RayButlerTD.
Birth Place/Date
Kells, Co. Meath, 30 December 1965.
Marital Status
Married to Marie. Four children.
Education
Kells Christian Brothers.
Occupation
Full-time public representative. Formerly
businessman.

Ray Butler is a new deputy.

Topped the poll in elections to Trim Town
Council in 2004 and 2009. Chairman of the
council in 2008 and 2010. Member of Meath
VEC. Director of Meath County Enterprise
Board. Member of the board of management
of the Aura Leisure Centre in Trim.

Meath West

Seats 3
Quota 10,045

	COUNT	Distribution of **Ball, Carolan, Irwin, MacMeanmain, McDonagh, Stevens** votes		Distribution of **Cassells** votes		Distribution of **Yore** votes		Distribution of **Brady** votes	
	1		2		3		4		5
BALL, Stephen (Ind)	475								
BRADY, Johnny* (FF)	3,789	(+85)	3,874	(+2,191)	6,065	(+372)	6,437		
BUTLER, Ray (FG)	5,262	(+152)	5,414	(+160)	5,574	(+2,305)	7,879	(+1,047)	8,926
CAROLAN, Ronan (Ind)	258								
CASSELLS, Shane (FF)	3,496	(+135)	3,631						
ENGLISH, Damien* (FG)	9,290	(+319)	9,609	(+513)	10,122				
IRWIN, Fiona (GP)	479								
MAC MEANMAIN, Manus (Ind)	234								
MCDONAGH, Seamus (Ind)	189								
MCHUGH, Jenny (Lab)	5,432	(+420)	5,852	(+188)	6,040	(+754)	6,794	(+1,004)	7,798
STEVENS, Daithi (Ind)	387								
TÓIBÍN, Peadar (SF)	6,989	(+432)	7,421	(+290)	7,711	(+444)	8,155	(+957)	9,112
YORE, Catherine (FG)	3,898	(+174)	4,072	(+136)	4,208				
NON-TRANSFERABLE			305		153		333		3,429

Eamon Gilmore addressing campaign workers and the media at the Labour Party election headquarters in Dublin after the dissolution of the 30th Dáil. Photograph: Bryan O'Brien.

Roscommon–South Leitrim

Statistics

Seats	3
Electorate	60,998
Total Poll	48,035
Turnout	78.7%
Spoiled	531
Total Valid Poll	47,504
Quota	11,877
Candidates	10

Party Share of Vote

1st Preferences	Number	%	Gain/Loss
Fine Gael	18,303	38.53	-0.60
Labour	4,455	9.38	7.57
Fianna Fáil	7,103	14.95	-23.89
Sinn Féin	4,637	9.76	1.35
United Left Alliance	0	0.00	0.00
Green Party	220	0.46	-1.35
Others	12,786	26.92	16.92

	Quotas	Seats
Fine Gael	1.5	2
Labour	0.4	–
Fianna Fáil	0.6	–
Sinn Féin	0.4	–
United Left Alliance	0	–
Green Party	0	–
Others	1.1	1

Ind gains 1 from FF.

Frank Feighan (FG)

Home Address
Bridge Street, Boyle, Co. Roscommon.
Constituency Office
Bridge Street, Boyle.
Contact Details
Office: (071) 966 2608; (071) 966 2115;
Fax: (071) 966 3956. Mobile: (086) 833 1234.
Marital Status
Single.
Birth Place/Date
Roscommon, 4 July 1962.
Education
St Joseph's N.S., Boyle. St Mary's College, Boyle.
Occupation
Public representative; businessman.

Fine Gael front bench spokesperson on Community, Equality and Gaeltacht Affairs, July 2010 to February 2011. Member of the Joint Oireachtas Committee on Education and Science 2007–11.

First elected to the Dáil in 2007. He was elected to Seanad Éireann on the Administrative Panel in 2002.

Took part in RTÉ's *You're A Star* in 2006 to help raise money for charity.

He was elected to Roscommon County Council in 1999, topping the poll in the Boyle electoral area, and served on the council until the ending of the dual mandate in 2003. Chairman of Roscommon VEC 2000–02. Member: West Region Authority; Roscommon County Enterprise Board; Roscommon GAA Supporters' Club. Chairman: Roscommon Adult Education Board; Lough Key Forest Park Action Group. President, North Roscommon Anglers' Association. Past president, Boyle Chamber of Commerce. Director: non-profit organisation Boyle 2000.com; Boyle Ledford Park Oval Car Racing Club. Member, Irish Kidney Association.

Luke 'Ming' Flanagan (Ind)

Home Address
Priory House, Barrack Street, Castlerea, Co. Roscommon.
Contact Details
Dáil Office: (01) 618 3058.
Mobile: (086) 368 5680.
Website: www.lukemingflanagan.ie.
Twitter: lukeming.
Birth Place/Date
Roscommon, 22 January 1972.
Marital Status
Married. Two children.
Education
Castlerea N.S. NUI Galway.
Occupation
Full-time public representative.

A new Dáil deputy, Flanagan first came to prominence as a campaigner for the legalisation of cannabis. He was an unsuccessful candidate in Roscommon in 2007 and in Galway West in 1997. He was also an unsuccessful candidate in the West constituency in the 1999 European elections. He was elected to Roscommon County Council in 2004 and again in 2009. Mayor of Roscommon in 2010.

Denis Naughten (FG)

Home Address
Abbey Street, Roscommon.
Constituency Offices
Abbey Street, Roscommon; Monksland,
Athlone, Co. Roscommon.
Contact Details
Home: (090) 662 7557. Constituency Offices:
(090) 662 7557; (090) 643 7324. Mobile: (087)
234 6115. Website: www.denisnaughten.ie.
Birth Place/Date
Drum, Athlone, 23 June 1973.
Marital Status
Married to Mary Tiernan. Two sons, one
daughter.
Education
St Aloysius College, Athlone. UCD (BSc).
UCC (Researcher in Food Microbiology).
Occupation
Full-time public representative. Formerly
research scientist.

First elected to Dáil Éireann in 1997, less than
six months after being elected to the Seanad
Agricultural Panel in a by-election in January
1997. Re-elected to the Dáil in all subsequent
general elections.

Fine Gael front bench spokesperson on:
Immigration and Integration 2007–10;
Agriculture and Food 2004–07; Transport
2002–04; Enterprise, Trade and Employment
2000–01; Youth Affairs, School Transport and
Adult Education from 1997–2000. Deputy
spokesperson on Public Enterprise 2001–02.

Member: Roscommon County Council
1997–2003; Western Health Board
1997–2003; Association of Health Boards
1997–99.

He is son of the late Liam Naughten: Dáil
deputy 1982–89; Senator, Agricultural Panel,
1981–82 and 1989–96; Leas-Chathaoirleach
of the Seanad 1989–95 and Cathaoirleach
1995–96.

Roscommon–South Leitrim

Seats 3
Quota 11,877

	COUNT	1	Distribution of **Kearns, Kilrane, McDaid** votes 2	Distribution of **McDermott** votes 3	Distribution of **Kelly** votes 4	Distribution of **Flanagan** surplus 5	Distribution of **Kenny** votes 6
CONNAUGHTON, Ivan	(FF)	4,070	(+1,309) 5,379	(+477) 5,856	(+398) 6,254	(+31) 6,285	(+749) 7,034
FEIGHAN, Frank*	(FG)	8,983	(+474) 9,457	(+445) 9,902	(+1,228) 11,130	(+109) 11,239	(+2,027) 13,266
FLANAGAN, Luke 'Ming'	(Ind)	8,925	(+326) 9,251	(+1,197) 10,448	(+1,701) 12,149		
KEARNS, Seán	(Ind)	91					
KELLY, John	(Lab)	4,455	(+162) 4,617	(+277) 4,894			
KENNY, Martin	(SF)	4,637	(+732) 5,369	(+157) 5,526	(+516) 6,042	(+66) 6,108	
KILRANE, Gerry	(FF)	3,033					
MCDAID, Garreth	(GP)	220					
MCDERMOTT, John	(Ind)	3,770	(+112) 3,882				
NAUGHTEN, Denis*	(FG)	9,320	(+109) 9,429	(+1,189) 10,618	(+731) 11,349	(+66) 11,415	(+707) 12,122
NON-TRANSFERABLE			120	140	320	0	2,625

The Green Party's Mary White picks up a souvenir while canvassing in Carlow. Photograph: Brenda Fitzsimons.

Sligo–North Leitrim

Statistics

Seats	3
Electorate	63,432
Total Poll	44,837
Turnout	70.7%
Spoiled	409
Total Valid Poll	44,428
Quota	11,108
Count Number	9
Candidates	13

Party Share of Vote

1st Preferences	Number	%	Gain/Loss
Fine Gael	16,378	36.86	-2.41
Labour	4,553	10.25	6.35
Fianna Fáil	9,708	21.85	-19.12
Sinn Féin	5,911	13.30	1.58
United Left Alliance	0	0.00	0.00
Green Party	432	0.97	-2.06
Others	7,446	16.76	15.65

	Quotas	Seats
Fine Gael	1.5	2
Labour	0.4	–
Fianna Fáil	0.9	–
Sinn Féin	0.5	1
United Left Alliance	0	–
Green Party	0	–
Others	0.7	–

FG gains 1, SF gains 1; from FF.

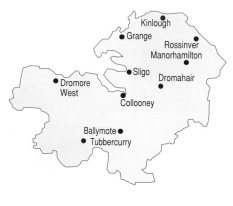

John Perry (FG)

Home Address
Grianán Iuda, Carrownanty, Ballymote, Co. Sligo.
Constituency Offices
Teeling Street, Ballymote; Westward Town Centre, Bridge Street, Sligo.
Contact Details
Constituency Office: (071) 918 9333.
Department Office: (01) 631 2243. Dáil Office: (01) 618 3765. Mobile: (087) 245 9407.
Birth Place/Date
Ballymote, 15 August 1956.
Marital Status
Married to Marie Mulvey. One son.
Education
Corran College, Ballymote.
Occupation
Full-time public representative. Formerly businessman.

John Perry was first elected to the Dáil in 1997. In March 2011 he was appointed Minister of State at the Department of Enterprise, with special responsibility for Small Business. He was Fine Gael spokesperson on Small Business prior to the 2011 General Election.

In the 29th Dáil, he was Vice-Chairman of the Oireachtas Joint Committee on Communications and Natural Resources and member of the Audit Committee of the Houses of the Oireachtas Commission. Chairman of the Public Accounts Committee, September 2002 to October 2004. Party spokesperson on: the Marine 2004–07; Science, Technology, Small Business and Enterprise, Border Counties 1997–02.

Elected to Sligo County Council, 1999. Chairman, Ballymote Community Enterprise. Chairman of Ballymote Cattle and Horse Show. Member of various community and development committees and organisations.

Irish Quality Business award in 1991 and 1992. Sligo Person of the Year award, 1993.

Tony McLoughlin (FG)

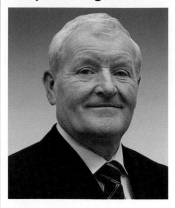

Home Address
Beechlawn, Barnasragh, Sligo.
Contact Details
Dáil Office: (01) 618 3537.
Mobile: (087) 663 3587.
Birth Place/Date
Sligo, January 1949.
Marital Status
Married to Paula. One son, one daughter.
Education
Mount St Joseph's College, Roscrea, Co. Tipperary.
Occupation
Full-time public representative. Formerly sales executive.

Tony McLoughlin is a new deputy.

He unsuccessfully contested the 1981 General Election and did not stand for the Dáil again until 2011.

He was elected to Sligo County Council in 1985 and was re-elected at every subsequent local election up to and including 2009.

His uncle Joe McLoughlin was a TD for Sligo–Leitrim from 1961 until 1977.

Michael Colreavy (SF)

Home Address
Main Street, Manorhamilton, Co. Leitrim.
Contact Details
Constituency Office: (071) 985 5716.
Dáil Office: (01) 618 3745.
Mobile: (087) 249 9476.
Birth Place/Date
Leitrim, September 1948.
Marital Status
Married to Alice. Four sons, four daughters.
Education
Summerhill College, Sligo. National
Computing Centre UK. Institute of Public
Administration (Diploma in Healthcare
Management).
Occupation
Full-time public representative. Formerly IT
projects manager with Health Service
Executive.

Michael Colreavy is a new deputy.

He is Sinn Féin spokesperson on Agriculture,
Food and Marine.

First elected to Leitrim County Council in 1999
and re-elected at the two subsequent local
elections.

Chairman of Leitrim County Council 2000–01.
He joined Sinn Féin in 1979 and was branch
secretary of the Impact trade union and
president of the Sligo Council of Trade
Unions.

Sligo–North Leitrim

Seats 3 **Quota 11,108**				Distribution of **Cahill, Gogan** votes		Distribution of **McSharry** votes		Distribution of **Cawley, Love Alywn** votes	
COUNT			**1**		**2**		**3**		**4**
BREE, Declan	(Ind)		2,284	(+50)	2,334	(+46)	2,380	(+383)	2,763
CAHILL, Dick	(Ind)		102						
CAWLEY, Veronica	(Ind)		1,119	(+21)	1,140	(+31)	1,171		
CLARKE, Michael Noel	(Ind)		2,415	(+16)	2,431	(+32)	2,463	(+144)	2,607
COLREAVY, Michael	(SF)		5,911	(+61)	5,972	(+260)	6,232	(+233)	6,465
GOGAN, Johnny	(GP)		432						
LOVE ALYWN, Robert	(Ind)		779	(+57)	836	(+45)	881		
MACSHARRY, Marc	(FF)		4,633	(+14)	4,647	(+39)	4,686	(+179)	4,865
MCLOUGHLIN, Tony	(FG)		7,715	(+63)	7,778	(+113)	7,891	(+236)	8,127
MCSHARRY, Gabriel	(Ind)		747	(+23)	770				
O KEEFFE, Susan	(Lab)		4,553	(+156)	4,709	(+60)	4,769	(+444)	5,213
PERRY, John*	(FG)		8,663	(+40)	8,703	(+38)	8,741	(+227)	8,968
SCANLON, Eamon*	(FF)		5,075	(+22)	5,097	(+68)	5,165	(+70)	5,235
NON-TRANSFERABLE					11		38		136

Distribution of **Clarke** votes		Distribution of **Bree** votes		Distribution of **MacSharry** votes		Distribution of **O Keeffe** votes		Distribution of **Perry** surplus	
5		6		7		8		9	
(+183)	2,946								
(+381)	6,846	(+929)	7,775	(+364)	8,139	(+1,477)	9,616	(+155)	9,771
(+437)	5,302	(+284)	5,586						
(+193)	8,320	(+379)	8,699	(+794)	9,493	(+1,488)	10,981	(+527)	11,508
(+217)	5,430	(+666)	6,096	(+550)	6,646				
(+580)	9,548	(+220)	9,768	(+651)	10,419	(+1,554)	11,973		
(+390)	5,625	(+74)	5,699	(+2,690)	8,389	(+553)	8,942	(+183)	9,125
226		394		537		1,574		0	

Tipperary North

Statistics

Seats	3
Electorate	63,235
Total Poll	48,789
Turnout	77.2%
Spoiled	516
Total Valid Poll	48,273
Quota	12,069
Candidates	8

Party Share of Vote

1st Preferences	Number	%	Gain/Loss
Fine Gael	11,425	23.67	7.78
Labour	9,559	19.80	9.53
Fianna Fáil	7,978	16.53	-17.78
Sinn Féin	3,034	6.29	2.53
United Left Alliance	0	0.00	0.00
Green Party	409	0.85	-0.26
Others	15,868	32.87	-0.36

	Quotas	Seats
Fine Gael	0.9	1
Labour	0.8	1
Fianna Fáil	0.7	–
Sinn Féin	0.3	–
United Left Alliance	0	–
Green Party	0	–
Others	1.3	1

Lab gain 1 from FF.

Michael Lowry (Ind)

Home Address
Glenreigh, Holycross, Thurles, Co. Tipperary.
Constituency Office
Abbey Road, Thurles.
Contact Details
Constituency Office: (0504) 22022. Mobile: (087) 232 3828. Website: www.michaellowry.ie.
Birth Place/Date
Holycross, 13 March 1954.
Marital Status
Married to Catherine McGrath. Two sons, one daughter.
Education
Thurles CBS.
Occupation
Public representative; company director.

Michael Lowry was first elected for Fine Gael to the Dáil in 1987. He was Minister for Transport, Energy and Communications from 1994 to November 1996 when he resigned after controversy over his business relationship with Ben Dunne. Subsequently resigned from the Fine Gael Parliamentary Party in 1997.

Topped the poll as an Independent and has been elected on the first count in all subsequent general elections, including 2011. The Dáil unanimously passed a motion of censure calling on him to resign his seat voluntarily following publication of the Moriarty Tribunal Report after the 2011 election. The report said he had 'secured the winning' of a mobile phone licence for Esat Digifone in 1995.

Chairman, Fine Gael Parliamentary Party 1993–94. Member of front bench 1993–94. Fine Gael Leader of the British–Irish Inter-Parliamentary Body 1994.

Member, Tipperary North County Council 1979–95 and 1999–2003. Former Chairman, Semple Stadium Management Committee. Former Chairman, County Tipperary GAA Board and Mid-Tipperary GAA Board.

Noel Coonan (FG)

Home Address
Gortnagoona, Roscrea, Co. Tipperary.
Constituency Office
Bank Street, Templemore, Co. Tipperary.
Contact Details
Constituency Office: (0504) 32544.
Mobile: (086) 242 7733.
Email: noel.coonan@oireachtas.ie.
Website: www.noelcoonan.com.
Facebook: noelcoonan.
Twitter: @NoelCoonantd.
Birth Place/Date
Roscrea, 6 January 1951.
Marital Status
Married to Pauline.
Education
Shanakill N.S. Templemore CBS.
Occupation
Full-time public representative.

First elected in 2007, having contested Tipperary North unsuccessfully in the 2002 General Election. Senator on the Cultural and Educational Panel from 2002–07.

Fine Gael deputy spokesperson on Agriculture, with special responsibility on CAP reform, from October 2010 to 2011. Deputy spokesperson on Communications, Energy and Natural Resources, with special responsibility for Telecommunications, 2007–10.

Chairperson of the Northern European Group which includes Hungary, Latvia, Lithuania and Poland.

Member, North Tipperary County Council 1991–2003 and Templemore Town Council 1994–2003. Former member Mid-Western Health Board. President, Collins 22 Society, which commemorates Michael Collins.

Alan Kelly (Lab)

Home Address
Loughrea, Ballina, Nenagh, Co. Tipperary.
Constituency Offices
1 Summerhill, Nenagh, Co. Tipperary;
Rosemary Square, Roscrea, Co. Tipperary;
Department of Transport, Tourism and Sport,
Kildare Street, Dublin 2.
Contact Details
Constituency Office: (067) 34190.
Mobile: (087) 679 2859.
Email: office@alankelly.ie
Website: www.alankelly.ie.
Facebook: AlanKellylabour.
Twitter: @alankellylabour.
Birth Place/Date
Limerick, 13 July 1975.
Marital Status
Married to Regina O'Connor. One daughter.
Education
Nenagh CBS. UCC (BA; MPhil). UCD (BA in
English and History; Mphil in Political History).
Boston College (Leadership certificate).
Smurfit Business School (MBS in
Ecommerce).
Occupation
Full-time public representative. Formerly e-
business manager with Fáilte Ireland.

Alan Kelly is a new deputy.

He is Minister of State at the Department of
Transport, Tourism and Sport. He was elected
to the Seanad on the Agricultural Panel in
2007. Elected to the European Parliament in
2009.

Founder of the Jim Kemmy branch of the
Labour Party in UCC in 1995. Chair, Labour
Youth, 2000; General Council 2001.

Author of *A Political History of County
Tipperary 1916–1997*.

Seats 3
Quota 12,069

			COUNT	Distribution of **Lowry** surplus		Distribution of **Bopp, Clancy, Morris, O'Malley** votes	
			1	2		3	
BOPP, Kate	(Ind)		322	(+30)	352		
CLANCY, Billy	(Ind)		1,442	(+211)	1,653		
COONAN, Noel*	(FG)		11,425	(+705)	12,130		
HOCTOR, Máire*	(FF)		7,978	(+378)	8,356	(+1,085)	9,441
KELLY, Alan	(Lab)		9,559	(+545)	10,104	(+1,961)	12,065
LOWRY, Michael*	(Ind)		14,104				
MORRIS, Seamus Seán	(SF)		3,034	(+146)	3,180		
O'MALLEY, Olwyn	(GP)		409	(+20)	429		
NON-TRANSFERABLE				0		2,568	

Tipperary South

Statistics

Seats	3
Electorate	57,420
Total Poll	41,793
Turnout	72.8%
Spoiled	432
Total Valid Poll	41,361
Quota	10,341
Candidates	8

Party Share of Vote

1st Preferences	Number	%	Gain/Loss
Fine Gael	14,298	34.57	13.43
Labour	4,525	10.94	2.17
Fianna Fáil	5,419	13.10	-33.32
Sinn Féin	1,860	4.50	1.41
United Left Alliance	8,818	21.32	21.32
Others	6,074	14.69	-2.97
Green Party	367	0.89	-0.63

	Quotas	Seats
Fine Gael	1.4	1
Labour	0.4	–
Fianna Fáil	0.5	–
Sinn Féin	0.2	–
United Left Alliance	0.9	1
Green Party	0	–
Others	0.6	1

ULA gain 1 from FF.

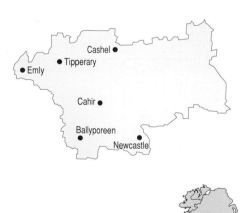

Seamus Healy (Ind)

Home Address
Scrouthea, Old Bridge, Clonmel, Co. Tipperary.
Constituency Office
56 Queen Street, Clonmel.
Contact Details
Home: (0502) 23184. Constituency Office: (052) 612 1883. Mobile: (087) 280 2199.
Birth Place/Date
Clonmel, August 1950.
Marital Status
Married. Four daughters.
Education
CBS High School Clonmel.
Occupation
Full-time public representative. Formerly hospital administrator.

Seamus Healy was elected as a United Left Alliance candidate in 2011. First elected to the Dáil at a by-election in 2000, after unsuccessful attempts in 1992 and 1997. He retained his seat in the 2002 General Election but lost it in 2007.

A member of Clonmel Borough Council from 1985 to 2004, he was elected to Tipperary South Riding County Council in 1991 and served until 2002. He was co-opted back on to the county council in 2007. Mayor of Clonmel, 1994–95. Former member of Clonmel Trades and Labour Council.

Tom Hayes (FG)

Home Address
Cahervillahow, Golden, Co. Tipperary.
Constituency Offices
Main Street, Cashel; Upper Gladstone Street, Clonmel; Upper Church Street, Tipperary Town.
Contact Details
Constituency Offices: (062) 62892; (052) 6180731. Mobile: (087) 810 5016.
Email: tom.hayes@oireachtas.ie.
Website: www.tomhayes.ie.
Facebook: TomHayesTipperaryTD.
Twitter: @tomhayestd.
Birth Place/Date
Golden, Co. Tipperary, 16 February 1952.
Marital Status
Married to Marian Hayes. Three sons.
Education
Thomastown N.S. Mount Mellary Secondary School. Vocational School, Tipperary Town. UCC (Diploma in Public Administration).
Occupation
Full-time public representative.

First elected to the Dáil at a by-election in July 2001 having been a member of the Seanad, elected to the Agricultural Panel, from 1997.

Member of: the Oireachtas Committee for the Constitution; Committee for Procedures and Privileges; and the Oireachtas Commission in the last Dáil.

Chairperson of the Fine Gael Parliamentary Party from September 2002 to March 2010. Appointed party spokesperson for Road Safety September 2010. Deputy party spokesperson for Environment, with special responsibility for Heritage and Rural Affairs, and member Committee of Public Accounts in 29th Dáil.

Member of Tipperary South Riding County Council 1991–2003. Served on Vocational Education Committee, County Enterprise Board, Cashel Heritage Committee. Member of GAA, Macra na Feirme and IFA.

Mattie McGrath (Ind)

Home Address
Mollough, Newcastle, Clonmel, Co. Tipperary.
Constituency Office
2 Joyce's Lane, The Quay, Clonmel.
Contact Details
Constituency Office: (052) 612 9155.
Mobile: (086) 818 4307.
Email: mattie.mcgrath@oireachtas.ie.
Website: www.mattiemcgrath.ie.
Facebook: MattieMcGrathTD.
Birth Place/Date
Newcastle, Clonmel, September 1958.
Marital Status
Married to Margaret Sherlock. Five daughters, three sons.
Education
St Joseph's College, Cahir. Kildalton Agriculture College, Co. Kilkenny. UCC (Diploma in Communications Skills).
Occupation
Full-time public representative. Formerly ran plant hire business.

First elected to the Dáil for Fianna Fáil but left the party over issues including stag hunting and the EU–IMF bailout. Re-elected as an Independent in 2011.

Member of South Tipperary County Council for the Cahir electoral area 1990–91 and 1999–2007. Chairperson of South Tipperary County Council 2004–05. Member of South Tipperary VEC 1991–99. Founder Member of the Lemass Forum of Fianna Fáil back benchers.

Director of: Muintir na Tíre; Ring a Link Rural Transport Service; and Clonmel Boxing Club. Member: board of management of Naionra Chaislean Nua Teoranta; board of Newcastle Voluntary Housing Association; British–Irish Inter-Parliamentary Association; Cahir Farmer Market; GAA; and many local organisations.

All Ireland set-dancing champion 1974.

Tipperary South

Seats 3
Quota 10,341

COUNT	1	Distribution of **Browne, McNally** votes		Distribution of **Prendergast** votes		Distribution of **Healy** surplus		Distribution of **Mansergh** votes	
	1		**2**		**3**		**4**		**5**
BROWNE, Michael (SF)	1,860								
HAYES, Tom* (FG)	8,896	(+318)	9,214	(+972)	10,186	(+277)	10,463		
HEALY, Seamus (Ind)	8,818	(+724)	9,542	(+1,723)	11,265				
MANSERGH, Martin* (FF)	5,419	(+169)	5,588	(+277)	5,865	(+83)	5,948		
MCGRATH, Mattie* (Ind)	6,074	(+275)	6,349	(+729)	7,078	(+335)	7,413	(+2,565)	9,978
MCNALLY, Paul (GP)	367								
MURPHY, Michael (FG)	5,402	(+161)	5,563	(+841)	6,404	(+229)	6,633	(+1,315)	7,948
PRENDERGAST, Phil (Lab)	4,525	(+441)	4,966						
NON-TRANSFERABLE			139		424		0		2,068

Enda Kenny talks to a young voter in Bray during a canvass in the Wicklow area. Photograph: David Sleator.

Waterford

Statistics

Seats	4
Electorate	78,435
Total Poll	54,298
Turnout	69.2%
Spoiled	578
Total Valid Poll	53,720
Quota	10,745
Candidates	15

Party Share of Vote

1st Preferences	Number	%	Gain/Loss
Fine Gael	20,416	38.00	10.64
Labour	10,192	18.97	7.65
Fianna Fáil	7,515	13.99	-32.50
Sinn Féin	5,342	9.94	3.23
United Left Alliance	0	0.00	0.00
Green Party	462	0.86	-1.26
Others	9,793	18.23	12.24

	Quotas	Seats
Fine Gael	1.9	2
Labour	0.9	1
Fianna Fáil	0.7	–
Sinn Féin	0.5	–
United Left Alliance	0	–
Green Party	0	–
Others	0.9	1

FG gain 1, Ind gains 1; from FF.

John Deasy (FG)

Home Address
Kilrush, Dungarvan, Co. Waterford.
Constituency Office
1 Coady's Quay, Dungarvan.
Contact Details
Constituency Office: (058) 43003.
Mobile: (087) 256 5620.
Email: john.deasy@oireachtas.ie.
Birth Place/Date
Abbeyside, Dungarvan, 8 October 1967.
Marital Status
Married to Maura Derrane.
Education
Coláiste na Rinne, Ring, Dungarvan. St Augustine's College, Dungarvan. Mercyhurst College, Erie, Pennsylvania, US (BA History/Communications). UCC (BCL).
Occupation
Public representative. Formerly US congressional aide.

John Deasy topped the poll in the Waterford constituency in 2011. He was first elected to the Dáil in 2002. He has been a vocal opponent of party leader Enda Kenny.

Deasy was Fine Gael's front bench spokesperson for Justice, Equality and Law Reform 2002–04, during his first term in the Dáil. Chairman of the Dáil's European Affairs Committee and member of the Public Accounts Committee 2004–07.

Member of Waterford County Council 1999–2003. Member, Dungarvan Town Council 1999–2003. Board member, Waterford Regional Airport. Manager of Public Affairs for multinational waste management company 1991–92. Legislative assistant to Senator John Heinz in US Senate, handling Trade and Foreign Affairs, 1990–91. Legislative assistant to Representative Ronald K. Machtley in US House of Representatives, 1993–95.

He is son of Austin Deasy: Dáil deputy 1977–2002; Senator 1973–77.

Paudie Coffey (FG)

Home Address
Mount Bolton, Portlaw, Co. Waterford.
Contact Details
Home: (051) 387295. Constituency Office: (051) 835 867. Dáil Office: (01) 618 3902.
Mobile: (087) 983 9940.
Facebook: PaudieCoffeyTD.
Twitter: @Paudie Coffey.
Birth Place/Date
Waterford, 15 May 1969.
Married
Married to Suzanne McAleenan. Two daughters, one son.
Education
St Declan's Community College, Kilmacthomas. Waterford Regional Technical College. UCD.
Occupation
Full-time public representative. Formerly ESB employee.

Paudie Coffey is a new deputy. He was elected to the Seanad in 2007. He was elected to Waterford County Council in 1999 and 2004. Former Deputy Mayor of Waterford.

He played hurling for Waterford at every level, including senior, and coached the Waterford Under-21 team.

Ciara Conway (Lab)

Constituency Office
36 Mary Street, Dungarvan, Co. Waterford.
Contact Details
Constituency Office: (058) 24514.
Dáil Office: (01) 618 4011.
Mobile: (086) 102 2958.
Email: ciara.conway@oireachtas.ie.
Website: www.labour.ie/ciaraconway.
Facebook: ciaraconwaylabour.
Birth Place/Date
Waterford, 13 August 1980.
Marital Status
Single. One child.
Education
NUI Galway (BA, Public and Social Policy).
UCC (Masters in Social Work). WIT (MBA).
Occupation
Full-time public representative.

Ciara Conway is a new deputy, elected at her first attempt.

She became involved in politics as a student at NUI Galway where she was elected to the Students' Union and joined the Labour Party. Involved in Labour Youth as its international officer. Elected to Dungarvan Town Council 2009.

Previously service design and development facilitator for children's charity Barnardos.

John Halligan (Ind)

Home Address
47 John's Hill, Waterford.
Contact Details
Dáil Office: (01) 618 3498.
Mobile: (086) 267 8622.
Website: www.johnhalligan.net.
Birth Place/Date
Waterford, January 1955.
Marital Status
Living with partner. Three daughters.
Education
St John's Manor School. Mount Sion CBS.
Waterford Technical College.
Occupation
Full-time public representative. Formerly radio operator for Bell Lines.

John Halligan is a new deputy. He was an unsuccessful candidate for the Workers' Party in the 2002 and 2007 general elections.

He was elected to Waterford City Council for the Workers' Party in 1999 and 2004 and topped the poll as an Independent candidate in 2009. Mayor of Waterford 2009–10.

Waterford

Seats 4 Quota 10,745		Distribution of **Kiersey** votes		Distribution of **Waters** votes		Distribution of **Nutty** votes		Distribution of **Power** votes	
COUNT	1		2		3		4		5
COFFEY, Paudie (FG)	9,698	(+7)	9,705	(+32)	9,737	(+37)	9,774	(+78)	9,852
COLLERY, Justin (Ind)	967	(+4)	971	(+12)	983	(+42)	1,025	(+50)	1,075
CONWAY, Ciara (Lab)	5,554	(+6)	5,560	(+5)	5,565	(+32)	5,597	(+111)	5,708
CONWAY, Joe (Ind)	725	(+4)	729	(+9)	738	(+13)	751	(+11)	762
CULLINANE, David (SF)	5,342	(+5)	5,347	(+14)	5,361	(+26)	5,387	(+27)	5,414
DEASY, John* (FG)	10,718	(+13)	10,731	(+20)	10,751				
HALLIGAN, John (Ind)	5,546	(+6)	5,552	(+17)	5,569	(+25)	5,594	(+45)	5,639
HIGGINS, Tom (Ind)	1,130	(+3)	1,133	(+17)	1,150	(+14)	1,164	(+37)	1,201
KENEALLY, Brendan* (FF)	7,515	(+6)	7,521	(+34)	7,555	(+12)	7,567	(+33)	7,600
KIERSEY, Gerard (Ind)	73								
NUTTY, Ben (Ind)	257	(+4)	261	(+15)	276				
POWER, Jody (GP)	462	(+)	462	(+3)	465	(+36)	501		
RYAN, Seamus (Lab)	4,638	(+6)	4,644	(+8)	4,652	(+12)	4,664	(+66)	4,730
TOBIN, Joe (Ind)	873	(+5)	878	(+11)	889	(+17)	906	(+19)	925
WATERS, Declan (Ind)	222	(+1)	223						
NON-TRANSFERABLE			3		26		10		24

Distribution of **Conway** votes		Distribution of **Tobin** votes		Distribution of **Collery, Higgins** votes		Distribution of **Ryan** votes		Distribution of **Cullinane** votes		Distribution of **Coffey, Deasy** surplus	
6		**7**		**8**		**9**		**10**		**11**	
(+147)	9,999	(+56)	10,055	(+648)	10,703	(+533)	11,236				
(+54)	1,129	(+37)	1,166								
(+159)	5,867	(+70)	5,937	(+487)	6,424	(+2,792)	9,216	(+1,966)	11,182		
(+44)	5,458	(+178)	5,636	(+232)	5,868	(+430)	6,298				
(+137)	5,776	(+275)	6,051	(+397)	6,448	(+925)	7,373	(+2,229)	9,602	(+216)	9,818
(+26)	1,227	(+19)	1,246								
(+72)	7,672	(+64)	7,736	(+232)	7,968	(+239)	8,207	(+575)	8,782	(+163)	8,945
(+61)	4,791	(+180)	4,971	(+142)	5,113						
(+12)	937										
50		58		274		194		1,528		118	

Wexford

Statistics

Seats	5
Electorate	111,063
Total Poll	76,351
Turnout	68.7%
Spoiled	812
Total Valid Poll	75,539
Quota	12,590
Candidates	14

Party Share of Vote

1st Preferences	Number	%	Gain/Loss
Fine Gael	26,034	34.46	2.90
Labour	15,462	20.47	6.70
Fianna Fáil	14,027	18.57	-23.62
Sinn Féin	4,353	5.76	-1.63
United Left Alliance	741	0.98	0.98
Green Party	391	0.52	-0.65
Others	14,531	19.24	18.46

	Quotas	Seats
Fine Gael	2.1	2
Labour	1.2	1
Fianna Fáil	1.1	1
Sinn Féin	0.3	–
United Left Alliance	0.1	–
Green Party	0	–
Others	1.2	1

Ind gains 1 from FF.

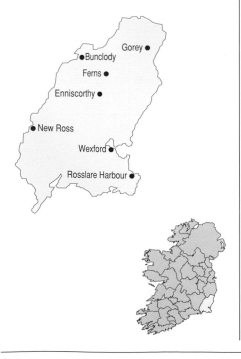

Mick Wallace (Ind)

Home Address
Wellingtonbridge, Co. Wexford.
Contact Details
Dáil Office: (01) 618 3287.
Mobile: (087) 245 4510.
Website: www.mickwallace.net.
Birth Place/Date
Wexford, November 1955.
Marital status
Divorced. Three sons, one daughter.
Education
Ballymitty N.S. St Augustine's College, Dungarven, Co. Waterford. Good Counsel College, New Ross, Co. Wexford.
Occupation
Public representative; builder.

Mick Wallace is a new TD. He was a well-known builder/developer responsible for Dublin's Italian Quarter. He made no secret of the fact that his companies owed a number of banks around €40 million at the time of the election. He stood in protest at the previous government's handling of the banking crisis. After the election a receiver was appointed by ACC Bank to Mr Wallace's main development company.

Brendan Howlin (Lab)

Home Address
Whiterock Hill, Wexford.
Constituency Office
Coolcotts, Wexford.
Contact Details
Constituency Office: (053) 912 4036.
Department Office: (01) 631 8102.
Email: brendan.howlin@oireachtas.ie;
brendan.howlin@per.gov.ie.
Website: www.brendanhowlin.ie.
Birth Place/Date
Wexford, 9 May 1956.
Marital Status
Single.
Education
Wexford CBS. St Patrick's College, Drumcondra, Dublin.
Occupation
Government Minister. Formerly national school teacher.

Brendan Howlin was appointed Minister for Public Expenditure and Reform on 9 March 2011.

Elected Leas-Cheann Comhairle of the Dáil in June 2007. He was appointed Labour Party spokesperson on Constitutional Matters and Law Reform in September 2007. Minister for the Environment 1994–97; Minister for Health 1993–94.

First elected to the Dáil in 1987 and elected Deputy Leader of the Labour Party in 1997. He was party spokesperson on: Finance, 2002; Justice, 1997–2002; Health and Youth Affairs, 1989–93; Health and Women's Rights, 1987–89.

Taoiseach's nominee to the Seanad 1982–87. Spokesperson on Education in Seanad 1983–87. Former member of the Houses of the Oireachtas Commission.

Member, Wexford County Council 1985–93; Wexford Borough Council 1981–93 (Alderman, 1985–93. Mayor, 1986–87).

John Browne (FF)

Home Address
3 Beech Park, Enniscorthy, Co. Wexford.
Constituency Office
Lower Church Street, Enniscorthy.
Contact Details
Constituency Office: (053) 923 5046.
Mobile: (087) 246 9234.
Email: john.browne@oireachtas.ie.
Website: www.johnbrowntd.ie.
Birth Place/Date
Marshalstown, Enniscorthy, August 1948.
Marital Status
Married to Judy Doyle. One son, three
daughters.
Education
St Mary's CBS, Enniscorthy.
Occupation
Full-time public representative.

Fianna Fáil spokesperson on Marine and
Fisheries.

First elected in 1982 and returned at all
subsequent general elections. Minister of
State at the Department of Communications,
the Marine and Natural Resources, 2002–04
and 2006–07; at the Department of
Agriculture and Food 2004–06.

Chairman of the Oireachtas Committee on
Agriculture, Food and the Marine 1997–2002.
Minister of State at the Department of the
Environment, with special responsibility for
Environmental Protection, 1993–94. Minister
of State at the Department of Agriculture and
Food, with special responsibility for the Food
Industry, 1992–93.

Assistant Party Chief Whip 1982–87.
Chairman of Fianna Fail Parliamentary Party
since 2010.

Former member: Wexford County Council;
Enniscorthy Urban District Council; Wexford
County Health Committee 1979–92.

Member of the GAA since 1965.

Liam Twomey (FG)

Home Address
Rosslare Medical Centre, Rosslare Strand,
Co. Wexford.
Constituency Office
Rosslare Medical Centre, Rosslare.
Contact Details
Constituency Office: (053) 32800.
Dáil Office: (01) 618 4299.
Mobile: (086) 626 7940.
Birth Place/Date
Cork, 3 April 1967.
Marital Status
Married to Elizabeth O'Sullivan. Two sons,
one daughter.
Education
St Finbarr's, Farenferris, Co. Cork. TCD (MB,
BCH, BAO, BA). MICGP. Diploma in Geriatric
Medicine.
Occupation
Public representative; medical doctor.

Liam Twomey was elected to the Dáil as an
Independent in 2002. He later joined Fine Gael
but lost his seat in the 2007 General Election.
He was elected to the Seanad in 2007 and
returned to the Dáil in 2011.

Member Irish Medical Organisation
(Chairperson of Wexford Branch). PRO for Co.
Wexford MICGP.

Paul Kehoe (FG)

Home Address
22 Greenville Court, Enniscorthy,
Co. Wexford.
Constituency Office
7 Weafer Street, Enniscorthy.
Contact Details
Home/Office: (053) 924 3558;
Fax: (053) 923 9562. Mobile: (087) 202 1383.
Birth Place/Date
Wexford, 11 January 1973.
Marital Status
Married to Brigid O'Connor.
Education
St Mary's CBS, Enniscorthy. Kildalton
Agricultural College
Occupation
Full-time public representative. Previously
worked in sales/marketing and farming.

Government Chief Whip and Minister of State
at the Departments of the Taoiseach and
Defence since 9 March 2011.

First elected in 2002. Fine Gael Chief Whip
from 2004. Previously deputy spokesperson
on Communications, Marine and Natural
Resources.

Former Chairman Macra na Feirme. Winner of
Macra National Leadership Award 2001.
Former County Youth Officer for Fine Gael
and Co. Wexford GAA.

Member: Fleadh Cheoil na hÉireann; and Irish
Handicapped Children's Pilgrimage Trust.

Wexford

Seats 5 Quota 12,590		COUNT	1	Distribution of **Wallace** surplus		Distribution of **De Valera, Dwyer, Forde, O'Brien, Roseingrave** votes	
			1	**2**		**3**	
BROWNE, John*	(FF)		7,352	(+42)	7,394	(+76)	7,470
CODY, Pat	(Lab)		4,457	(+48)	4,505	(+247)	4,752
CONNICK, Seán*	(FF)		6,675	(+69)	6,744	(+270)	7,014
D'ARCY, Michael*	(FG)		8,418	(+48)	8,466	(+129)	8,595
DE VALERA, Ruairí	(Ind)		119	(+10)	129		
DWYER, John	(Ind)		908	(+35)	943		
FORDE, Danny	(GP)		391	(+8)	399		
HOWLIN, Brendan*	(Lab)		11,005	(+161)	11,166	(+496)	11,662
KEHOE, Paul*	(FG)		8,386	(+73)	8,459	(+168)	8,627
KELLY, Anthony	(SF)		4,353	(+69)	4,422	(+479)	4,901
O'BRIEN, Seamus	(ULA)		741	(+37)	778		
ROSEINGRAVE, Siobhán	(Ind)		175	(+20)	195		
TWOMEY, Liam	(FG)		9,230	(+119)	9,349	(+176)	9,525
WALLACE, Mick	(Ind)		13,329				
NON-TRANSFERABLE				0		403	

Distribution of **Cody** votes		Distribution of **Kelly** votes		Distribution of **Howlin** surplus		Distribution of **Connick** votes	
	4		5		6		7
(+279)	7,749	(+426)	8,175	(+225)	8,400	(+4,357)	12,757
(+130)	7,144	(+252)	7,396	(+119)	7,515		
(+365)	8,960	(+532)	9,492	(+494)	9,986	(+424)	10,410
(+2,852)	14,514						
(+498)	9,125	(+549)	9,674	(+582)	10,256	(+790)	11,046
(+280)	5,181						
(+168)	9,693	(+760)	10,453	(+421)	10,874	(+722)	11,596
180		2,662		83		1,222	

Wicklow

Statistics

Seats	5
Electorate	95,339
Total Poll	71,311
Turnout	74.8%
Spoiled	811
Total Valid Poll	70,500
Quota	11,751
Candidates	24

Party Share of Vote

1st Preferences	Number	%	Gain/Loss
Fine Gael	27,926	39.61	16.46
Labour	12,087	17.14	0.80
Fianna Fáil	7,467	10.59	-27.46
Sinn Féin	7,089	10.06	5.08
United Left Alliance	0	0.00	0.00
Green Party	1,026	1.46	-5.92
Others	14,905	21.14	12.44

	Quotas	Seats
Fine Gael	2.4	3
Labour	1	1
Fianna Fáil	0.6	–
Sinn Féin	0.6	–
United Left Alliance	0	–
Green Party	0.1	–
Others	1.3	1

FG gain 1, Ind gains 1; from FF.

Andrew Doyle (FG)

Home Address
Lickeen, Roundwood, Co. Wicklow.
Constituency Office
2a, The Lower Mall, Wicklow Town.
Contact Details
Home: (0404) 45404. Office: (0404) 66622. Mobile: (086) 837 0088.
Email: andrew.doyle@oireachtas.ie.
Website: www.andrewdoyle.ie.
Facebook: andrewdoyle.
Birth Place/Date
Dublin, 2 July 1960.
Marital Status
Married to Ann Smith. Three sons, one daughter.
Education
Trooperstown and Rathdrum national schools. De La Salle, Wicklow Town. Rockwell Agricultural College.
Occupation
Public representative; farmer.

Andrew Doyle was first elected to the Dáil in 2007.

He was a member of the Oireachtas Committee on Agriculture and Food in the 30th Dáil.

He was a member of Wicklow County Council, representing East Wicklow electoral area, from 1999 until his election to the Dáil. Chairman of Wicklow County Council, 2005–06.

Billy Timmins (FG)

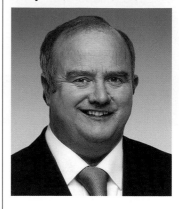

Home Address
Sruhaun, Baltinglass, Co. Wicklow.
Constituency Office
Weaver Square, Baltinglass.
Contact Details
Constituency Office: (059) 648 1016. Mobile: (087) 815 9090.
Website: www.billytimmins.finegael.ie.
Twitter: twitter.com/Billy_Timmins.
Birth Place/Date
Baltinglass, 1 October 1959.
Marital Status
Married to Madeleine Hyland. Two sons, three daughters.
Education
Patrician College, Ballyfin, Co. Laois. NUI Galway (BA; Diploma in Public Relations, Marketing and Advertising).
Occupation
Full-time public representative. Formerly army officer; served with the United Nations in Lebanon and Cyprus.

First elected to the Dáil in 1997, winning the seat previously held by his father Godfrey Timmins.

Party spokesperson on Foreign Affairs 2007–10. He opposed Enda Kenny's leadership in the attempted heave of June 2010 and was dismissed from the front bench. Previously he was spokesperson on Defence 2004–07 and Agriculture and Food 2002–04. Party spokesperson on: Defence, Peacekeeping and Humanitarian Relief 1997–2000; and Housing 2000–01. Deputy spokesperson: Justice and Defence 2001–02.

Member, National Economic and Social Forum 2000–02. Member, Wicklow County Council 1999–2004. Won Leinster and All-Ireland club championship medals in 1990. Hobbies are sports, reading, hill-walking and history.

His father, Godfrey Timmins, was a TD for Wicklow 1968–87 and 1989–97.

Simon Harris (FG)

Home Address
79 Redford Park, Greystones, Co. Wicklow.
Contact Details
Dáil Office: (01) 618 3805.
Email: simon.harris@oireachtas.ie.
Website: www.simonharris.ie.
Facebook: cllrsimonharris.
Twitter: @simonharristd.
Birth Place/Date
Dublin, 17 December 1986.
Marital Status
Single.
Education
St David's Secondary School, Greystones. DIT (Journalism).
Occupation
Public representative.

Simon Harris is a new deputy.

Elected to the Dáil at his first attempt. Elected to Wicklow County Council in 2009 and Greystones Town Council. Formerly political advisor to Minister for Children and Youth Affairs Frances Fitzgerald, when she was in the Seanad 2007–11.

Anne Ferris (Lab)

Home Address
10 Seapoint Court, Bray, Co. Wicklow.
Constituency Office
115 Main Street, Bray.
Contact Details
Home: (01) 286 5144. Constituency Office: (01) 276 4699. Dáil Office: (01) 618 3539.
Mobile: (086) 236 4780.
Email: anne.ferris@oireachtas.ie.
Website: www.labour.ie/anneferris.
Birth Place/Date
Dublin, 24 September 1954.
Marital Status
Divorced; in long-term relationship. Three daughters.
Education
Convent of Mercy, Goldenbridge, Inchicore, Dublin. St Patrick's College, Maynooth (Diploma in Women's Studies).
Occupation
Full-time public representative.

Anne Ferris is a new deputy, elected on her first attempt.

Cathaoirleach of Wicklow County Council 2007–08, the second woman to hold the position. Cathaoirleach, Bray Town Council 2001–02 and 2004–05.

Former personal assistant to Liz McManus: Democratic Left TD for Wicklow 1992–1999; Labour Party TD for Wicklow 1999–2011; and deputy leader of the Labour Party 2002–07.

Stephen Donnelly (Ind)

Home Address
Greystones, Co. Wicklow.
Contact Details
Dáil Office: (01) 618 4293.
Mobile: (086) 051 3493.
Email: stephen.donnelly@oireachtas.ie.
Website: www.stephendonnelly.ie.
Facebook: donnellyforwicklow.
Twitter: @donnellystephen.
Birth Place/Date
Dublin, 1975.
Marital Status
Married to Susan Leavy. Two sons.
Education
St David's Secondary School Greystones. UCD (B.E. Mechanical Engineering). Harvard's Kennedy School of Government (Masters in Public Administration and International Development).
Occupation
Full-time public representative.

Stephen Donnelly is a new deputy. Formerly a management consultant with McKinsey and Eden McCallum in London and Dublin. Decided to stand as Independent the day the IMF came to Ireland in 2010.

Wicklow

Seats 5
Quota 11,751

COUNT		Distribution of **Carroll** votes		Distribution of **Clarke** votes		Distribution of **Tallon** votes		Distribution of **Fitzgerald** votes		Distribution of **Mulvihill** votes		Distribution of **Keddy** votes		Distribution of **Finnegan** votes	
	1		**2**		**3**		**4**		**5**		**6**		**7**		**8**
BEHAN, Joe* (Ind)	4,197	(+3)	4,200	(+7)	4,207	(+3)	4,210	(+13)	4,223	(+8)	4,231	(+14)	4,245	(+32)	4,277
BRADY, John (SF)	7,089	(+1)	7,090	(+9)	7,099	(+16)	7,115	(+5)	7,120	(+24)	7,144	(+19)	7,163	(+24)	7,187
BYRNE, Niall (GP)	1,026	(+1)	1,027	(+4)	1,031	(+2)	1,033	(+5)	1,038	(+4)	1,042	(+3)	1,045	(+9)	1,054
CARROLL, Kevin (Ind)	74														
CLARKE, Thomas (Ind)	103	(+22)	125												
DEMPSEY, Peter (Ind)	1,409	(+6)	1,415	(+19)	1,434	(+20)	1,454	(+6)	1,460	(+8)	1,468	(+10)	1,478	(+8)	1,486
DONNELLY, Stephen (Ind)	6,530	(+6)	6,536	(+21)	6,557	(+14)	6,571	(+33)	6,604	(+20)	6,624	(+23)	6,647	(+45)	6,692
DOYLE, Andrew* (FG)	10,035	(+3)	10,038	(+2)	10,040	(+16)	10,056	(+14)	10,070	(+36)	10,106	(+11)	10,117	(+16)	10,133
FERRIS, Anne (Lab)	5,436	(+3)	5,439	(+13)	5,452	(+4)	5,456	(+13)	5,469	(+7)	5,476	(+5)	5,481	(+33)	5,514
FINNEGAN, Eugene (Ind)	286	(+2)	288	(+5)	293	(+2)	295	(+8)	303	(+2)	305	(+4)	309		
FITZGERALD, Anthony (Ind)	184	(+)	184	(+1)	185	(+1)	186								
FITZGERALD, Pat (FF)	3,576	(+)	3,576	(+)	3,576	(+16)	3,592	(+6)	3,598	(+6)	3,604	(+7)	3,611	(+2)	3,613
FORTUNE, Tom (Lab)	3,420	(+1)	3,421	(+2)	3,423	(+)	3,423	(+4)	3,427	(+8)	3,435	(+33)	3,468	(+14)	3,482
HARRIS, Simon (FG)	8,726	(+3)	8,729	(+6)	8,735	(+6)	8,741	(+11)	8,752	(+3)	8,755	(+37)	8,792	(+46)	8,838
KAVANAGH, Conal (Lab)	3,231	(+3)	3,234	(+3)	3,237	(+6)	3,243	(+6)	3,249	(+11)	3,260	(+12)	3,272	(+8)	3,280
KAVANAGH, Pat (Ind)	291	(+2)	293	(+5)	298	(+2)	300	(+2)	302	(+11)	313	(+9)	322	(+5)	327
KEDDY, Charlie (Ind)	233	(+3)	236	(+5)	241	(+20)	261	(+1)	262	(+4)	266				
KELLY, Nicky (Ind)	518	(+4)	522	(+1)	523	(+11)	534	(+2)	536	(+6)	542	(+7)	549	(+7)	556
KIERNAN, Donal (Ind)	403	(+2)	405	(+)	405	(+1)	406	(+9)	415	(+4)	419	(+14)	433	(+11)	444
KINSELLA, Gerry (Ind)	324	(+1)	325	(+2)	327	(+4)	331	(+4)	335	(+11)	346	(+13)	359	(+3)	362
MULVIHILL, Michael (Ind)	187	(+1)	188	(+3)	191	(+4)	195	(+1)	196						
ROCHE, Dick* (FF)	3,891	(+)	3,891	(+4)	3,895	(+3)	3,898	(+23)	3,921	(+5)	3,926	(+18)	3,944	(+20)	3,964
TALLON, Jim (Ind)	166	(+)	166	(+3)	169										
TIMMINS, Billy* (FG)	9,165	(+2)	9,167	(+4)	9,171	(+10)	9,181	(+13)	9,194	(+8)	9,202	(+11)	9,213	(+11)	9,224
NON-TRANSFERABLE			5		6		8		7		10		16		15

Distribution of **Kavanagh** votes	Distribution of **Kinsella** votes	Distribution of **Kelly, Kiernan** votes	Distribution of **Byrne, Dempsey** votes	Distribution of **Kavanagh** votes	Distribution of **Roche** votes	Distribution of **Behan** votes	Distribution of **Fortune** votes	Distribution of **Fitzgerald** votes	Distribution of **Doyle** surplus	Distribution of **Timmins** surplus
9	10	11	12	13	14	15	16	17	18	19
(+13) 4,290	(+22) 4,312	(+95) 4,407	(+144) 4,551	(+80) 4,631	(+286) 4,917					
(+33) 7,220	(+49) 7,269	(+135) 7,404	(+272) 7,676	(+211) 7,887	(+140) 8,027	(+599) 8,626	(+411) 9,037	(+760) 9,797	(+42) 9,839	(+15) 9,854
(+19) 1,073	(+19) 1,092	(+21) 1,113								
(+11) 1,497	(+19) 1,516	(+157) 1,673								
(+40) 6,732	(+60) 6,792	(+127) 6,919	(+470) 7,389	(+119) 7,508	(+162) 7,670	(+906) 8,576	(+404) 8,980	(+929) 9,909	(+37) 9,946	(+20) 9,966
(+18) 10,151	(+56) 10,207	(+57) 10,264	(+302) 10,566	(+316) 10,882	(+205) 11,087	(+535) 11,622	(+369) 11,991			
(+45) 5,559	(+18) 5,577	(+80) 5,657	(+340) 5,997	(+928) 6,925	(+111) 7,036	(+677) 7,713	(+2,530) 10,243	(+705) 10,948	(+94) 11,042	(+28) 11,070
(+3) 3,616	(+2) 3,618	(+54) 3,672	(+388) 4,060		(+80) 4,140	(+2,296) 6,436	(+462) 6,898	(+106) 7,004		
(+13) 3,495	(+12) 3,507	(+44) 3,551	(+108) 3,659	(+1,148) 4,807	(+124) 4,931	(+351) 5,282				
(+9) 8,847	(+25) 8,872	(+66) 8,938	(+195) 9,133	(+120) 9,253	(+191) 9,444	(+690) 10,134	(+767) 10,901	(+491) 11,392	(+67) 11,459	(+53) 11,512
(+16) 3,296	(+21) 3,317	(+52) 3,369	(+134) 3,503							
(+15) 571	(+14) 585									
(+12) 456	(+16) 472									
(+32) 394										
(+3) 3,967	(+10) 3,977	(+33) 4,010	(+47) 4,057	(+72) 4,129						
(+17) 9,241	(+12) 9,253	(+67) 9,320	(+147) 9,467	(+289) 9,756	(+428) 10,184	(+266) 10,450	(+279) 10,729	(+1,138) 11,867		
28	39	69	239	140	186	431	416	2,981	0	0

Summary of Returns (Dáil General Election 2011)

Note: all percentages have been rounded to one decimal place.

	Fine Gael				Labour				Fianna Fáil			
	No. of 1st pref.	% of 1st pref.	% + or –	Seats	No. of 1st pref.	% of 1st pref.	% + or –	Seats	No. of 1st pref.	% of 1st pref.	% + or –	Seats
Carlow–Kilkenny	28,924	39.2%	9.6%	3	11,980	16.2%	6.9%	1	20,721	28.1%	-19.6%	1
Cavan–Monaghan	28,199	39.6%	8.4%	3	4,011	5.6%	4.4%	0	14,360	20.1%	-17.6%	1
Clare	24,524	42.3%	7.1%	2	8,572	14.8%	13.2%	1	12,804	22.1%	-21.9%	1
Cork East	20,847	36.6%	5.8%	2	17,563	30.8%	9.9%	1	9,642	16.9%	-21.0%	0
Cork North-Central	13,669	26.2%	-1.4%	1	13,801	26.5%	14.1%	1	7,896	15.1%	-20.6%	1
Cork North-West	22,321	48.8%	10.4%	2	6,421	14.0%	9.1%	0	11,390	24.9%	-28.1%	1
Cork South-Central	22,225	34.7%	6.3%	2	11,869	18.5%	9.3%	1	17,936	28.0%	-16.3%	2
Cork South-West	22,162	48.5%	12.5%	2	6,533	14.3%	4.7%	1	10,787	23.6%	-18.9%	0
Donegal North-East	11,987	31.6%	9.0%	1	4,090	10.8%	9.0%	0	6,613	17.4%	-32.8%	1
Donegal South-West	8,589	19.9%	-3.1%	1	2,209	5.1%	2.3%	0	9,745	22.5%	-28.0%	0
Dublin Central	6,903	19.9%	10.4%	1	9,787	28.3%	15.7%	1	5,141	14.9%	-29.6%	0
Dublin Mid-West	13,214	30.9%	18.9%	2	13,138	30.8%	19.8%	2	5,043	11.8%	-21.2%	0
Dublin North	15,488	31.4%	17.3%	2	13,014	26.4%	16.8%	1	7,634	15.5%	-26.6%	0
Dublin North-Central	14,644	37.8%	12.2%	1	8,731	22.5%	15.2%	1	5,017	12.9%	-31.1%	0
Dublin North-East	12,332	29.5%	6.5%	1	14,371	34.3%	19.2%	2	4,794	11.5%	-28.2%	0
Dublin North-West	5,496	16.8%	6.8%	0	14,158	43.2%	22.8%	2	3,869	11.8%	-37.1%	0
Dublin South	26,404	36.3%	9.1%	3	13,059	18.0%	7.5%	1	6,844	9.4%	-31.9%	0
Dublin South-Central	11,956	23.5%	9.1%	1	18,032	35.4%	14.3%	2	4,837	9.5%	-23.6%	0
Dublin South-East	12,402	35.5%	16.9%	2	8,857	25.4%	8.7%	2	3,922	11.2%	-17.5%	0
Dublin South-West	13,044	27.8%	7.7%	1	17,032	36.3%	16.3%	2	5,059	10.8%	-28.5%	0
Dublin West	11,549	27.2%	6.8%	1	12,313	29.0%	11.9%	1	7,044	16.6%	-20.9%	1
Dún Laoghaire	19,591	34.6%	11.0%	2	17,217	30.4%	14.4%	1	8,632	15.2%	-19.6%	0
Galway East	25,409	42.9%	3.7%	2	7,831	13.2%	10.1%	1	10,694	18.0%	-21.6%	1
Galway West	18,627	30.7%	10.3%	2	7,489	12.4%	1.3%	1	12,703	21.0%	-16.2%	1
Kerry North–Limerick West	18,599	40.8%	N/A	1	9,159	20.1%	N/A	1	5,230	11.5%	N/A	0
Kerry South	14,482	32.6%	7.5%	1	4,926	11.1%	-2.4%	0	5,917	13.3%	-27.3%	0
Kildare North	17,050	33.3%	12.1%	2	14,979	29.2%	11.8%	1	7,436	14.5%	-25.0%	0
Kildare South	12,755	33.3%	16.2%	1	10,645	27.8%	7.1%	1	8,307	21.7%	-28.7%	1
Laois–Offaly	25,032	33.8%	6.4%	2	5,802	7.8%	5.4%	0	19,860	26.8%	-29.6%	2
Limerick City	18,696	43.3%	N/A	2	8,764	20.3%	N/A	1	9,259	21.4%	N/A	1
Limerick	21,925	48.7%	N/A	2	7,910	17.6%	N/A	0	9,361	20.8%	N/A	1
Longford–Westmeath	21,887	38.0%	7.1%	2	15,366	26.7%	9.1%	1	11,197	19.5%	-21.7%	1
Louth	21,825	31.5%	2.1%	2	13,264	19.1%	14.2%	1	10,858	15.7%	-26.5%	1
Mayo	48,170	65.0%	10.9%	4	3,644	4.9%	3.7%	0	11,920	16.1%	-8.5%	1
Meath East	17,471	40.9%	15.0%	2	8,994	21.0%	9.1%	1	8,384	19.6%	-23.9%	0
Meath West	18,450	45.9%	16.9%	2	5,432	13.5%	9.5%	0	7,285	18.1%	-33.5%	0
Roscommon–South Leitrim	18,303	38.5%	-0.6%	2	4,455	9.4%	7.6%	0	7,103	15.0%	-23.9%	0
Sligo–North Leitrim	16,378	36.9%	-2.4%	2	4,553	10.2%	6.4%	0	9,708	21.9%	-19.1%	0
Tipperary North	11,425	23.7%	7.8%	1	9,559	19.8%	9.5%	1	7,978	16.5%	-17.8%	0
Tipperary South	14,298	34.6%	13.4%	1	4,525	10.9%	2.2%	0	5,419	13.1%	-33.3%	0
Waterford	20,416	38.0%	10.6%	2	10,192	19.0%	7.6%	1	7,515	14.0%	-32.5%	0
Wexford	26,034	34.5%	2.9%	2	15,462	20.5%	6.7%	1	14,027	18.6%	-23.6%	1
Wicklow	27,926	39.6%	16.5%	3	12,087	17.1%	0.8%	1	7,467	10.6%	-27.5%	0
Regional Totals												
Connacht–Ulster	175,662	40.1%	5.2%	17	38,282	8.7%	5.4%	2	82,846	18.9%	-19.6%	5
Dublin	163,023	29.9%	11.2%	17	159,709	29.3%	14.8%	18	67,836	12.5%	-26.3%	1
Rest of Leinster	217,354	36.6%	9.6%	21	114,011	19.2%	7.8%	8	115,542	19.5%	-25.8%	7
Munster	245,589	38.1%	8.5%	21	119,794	18.6%	8.7%	9	121,134	18.8%	-23.9%	7
Total	**801,628**	**36.1%**	**8.8%**	**76**	**431,796**	**19.4%**	**9.3%**	**37**	**387,358**	**17.4%**	**-24.1%**	**20**

Sinn Féin				ULA				Green Party				Others			
No. of 1st pref.	% of 1st pref.	% + or −	Seats	No. of 1st pref.	% of 1st pref.	% + or −	Seats	No. of 1st pref.	% of 1st pref.	% + or −	Seats	No. of 1st pref.	% of 1st pref.	% + or −	Seats
7,033	9.5%	5.7%	0	1,135	1.5%	N/A	0	2,072	2.8%	-5.2%	0	1,878	2.5%	2.5%	0
18,452	25.9%	5.9%	1	0	0.0%	N/A	0	530	0.7%	-2.9%	0	5,723	8.0%	1.8%	0
0	0.0%	-3.4%	0	0	0.0%	N/A	0	1,154	2.0%	-3.1%	0	10,862	18.8%	9.5%	0
6,292	11.1%	4.2%	1	0	0.0%	N/A	0	635	1.1%	-1.8%	0	1,954	3.4%	2.9%	0
7,923	15.2%	7.0%	1	4,803	9.2%	N/A	0	524	1.0%	-2.5%	0	3,521	6.8%	-5.9%	0
3,405	7.4%	7.4%	0	1,552	3.4%	N/A	0	651	1.4%	-2.2%	0	0	0.0%	0.0%	0
5,250	8.2%	3.1%	0	0	0.0%	N/A	0	1,640	2.6%	-5.8%	0	5,120	8.0%	6.1%	0
3,346	7.3%	2.3%	0	0	0.0%	N/A	0	765	1.7%	-5.1%	0	2,065	4.5%	4.5%	0
9,278	24.5%	7.0%	1	0	0.0%	N/A	0	206	0.5%	-0.8%	0	5,744	15.1%	8.7%	0
14,262	33.0%	11.7%	1	0	0.0%	N/A	0	527	1.2%	-0.3%	0	7,931	18.3%	17.4%	1
4,526	13.1%	3.9%	1	0	0.0%	N/A	0	683	2.0%	-3.8%	0	7,572	21.9%	3.9%	1
5,060	11.8%	2.6%	0	3,093	7.2%	N/A	0	1,484	3.5%	-7.4%	0	1,690	4.0%	-7.5%	0
0	0.0%	-2.7%	0	7,513	15.2%	N/A	1	4,186	8.5%	-8.2%	0	1,512	3.1%	-9.3%	0
2,140	5.5%	1.7%	0	1,424	3.7%	N/A	0	501	1.3%	-3.9%	0	6,317	16.3%	2.1%	1
5,032	12.0%	-1.3%	0	869	2.1%	N/A	0	792	1.9%	-4.8%	0	3,649	8.7%	8.7%	0
7,115	21.7%	5.9%	1	677	2.1%	N/A	0	328	1.0%	-1.8%	0	1,168	3.6%	1.2%	0
1,915	2.6%	-0.4%	0	1,277	1.8%	N/A	0	4,929	6.8%	-4.3%	0	18,218	25.1%	24.8%	1
6,804	13.4%	3.2%	1	6,574	12.9%	N/A	1	1,015	2.0%	-3.8%	0	1,709	3.4%	-10.2%	0
1,272	3.6%	-1.1%	0	629	1.8%	N/A	0	2,370	6.8%	-7.1%	0	5,467	15.7%	11.4%	0
8,064	17.2%	5.0%	1	2,462	5.2%	N/A	0	480	1.0%	-2.7%	0	823	1.8%	-3.1%	0
2,597	6.1%	1.3%	0	8,084	19.0%	N/A	1	605	1.4%	-2.4%	0	280	0.7%	-14.3%	0
0	0.0%	-2.2%	0	6,206	10.9%	N/A	1	2,156	3.8%	-3.9%	0	2,874	5.1%	-3.8%	0
3,635	6.1%	2.9%	0	0	0.0%	N/A	0	402	0.7%	-1.2%	0	11,305	19.1%	12.1%	0
3,808	6.3%	3.3%	0	0	0.0%	N/A	0	1,120	1.8%	-3.6%	0	16,878	27.8%	21.0%	1
9,282	20.3%	N/A	1	0	0.0%	N/A	0	239	0.5%	N/A	0	3,105	6.8%	N/A	0
0	0.0%	-3.5%	0	0	0.0%	N/A	0	401	0.9%	-1.0%	0	18,654	42.0%	26.7%	2
2,896	5.7%	3.2%	0	0	0.0%	N/A	0	905	1.8%	-3.1%	0	7,956	15.5%	3.2%	1
2,308	6.0%	6.0%	0	0	0.0%	N/A	0	523	1.4%	-4.8%	0	3,732	9.8%	8.5%	0
8,032	10.8%	5.7%	1	561	0.8%	N/A	0	306	0.4%	-0.7%	0	14,565	19.6%	17.9%	0
3,711	8.6%	N/A	0	721	1.7%	N/A	0	490	1.1%	N/A	0	1,547	3.6%	N/A	0
0	0.0%	N/A	0	0	0.0%	N/A	0	354	0.8%	N/A	0	5,491	12.2%	N/A	0
4,339	7.5%	3.7%	0	0	0.0%	N/A	0	309	0.5%	-1.2%	0	4,427	7.7%	7.3%	0
15,072	21.7%	6.7%	1	0	0.0%	N/A	0	3,244	4.7%	-2.9%	0	5,056	7.3%	6.4%	0
4,802	6.5%	1.4%	0	0	0.0%	N/A	0	266	0.4%	-0.5%	0	5,352	7.2%	-7.1%	0
3,795	8.9%	4.9%	0	0	0.0%	N/A	0	461	1.1%	-2.0%	0	3,647	8.5%	-0.8%	0
6,989	17.4%	6.1%	1	0	0.0%	N/A	0	479	1.2%	-1.3%	0	1,543	3.8%	2.3%	0
4,637	9.8%	1.3%	0	0	0.0%	N/A	0	220	0.5%	-1.4%	0	12,786	26.9%	16.9%	1
5,911	13.3%	1.6%	1	0	0.0%	N/A	0	432	1.0%	-2.1%	0	7,446	16.8%	15.7%	0
3,034	6.3%	2.5%	0	0	0.0%	N/A	0	409	0.8%	-0.3%	0	15,868	32.9%	-0.4%	1
1,860	4.5%	1.4%	0	8,818	21.3%	N/A	1	367	0.9%	-0.6%	0	6,074	14.7%	-3.0%	1
5,342	9.9%	3.2%	0	0	0.0%	N/A	0	462	0.9%	-1.3%	0	9,793	18.2%	12.2%	1
4,353	5.8%	-1.6%	0	741	1.0%	N/A	0	391	0.5%	-0.7%	0	14,531	19.2%	18.5%	1
7,089	10.1%	5.1%	0	0	0.0%	N/A	0	1,026	1.5%	-5.9%	0	14,905	21.1%	12.4%	1
64,785	14.8%	4.1%	4	0	0.0%	N/A	0	3,703	0.8%	-1.6%	0	73,165	16.7%	9.4%	3
44,525	8.2%	1.2%	4	38,808	7.1%	N/A	4	19,529	3.6%	-4.7%	0	51,279	9.4%	0.8%	3
61,906	10.4%	4.5%	3	2,437	0.4%	N/A	0	9,716	1.6%	-2.7%	0	72,240	12.2%	8.7%	3
49,445	7.7%	2.4%	3	15,894	2.5%	N/A	1	8,091	1.3%	-2.3%	0	84,054	13.1%	5.6%	5
220,661	**9.9%**	**3.0%**	**14**	**57,139**	**2.6%**	**N/A**	**5**	**41,039**	**1.8%**	**-2.8%**	**0**	**280,738**	**12.6%**	**6.0%**	**14**

Statistics

A record 76 new deputies were elected to the 31st Dáil in February 2011, along with 8 former members who were not in the outgoing Dáil. The remaining 82 deputies, including two elected at by-elections, were members of the 30th Dáil.

New Deputies

Candidate	Constituency
Adams, Gerry (SF)	Louth
Barry, Tom (FG)	Cork East
Boyd Barrett, Richard (ULA)	Dún Laoghaire
Butler, Ray (FG)	Meath West
Buttimer, Jerry (FG)	Cork South-Central
Cannon, Ciarán (FG)	Galway East
Coffey, Paudie (FG)	Waterford
Collins, Áine (FG)	Cork North-West
Collins, Joan (ULA)	Dublin South-Central
Colreavy, Michael (SF)	Sligo–North Leitrim
Conaghan, Michael (Lab)	Dublin South-Central
Conlan, Sean (FG)	Cavan–Monaghan
Connaughton Jnr, Paul (FG)	Galway East
Conway, Ciara (Lab)	Waterford
Corcoran Kennedy, Marcella (FG)	Laois–Offaly
Cowen, Barry (FF)	Laois–Offaly
Daly, Clare, (ULA)	Dublin North
Daly, Jim (FG)	Cork South-West
Deering, Pat (FG)	Carlow–Kilkenny
Doherty, Regina (FG)	Meath East
Donnelly, Stephen (Ind)	Wicklow
Donohoe, Paschal, (FG)	Dublin Central
Dowds, Robert (Lab)	Dublin Mid-West
Ellis, Dessie (SF)	Dublin North-West
Farrell, Alan (FG)	Dublin North
Ferris, Anne (Lab)	Wicklow
Fitzpatrick, Peter (FG)	Louth
Flanagan, Luke 'Ming' (Ind)	Roscommon–South Leitrim
Fleming, Tom (Ind)	Kerry South
Griffin, Brendan (FG)	Kerry South
Halligan, John (Ind)	Waterford
Hannigan, Dominic (Lab)	Meath East
Harrington, Noel (FG)	Cork South-West
Harris, Simon (FG)	Wicklow
Healy-Rae, Michael (Ind)	Kerry South
Heydon, Martin (FG)	Kildare South
Humphreys, Heather (FG)	Cavan–Monaghan
Humphreys, Kevin (Lab)	Dublin South-East
Keating, Derek (FG)	Dublin Mid-West
Keaveney, Colm (Lab)	Galway East
Kelly, Alan (Lab)	Tipperary North
Kyne, Seán (FG)	Galway West
Lawlor, Anthony (FG)	Kildare North
Lyons, John (Lab)	Dublin North-West
McCarthy, Michael (Lab)	Cork South-West
McConalogue, Charlie (FF)	Donegal North-East
McDonald, Mary Lou (SF)	Dublin Central
McFadden, Nicky (FG)	Longford–Westmeath
McLellan, Sandra (SF)	Cork East
McLoughlin, Tony (FG)	Sligo–North Leitrim
McNamara, Michael (Lab)	Clare
Mac Lochlainn, Pádraig (SF)	Donegal North-East
Maloney, Eamonn (Lab)	Dublin South-West
Mathews, Peter (FG)	Dublin South
Mitchell O'Connor, Mary (FG)	Dún Laoghaire
Mulherin, Michelle (FG)	Mayo
Murphy, Dara (FG)	Cork North-Central
Murphy, Eoghan (FG)	Dublin South-East
Nash, Gerald (Lab)	Louth
Nolan, Derek (Lab)	Galway West
O'Brien, Jonathan (SF)	Cork North-Central
O'Donovan, Patrick (FG)	Limerick
O'Reilly, Joe (FG)	Cavan–Monaghan
Ó Ríordáin, Aodhán (Lab)	Dublin North-Central
Phelan, Ann (Lab)	Carlow–Kilkenny
Phelan, John Paul (FG)	Carlow–Kilkenny
Pringle, Thomas (Ind)	Donegal South-West
Ross, Shane (Ind)	Dublin South
Ryan, Brendan (Lab)	Dublin North
Spring, Arthur (Lab)	Kerry North–Limerick West
Stanley, Brian (SF)	Laois–Offaly
Tóibín, Peadar (SF)	Meath West
Troy, Robert (FF)	Longford–Westmeath
Wallace, Mick (Ind)	Wexford
Walsh, Brian (FG)	Galway West
White, Alex (Lab)	Dublin South

Ex-TDs Re-elected

Eight former deputies were elected. They are:

Candidate	Constituency
Byrne, Eric (Lab)	Dublin South-Central
Crowe, Seán (SF)	Dublin South-West
Fitzgerald, Frances (FG)	Dublin Mid-West
Healy, Seamus (ULA)	Tipperary South
Higgins, Joe (ULA)	Dublin West
Kenny, Sean (Lab)	Dublin North-East
Murphy, Catherine (Ind)	Kildare North
Twomey, Liam (FG)	Wexford

Senators Elected

There were 14 members of the last Seanad elected to the 31st Dáil. They are:

Candidate	Constituency
Buttimer, Jerry (FG)	Cork South-Central
Cannon, Ciarán (FG)	Galway East
Coffey, Paudie (FG)	Waterford
Donohoe, Paschal (FG)	Dublin Central
Hannigan, Dominic (Lab)	Meath East
*Kelly, Alan (Lab)	Tipperary North
McCarthy, Michael (Lab)	Cork South-West
McFadden, Nicky (FG)	Longford–Westmeath
O'Reilly, Joe (FG)	Cavan–Monaghan
Phelan, John Paul (FG)	Carlow–Kilkenny
Ross, Shane (Ind)	Dublin South
Ryan, Brendan (Lab)	Dublin North
Twomey, Liam (FG)	Wexford
White, Alex (Lab)	Dublin South

* Alan Kelly was elected to the Seanad in 2007 but was subsequently elected to the European Parliament and resigned his Seanad seat.

Women Elected

A total of 25 women were elected in 2011, 3 more than in 2007 and 2002. It is the highest number of women ever elected. They are:

Candidate	Constituency
Burton, Joan (Lab)	Dublin West
Byrne, Catherine (FG)	Dublin South-Central
Collins, Áine (FG)	Cork North-West
Collins, Joan (ULA)	Dublin South-Central
Conway, Ciara (Lab)	Waterford
Corcoran Kennedy, Marcella (FG)	Laois–Offaly
Creighton, Lucinda (FG)	Dublin South-East
Daly, Clare (ULA)	Dublin North
Doherty, Regina (FG)	Meath East
Ferris, Anne (Lab)	Wicklow
Fitzgerald, Frances (FG)	Dublin Mid-West
Humphreys, Heather (FG)	Cavan–Monaghan
Lynch, Kathleen (Lab)	Cork North-Central
McDonald, Mary Lou (SF)	Dublin Central
McFadden, Nicky (FG)	Longford–Westmeath
McLellan, Sandra (SF)	Cork East
Mitchell, Olivia (FG)	Dublin South
Mitchell O'Connor, Mary (FG)	Dún Laoghaire
Mulherin, Michelle (FG)	Mayo
Murphy, Catherine (Ind)	Kildare North
O'Sullivan, Jan (Lab)	Limerick City
O'Sullivan, Maureen (Ind)	Dublin Central
Phelan, Ann (Lab)	Carlow–Kilkenny
Shortall, Róisín (Lab)	Dublin North-West
Tuffy, Joanna (Lab)	Dublin Mid-West

Lost Seats

A total of 45 outgoing TDs lost their seats. Thirty-five of those who lost were Fianna Fáil and all 6 Green TDs lost their seats. Three Fine Gael TDs lost their seats to party colleagues. Joe Behan, the one Independent who lost his seat, was elected for Fianna Fáil in 2007 but left the party in protest at the Budget measures enacted in 2009.

Candidate	Constituency
Ahern, Michael (FF)	Cork East
Andrews, Barry (FF)	Dún Laoghaire
Andrews, Chris (FF)	Dublin South-East
Aylward, Bobby (FF)	Carlow–Kilkenny
Behan, Joe (Ind)	Wicklow
Brady, Áine (FF)	Kildare North
Brady, Cyprian (FF)	Dublin Central
Brady, Johnny (FF)	Meath West
Byrne, Thomas (FF)	Meath East
Carey, Pat (FF)	Dublin North-West
Clune, Deirdre (FG)	Cork South-Central
Conlon, Margaret (FF)	Cavan–Monaghan
Connick, Seán (FF)	Wexford
Coughlan, Mary (FF)	Donegal South-West
Cuffe, Ciaran, (GP)	Dún Laoghaire
Curran, John (FF)	Dublin Mid-West
D'Arcy, Michael W. (FG)	Wexford
Fahey, Frank (FF)	Galway West
Fitzpatrick, Michael (FF)	Kildare North
Gogarty, Paul (GP)	Dublin Mid-West
Gormley, John (GP)	Dublin South-East
Hanafin, Mary (FF)	Dún Laoghaire
Haughey, Seán (FF)	Dublin North-Central
Hoctor, Máire (FF)	Tipperary North
Kelly, Peter (FF)	Longford–Westmeath
Kenneally, Brendan (FF)	Waterford
Kennedy, Michael (FF)	Dublin North
Lenihan, Conor (FF)	Dublin South-West
McEllistrim, Tom, (FF)	Kerry North
Mansergh, Martin (FF)	Tipperary South
Moloney, John Anthony (FF)	Laois–Offaly
Mulcahy,Michael (FF)	Dublin South-Central
O'Brien, Darragh (FF)	Dublin North
O'Connor, Charlie (FF)	Dublin South-West
O'Donoghue, John (FF)	Kerry South
O'Rourke, Mary (FF)	Longford–Westmeath
O'Sullivan, Christy (FF)	Cork South-West
Power, Peter (FF)	Limerick City
Power, Seán (FF)	Kildare South
Roche, Dick (FF)	Wicklow
Ryan, Eamon (GP)	Dublin South
Sargent, Trevor (GP)	Dublin North
Scanlon, Eamon (FF)	Sligo–North Leitrim
Sheahan, Tom (FG)	Kerry North
White, Mary (GP)	Carlow–Kilkenny

Retiring Deputies

Thirty-six deputies who were members of the 30th Dáil on its dissolution did not seek re-election in 2011. Twenty-one of those who didn't stand again were Fianna Fáil TDs, 8 were Fine Gael, 4 Labour, 1 Sinn Féin and 2 Independents. One of the Independents, Joe Behan, was elected for Fianna Fáil in 2007 but left the party in protest at Budget cuts in 2009.

Candidate	Constituency
Ahern, Bertie (FF)	Dublin Central
Ahern, Dermot (FF)	Louth
Ahern, Noel (FF)	Dublin North-West
Allen, Bernard (FG)	Cork North-Central
Ardagh, Seán (FF)	Dublin South-Central
Blaney, Niall (FF)	Donegal North-East
Burke, Ulick (FG)	Galway East
Connaughton, Paul (FG)	Galway East
Cowen, Brian (FF)	Laois–Offaly
Crawford, Seymour (FG)	Cavan–Monaghan
Cregan, John (FF)	Limerick West
Dempsey, Noel (FF)	Meath West
Devins, Jimmy (FF)	Sligo–North Leitrim
Enright, Olwyn (FG)	Laois–Offaly
Finneran, Michael (FF)	Roscommon–South Leitrim
Flynn, Beverley (FF)	Mayo
Harney, Mary (Ind)	Dublin Mid-West
Healy-Rae, Jackie (Ind)	Kerry South
Higgins, Michael D. (Lab)	Galway West
Killeen, Tony (FF)	Clare
Kitt, Tom (FF)	Dublin South
McCormack, Pádraic (FG)	Galway West
McManus, Liz (Lab)	Wicklow
Morgan Arthur (SF)	Louth
Nolan, M.J. (FF)	Carlow–Kilkenny
O'Flynn, Noel (FF)	Cork North-Central
O'Hanlon, Rory (FF)	Cavan–Monaghan
O'Keeffe, Batt (FF)	Cork North–West
O'Keeffe, Jim (FG)	Cork South-West
O'Keeffe, Ned (FF)	Cork East
O'Shea, Brian (Lab)	Waterford
Sheehan, P.J. (FG)	Cork South-West
Treacy, Noel (FF)	Galway East
Upton, Mary (Lab)	Dublin South-Central
Wallace, Mary (FF)	Meath East
Woods, Michael J. (FF)	Dublin North-East

Resignations

Three TDs resigned from the 30th Dáil but by-elections to fill the resulting vacancies were never held. The three were:

George Lee, (FG) Dublin South, who was elected at a by-election in June 2009 to fill the vacancy caused by Seamus Brennan's death. He resigned from the Dáil on 8 February 2010.

Martin Cullen, (FF) Waterford, who resigned in March 2010.

Jim McDaid, (FF) Donegal North-East, who resigned in November 2010

Deceased Deputies

Seamus Brennan, former Fianna Fáil Minister, died on 9 July 2008. He had been a TD for Dublin South since June 1981.

Independent TD Tony Gregory died on 2 January 2009. He had been a TD for Dublin Central since February 1982.

Brian Lenihan, former Minister for Finance, died on 10 June 2011. He had been a TD for Dublin West since the 1996 by-election caused by the death of his father, Brian Lenihan Snr TD.

Leading Vote-Getters

The leading vote-getter in the country in 2011 was Fine Gael leader Enda Kenny, who went on to be elected Taoiseach when the 31st Dáil met. However, the person who won the highest percentage of a quota was Michael Noonan of Fine Gael, who was appointed Minister for Finance on 9 March.

The top ten by votes won were:

Candidate	Votes
Enda Kenny (FG) Mayo	**17,472**
Shane Ross (Ind) Dublin South	**17,075**
Gerry Adams (SF) Louth	**15,072**
Pearse Doherty (SF) Donegal South-West	**14,262**
Michael Lowry (Ind) Tipperary North	**14,104**
Mick Wallace (Ind) Wexford	**13,329**
Michael Noonan (FG) Limerick City	**13,291**
Michael Ring (FG) Mayo	**13,180**
Pat Rabbitte (Lab) Dublin South-West	**12,867**
Martin Heydon (FG) Kildare South	**12,755**

Statistics

The top ten in proportions of a quota were:

Candidate	Quotas
Michael Noonan (FG)	**1.54**
Limerick City	
Enda Kenny (FG)	**1.41**
Mayo	
Shane Ross (Ind)	**1.41**
Dublin South	
Pat Rabbitte (Lab)	**1.37**
Dublin South-West	
Martin Heydon (FG)	**1.33**
Kildare South	
Pearse Doherty (SF)	**1.32**
Donegal South-West	
Terence Flanagan (FG)	**1.18**
Dublin North-East	
Michael Lowry (Ind)	**1.17**
Tipperary North	
Gerry Adams (SF)	**1.09**
Louth	
Jimmy Deenihan (FG)	**1.08**
Kerry North–Limerick West	

Transfers

Of the 2,243,176 votes cast, a total of 812,414 (36.6 per cent) ended up being transferred. The biggest beneficiary of those transfers was Fine Gael, which received 29 per cent of them. Labour got 17.7 per cent; Fianna Fáil got 17 per cent; and Sinn Féin got 7 per cent.

The transfers to Fine Gael helped the party to win 45.8 per cent of the seats with 36.1 per cent of the first preference vote.

Occupations of Deputies

A number of TDs describe themselves as full-time public representatives. The following list is based on the information they supplied about their occupations before they became involved in politics. Teachers remain the biggest single group in the Dáil but their numbers have fallen since the 2007 election, while the number of those engaged in business has increased.

Education	32
Secondary teachers	*20*
National teachers	*10*
Pre-school	*1*
Third level	*1*
Business	25
Public service	15
Farmers	14
Industry/employees	12
Lawyers	11
Barristers	*6*
Solicitors	*5*
Accountants	8
Clerical	6
Doctors	3

Engineering/Science	3
Publicans	3
Trade union officials	3
Voluntary sector	3
Architects	1
Journalists	1

Would You Believe

Two members of the Oireachtas are chocolate makers, one is a former All-Ireland set dancing champion, another is an international karaoke judge and another a member of Ireland's most famous brass band. The captain of the greatest team in the history of Gaelic football is also a member of the current Dáil.

The chocolate makers are both members of the Upper House. Mary White of Fianna Fáil, who was elected on the Industrial and Commercial Panel, is the founder of Lir Chocolates; while Mary Ann O'Brien, the founder of Lily O'Brien's Chocolates was a Taoiseach's nominee.

Tipperary South TD Mattie McGrath was an All-Ireland set dancing champion in 1974.

Cork North-Central TD Kathleen Lynch, who is Minister of State with responsibility for Disability, Older People, Equality and Mental Health, was a prominent judge in Irish and international karaoke competitions while she was a member of the previous Dáil.

Dublin North-East TD Terence Flanagan is a percussion player with the Artane Senior Band and is a former member of the Artane Boys' Band.

Jimmy Deenihan, Minister for Arts, won five All-Ireland medals playing for Kerry between 1975 and 1981. He was captain of the 1981 winning team.

Family Seats

One of the by-products of the Fianna Fáil rout in the 2011 election was that the 31st Dáil contains far fewer children of former TDs than the previous Dáil. The number of offspring of former TDs was cut to 15 from 31 in the last Dáil, 25 in the 29th Dáil, 30 in the 28th Dáil and 24 in the 27th Dáil.

There were 15 children (all sons) of TDs elected to the 31st Dáil. They were:

Candidate	Constituency
Calleary, Dara (FF)	Mayo
Carey, Joe (FG)	Clare
Connaughton Jnr, Paul (FG)	Galway East
Coveney, Simon (FG)	Cork South-Central
Cowen, Barry (FF)	Laois–Offaly

Candidate	Constituency
Creed, Michael (FG)	Cork North-West
Deasy, John (FG)	Waterford
Flanagan, Charles (FG)	Laois–Offaly
Healy-Rae, Michael (Ind)	Kerry South
Kenny, Enda (FG)	Mayo
Kitt, Micheal P. (FF)	Galway East
Lenihan, Brian (FF)	Dublin West
Naughten, Denis (FG)	Roscommon–South Leitrim
Sherlock, Sean (Lab)	Cork East
Timmins, Billy (FG)	Wicklow

Four TDs are grandsons of deputies:

Candiate	Constituency
Collins, Niall (FF)	Limerick
Lenihan, Brian (FF)	Dublin West
Ó Cuív, Éamon (FF)	Galway West
Spring, Arthur (Lab)	Kerry North–Limerick West

While there are no sets of brothers in the 31st Dáil, compared with three sets of siblings in the last Dáil, four deputies are brothers of former TDs. They are:

Candidate	Constituency
Bruton, Richard (FG)	Dublin North-Central
Cowen, Barry (FF)	Laois–Offaly
Kitt, Micheal P. (FF)	Galway East
Ryan, Brendan (Lab)	Dublin North

Four TDs are nephews of former deputies:

Candidate	Constituency
Browne, John (FF)	Wexford
McLoughlin, Tony (FG)	Sligo–North Leitrim
O'Donnell, Kieran (FG)	Limerick City
Spring, Arthur (Lab)	Kerry North–Limerick West

Labour Cork North-Central TD Kathleen Lynch and Labour Cork South-Central TD Ciarán Lynch are brother- and sister-in-law.

Long-serving Deputies

Taoiseach Enda Kenny is the longest-serving deputy in the 31st Dáil, although he is by no means the oldest. He was first elected to the Dáil in November 1975 at the age of twenty-four at a by-election caused by the death of his father Henry and was successfully returned at the 1977 General Election and the ten subsequent general elections. Not one of the TDs elected along with Kenny in 1977 now remains in the Dáil.

Kenny came very close to losing his seat in the 2002 election, when he was 24 votes behind his running mate Jim Higgins on the first count. By the eighth count, he had pulled 87 votes ahead of Higgins, who was eliminated. Higgins' transfers then elected him. Michael Ring topped the poll in Mayo in 2002 (more than 4,000 votes ahead of Kenny) and Fine Gael won two seats. In 2011 the party won a remarkable four out of five seats there.

Galway East Fianna Fáil TD Micheal P. Kitt was first elected to the Dáil eight months before Kenny in March 1975, but Kitt does not have Kenny's unbroken service. Kitt lost his seat in 1977, returned to the Dáil in 1981, lost his seat again in 2002, but made it back in 2007. He was a senator during those two periods out of the Dáil. Kenny and Kitt are almost the same age and studied to be national teachers in St Patrick's, Drumcondra. They both stood for the Dáil in by-elections in 1975 on the deaths of their fathers, who were both TDs. In 2011 Kenny as Taoiseach appointed Kitt as Leas-Cheann Comhairle of the 31st Dáil.

After Kenny, the next longest-serving deputy with continuous service is Minister for Finance Michael Noonan, who was first elected in June 1981. Ceann Comhairle Sean Barrett, Minister for Justice Alan Shatter and Kildare North TD Bernard Durkan were also elected in June 1981, but each of them missed one Dáil term.

Minister for Jobs, Enterprise and Innovation, Richard Bruton, is the deputy with the third-longest continuous service. He was first elected to the Dáil in February 1982.

Life After Death For the PDs

There are more former Progressive Democrats in the 31st Dáil than Progressive Democrats elected in 2002, when the party was reduced to two seats.

Three former PD public representatives were elected to the 31st Dáil. Noel Grealish was re-elected as a TD for Galway West, standing as an Independent. Ciarán Cannon, leader of the PDs and a senator when the party was wound up, was elected as a Fine Gael TD for Galway East. Mary Mitchell O'Connor, who had been a PD councillor in Dún Laoghaire–Rathdown was elected as a Fine Gael TD in Dún Laoghaire.

Another Fine Gael TD, Peter Matthews, was a member of the PDs in the late 1980s but was never elected to public office for the party.

Cáit Keane, a former PD councillor and Dáil candidate, was elected to the Seanad for Fine Gael in 2011.

Changed Seats

There were changes in party representation in every single constituency except Cork South-Central in 2011. Fianna Fáil was left without a seat in 25 of the 43 constituencies. In all previous elections since 1927 the party won at least one seat in every constituency in the country.

There were a number of constituency boundary changes since 2007. Kerry North was redrawn to become Kerry North–Limerick West, while Limerick East and Limerick West were redrawn to become Limerick City and Limerick. Two constituencies, Dublin West and Louth, gained an extra seat each, while the Dún Laoghaire constituency lost a seat.

The changed seats in 39 constituencies were:

Constituency	Changes
Carlow–Kilkenny	FG gain 2; Lab gain 1. FF lose 2; GP lose 1.
Cavan–Monaghan	FG gain 2. FF lose 2.
Clare	Lab gain 1. FF lose 1.
Cork East	FG and SF gain 1 each. FF lose 2.
Cork North-Central	SF gain 1. FF lose 1.
Cork North-West	FG gain 1. FF lose 1.
Cork South-West	Lab gain 1. FF lose 1.
Donegal North-East	SF gain 1. FF lose 1.
Donegal South-West	Ind gains 1. FF lose 1.
Dublin Central	FG and SF gain 1 each. FF lose 2.
Dublin Mid-West	FG gain 2; Lab gain 1. FF, GP and Ind lose 1 each.
Dublin North	FG, Lab and ULA gain 1 each. FF lose 2; GP lose 1.
Dublin North-Central	Lab gain 1. FF lose 1.
Dublin North-East	Lab gain 1. FF lose 1.
Dublin North-West	Lab gain 1; SF gain 1. FF lose 2.
Dublin South	Lab and Ind gain 1 each. FF and GP lose 1 each.
Dublin South-Central	Lab and ULA gain 1 each. FF lose 2.
Dublin South-East	FG and Lab gain 1 each. FF and GP lose 1 each.
Dublin South-West	Lab and SF gain 1 each. FF lose 2.
Dublin West	ULA gain 1 (constituency has 1 extra seat since 2007).
Dún Laoghaire	FG and ULA gain 1 each. FF lose 2; GP lose 1 (constituency has 1 less seat since 2007).
Galway East	Lab gain 1. FF lose 1.
Galway West	FG gain 1. FF lose 1.
Kerry South	Ind gains 1. FF lose 1.
Kildare North	FG and Ind gain 1 each. FF lose 2.
Kildare South	FG gain 1. FF lose 1.
Laois–Offaly	SF gain 1. FF lose 1.
Longford–Westmeath	FG gain 1. FF lose 1.
Louth	FG and Lab gain 1 each; FF lose 1 (constituency has 1 extra seat since 2007).
Mayo	FG gain 1. FF lose 1.
Meath East	FG and Lab gain 1 each. FF lose 2.
Meath West	FG and SF gain 1 each. FF lose 2.
Roscommon–South Leitrim	Ind gains 1. FF lose 1.
Sligo–North Leitrim	FG and SF gain 1 each. FF lose 2.
Tipperary North	Lab gain 1. FF lose 1.
Tipperary South	ULA gain 1. FF lose 1.
Waterford	FG and Ind gain 1 each. FF lose 2.
Wexford	Ind gains 1. FF lose 1.
Wicklow	FG and Ind gain 1 each. FF lose 2.

The 24th Seanad (elected August 2011)

Fine Gael	19	Independent nominees	7
Fianna Fáil	14	University Independents	5
Labour	12		
Sinn Féin	3		

Senator	Whip	Panel/Constituency
Bacik, Ivana	Lab	University of Dublin
• Barrett, Sean	Ind	University of Dublin
Bradford, Paul	FG	Agricultural
• Brennan, Terry	FG	Labour
• Burke, Colm	FG	Industrial and Commercial
Burke, Paddy	FG	Agricultural
• Byrne, Thomas	FF	Cultural and Educational
• Clune, Deirdre	FG	Cultural and Educational
• Coghlan, Eamonn	Ind	Taoiseach's nominee
Coghlan, Paul	FG	Industrial and Commercial
• Comiskey, Michael	FG	Agricultural
• Conway, Martin	FG	Administrative
• Crown, John	Ind	National University of Ireland
• Cullinane, David	SF	Labour
Cummins, Maurice	FG	Labour
Daly, Mark	FF	Administrative
• D'Arcy, Jim	FG	Taoiseach's nominee
• D'Arcy, Michael	FG	Administrative
• Gilroy, John	Lab	Cultural and Educational
• Harte, Jimmy	Lab	Industrial and Commercial
• Hayden, Aideen	Lab	Taoiseach's nominee
Healy-Eames, Fidelma	FG	Labour
• Heffernan, James	Lab	Agricultural
• Henry, Imelda	FG	Industrial and Commercial
• Higgins, Lorraine	Lab	Taoiseach's nominee
• Keane, Cáit	FG	Labour
• Kelly, John	Lab	Administrative
• Landy, Denis	Lab	Administrative
Leyden, Terry	FF	Labour
• McAleese, Martin	Ind	Taoiseach's nominee
• Mac Conghail, Fiach	Ind	Taoiseach's nominee
MacSharry, Marc	FF	Industrial and Commercial
• Moloney, Marie	Lab	Labour
• Mooney, Paschal	FF	Agricultural
• Moran, Mary	Lab	Taoiseach's nominee
• Mulcahy, Tony	FG	Labour
Mullen, Rónán	Ind	National University of Ireland
• Mullins, Michael	FG	Cultural and Educational
• Noone, Catherine	FG	Industrial and Commercial
Norris, David Patrick Bernard	Ind	University of Dublin
• O'Brien, Darragh	FF	Labour
• O'Brien, Mary Ann	Ind	Taoiseach's nominee
• Ó Clochartaigh, Trevor	SF	Agricultural
Ó Domhnaill, Brian	FF	Agricultural
• O'Donnell, Marie-Louise	Ind	Taoiseach's nominee
O'Donovan, Denis	FF	Agricultural
• O'Keeffe, Susan	Lab	Agricultural
Ó Murchú, Labhrás	FF	Cultural and Educational
• O'Neill, Pat	FG	Agricultural
• O'Sullivan, Ned	FF	Labour
• Power, Averil	FF	Industrial and Commercial
Quinn, Feargal	Ind	National University of Ireland
• Reilly, Kathryn	SF	Industrial and Commercial
• Sheahan, Tom	FG	Administrative
• van Turnhout, Jillian	Ind	Taoiseach's nominee
Walsh, Jim	FF	Agricultural
• Whelan, John	Lab	Labour
White, Mary	FF	Industrial and Commercial
Wilson, Diarmuid	FF	Administrative
• Zappone, Katherine	Ind	Taoiseach's nominee

The 23rd Seanad was elected on 26 April 2011 and held its first meeting on 25 May 2011. The party strengths in the 60-member House were: Fine Gael 19, Fianna Fáil 14, Labour 12, Sinn Féin 3, and Independents 12. Seven of the Independents were among the 11 Taoiseach's nominees; the other five Independents were elected by the university constituencies.

The programme of the incoming Fine Gael–Labour government ('Towards Recovery 2011–2016') promised to prioritise the holding of a referendum to abolish the Seanad.

Labour Party Leader Eamon Gilmore with his team at the launch of Labour's Manifesto in The Aviva Stadium. Photograph: David Sleator.

Administrative Panel

Elected (7 Seats)

Mark Daly (FF)*	9th count
John Kelly (Lab)	12th count
Diarmuid Wilson (FF)*	13th count
Tom Sheahan (FG)	15th count
Michael D'Arcy (FG)	15th count
Martin Conway (FG)	15th count
Denis Landy (Lab)	16th count
Quota	133.001

Candidates

Name	(County, Party)	Vote (1st Pref)

Nominating Bodies Sub-Panel

Name	(County, Party)	Vote (1st Pref)
Boland, Seamus	Offaly, Ind	30
Buckley, Molly	Offaly, FG	23
Bugler, Phyll	Tipperary, FG	19
Conway, Martin	Clare, FG	86
Daly, Mark	Kerry, FF	121
Landy, Denis	Tipperary, Lab	75
McGloin, Enda	Leitrim, FG	70
Moran, Mary	Louth, Lab	63
O'Grady, Sean	Kerry, Lab	22
Ward, Barry	Dublin FG	27

Oireachtas Sub-Panel

Name	(County, Party)	Vote (1st Pref)
Brady, Martin	Dublin FF	12
D'Arcy, Michael	Wexford, FG	89
Dennison, Kevin	Dublin FG	26
Fitzpatrick, Mary	Dublin, FF	105
Hourigan, Mary Hanna	Tipperary, FG	32
Kelly, John	Roscommon, Lab	73
Lyons, Sean	Dublin, Ind	19
Sheahan, Tom	Kerry, FG	62
Wilson, Diarmuid	Cavan, FF	110

Mark Daly (FF)

Home Address: 34 Henry Street, Kenmare, Co. Kerry.
Contact Details: Seanad Office: (01) 618 3830. Mobile: (086) 803 2612. Email: mark.daly@oireachtas.ie.
Birth Place/Date: Cork, 12 March 1973.
Marital Status: Single.
Education: Holy Cross College, Kenmare. Dublin Institute of Technology (Diploma in Valuations). Greenwich University, London (BSc in Management). Harvard Kennedy School.
Occupation: Senator; auctioneer.

Senator since 2007. Former assistant to MEP Brian Crowley.

John Kelly (Lab)

Home Address: Castlemore, Ballaghaderreen, Co. Roscommon.
Contact Details: Seanad Office: (01) 618 3049. Mobile: (086) 809 4698. Email: john.kelly@oireachtas.ie.
Birth Place/Date: Ballintubber, Co. Roscommon, 21 February 1960.
Marital Status: Married to Brid. One daughter, two sons.
Education: Ballintubber N.S. CBS, Roscommon.
Occupation: Senator.

New senator. Elected to Roscommon County Council in 2004 and re-elected in 2009 as an

Independent. Joined the Labour Party in 2010. Former community welfare officer in Ballaghadereen area.

Diarmuid Wilson (FF)

Home Address: 46 Carrickfern, Cavan.
Contact Details: Seanad Office: (01) 618 3561. Mobile: (087) 232 3959.
Email: diarmuid.wilson@oireachtas.ie.
Birth Place/Date: Cavan town, 20 November 1965.
Marital Status: Married. Four children.
Education: Ballinagh N.S., Cavan. Cavan Vocational School. St Patrick's College, Maynooth. Brunel University, London (extern graduate).
Occupation: Senator.

Fianna Fáil Whip in the Seanad. Senator since 2002. Former member, Cavan County Council, 1999–2003.

Tom Sheahan (FG)

Home Address: Rathbeg, Rathmore, Co. Kerry.
Contact Details: Constituency Office: (064) 775 8102. Mobile: (087) 202 1661.
Email: tom.sheahan@oireachtas.ie.
Birth Place/Date: Killarney, 5 September 1968.
Marital Status: Married to Mary Lenihan. Two daughters, one son.

Education: Glenbeigh N.S. De La Salle Brothers. Coláiste Iosagáin, Ballyvourney.
Occupation: Public representative.

New senator. Former Fine Gael TD for Kerry South 2007–11 but lost seat in the 2011 General Election to party colleague. Former member of Kerry County Council.

Michael D'Arcy (FG)

Home Address: Annagh, Gorey, Co. Wexford.
Contact Details: Constituency Office: (053) 948 3966. Mobile: (087) 990 1055.
Email: michaelwdarcy@gmail.com; michael.darcy@oireachtas.ie.
Birth Place/Date: Wexford, 26 February 1970.
Marital Status: Married to Shelley Vaughan. Two children.
Education: Ballythomas N.S. Gorey CBS. University of London (Diploma in Law).
Occupation: Public representative; farmer.

New senator. Fine Gael TD for Wexford 2007–11 but lost seat in 2011 General Election. Member Wexford County Council 2004–07. Son of Michael D'Arcy: TD for Wexford 1977–1992 and 1997–2002; Senator 1992–97.

Martin Conway (FG)

Home Address: Woodmount, Ennistymon, Co. Clare.

Contact Details: Constituency Office: (065) 707 2222. Mobile: (087) 261 2977. Email: martin.conway@oireachtas.ie.
Birth Place/Date: Ennistymon, 8 April 1974.
Marital Status: Married to Breege Hannify.
Education: Ennistymon CBS, primary and secondary. UCD (BA in Economics and Politics).
Occupation: Public representative.

New senator. Elected to Clare County Council in 2004 and re-elected in 2009 for North Clare area. Founder member of AHEAD, which aims to improve third-level access for people with disabilities.

Denis Landy (Lab)

Home Address: Mainstown, Carrick-on-Suir, Co. Tipperary.
Contact Details: Seanad Office: (01) 618 3351. Mobile: (087) 232 6138. Email: denis.landy@oireachtas.ie.
Birth Place/Date: Carrick-on-Suir, 28 February 1962.
Marital Status: Married to Nancy. One son.
Education: CBS, Carrick-on-Suir. UCC (Diploma in Rural Development; Certificate in Local Government). IPA.
Occupation: Public representative.

New senator. Member of Carrick-on-Suir Council from 1988 and South Tipperary County Council from 1991. Mayor of Carrick-on-Suir, 1996 and 2006.

Agricultural Panel

Elected (11 Seats)

James Heffernan (Lab)	1st count
Paddy Burke (FG)*	8th count
Trevor O'Clochartaigh (SF)	14th count
Paul Bradford (FG)*	16th count
Brian Ó Domhnaill (FF)*	19th count
Michael Commiskey (FG)	21st count
Pat O'Neill (FG)	21st count
Jim Walsh (FF)*	24th count
Susan O'Keeffe (Lab)	25th count
Denis O'Donovan (FF)*	25th count
Paschal Mooney (FF)	25th count
Quota	88.834

Candidates

Name	(County, Party)	Vote (1st Pref)
Nominating Bodies Sub-Panel		
Bradford, Paul	Cork, FG	63
Brennan, Joseph	Tipperary, FG	11
Burke, Paddy	Mayo, FG	82
Clarke, Michael	Sligo, Ind	32
Coleman, Alan	Cork, FF	3
Connick, Seán	Wexford, FF	25
Dillon, John	Limerick, Ind	12
Doocey, Declan	Waterford, FG	24
Hogan, John	Tipperary, FF	23
McDermott, Frank	Westmeath, FG	21
Mansergh, Dr Martin	Tipperary, FF	9
Mooney, Paschal	Leitrim, FF	40
Ó Domhnaill, Brian	Donegal, FF	53
O'Donovan, Denis	Cork, FF	42
O'Neill, Pat	Kilkenny, FG	40
Phelan, Martin	Laois, FG	26
Sheahan, John	Limerick, FG	38
Walsh, Jim	Wexford, FF	53
Oireachtas Sub-Panel		
Bailey, John	Dún Laoghaire–Rathdown, FG	19
Burton, Pat	Cork, FG	25
Carroll, James	Louth, FF	34
Comiskey, Michael	Leitrim, FG	40
Feeney, Peter	Galway, FG	29
Heffernan, James	Limerick, Lab	97
Markey, Colm	Louth, FG	27
Ó Clochartaigh, Trevor	Galway, SF	82
O'Keeffe, Susan	Sligo, Lab	69
Scanlon, Eamon	Sligo, FF	47

James Heffernan (Lab)

Home Address: Main Street, Kilfinane, Co. Limerick.
Contact Details: Seanad Office: (01) 618 3057. Mobile: (087) 324 3315. Email: james.heffernan@oireachtas.ie.
Birth Place/Date: Limerick, 3 October 1979.
Marital Status: Single.
Education: University of Limerick (BA in History, Politics, Sociology and Social Studies; post graduate Certificate in Primary Education).
Occupation: Public representative; primary school teacher.

New senator. Unsuccessful Dáil candidate in Limerick in 2011 and 2007. Elected to Limerick County Council for Kilmallock area, 2009.

Paddy Burke (FG)

Home Address: Annagh, Castlebar, Co. Mayo.
Contact Details: Constituency Office: (094) 902 2568. Mobile: (087) 244 1802. Email: paddy.burke@oireachtas.ie.
Birth Place/Date: Castlebar, 15 January 1955.
Marital Status: Married to Dolores Barrett.
Education: Ballinafad College, Castlebar. Rockwell Agricultural College, Co. Tipperary.

Franciscan Brothers Agricultural College, Mount Bellew, Co. Galway.
Occupation: Public representative.

Elected unopposed as Cathaoirleach of the Seanad in May 2011. Leas-Chathaoirleach of the 22nd and 23rd Seanad from 2002 to 2011. Member of the Seanad's Agricultural Panel since 1993. Member, Mayo County Council, 1993–2003.

Trevor Ó Clochartaigh (SF)

Home Address: An Caorán Beag, An Cheathrú Rua, Co. na Gaillimhe.
Contact Details: Seanad Office: (01) 618 4069. Mobile: (087) 247 6624. Email: trevor.oclochartaigh@oireachtas.ie.
Birth Place/Date: Huddersfield, England, 14 March 1968.
Marital Status: Married to Mali. Four children.
Education: NUI Galway (B.Comm).
Occupation: Senator.

New senator. Unsuccessful candidate in Galway West in 2011 General Election. Also ran for Galway County Council for Connemara in 2009 local elections. Former manager and artistic director of An Taibhdhearc in Galway and producer/director on *Ros na Rún* and *Fair City* TV soap operas.

Paul Bradford (FG)

Home Address: Ballyphilibeen, Mourne Abbey, Mallow, Co. Cork.
Contact Details: Constituency Office: (022) 29375. Mobile: (087) 259 6204. Email: paul.bradford@oireachtas.ie.
Birth Place/Date: Mallow, December 1963.
Marital Status: Married to Lucinda Creighton.
Education: Patrician Academy, Mallow.
Occupation: Public representative; farmer.

Senator since 2002 and previously 1987–89. TD for Cork East, 1989–2002. Contested Cork-East Dáil constituency in 2007 and 2002.

Brian Ó Domhnaill (FF)

Home Address: Killult, Falcarragh, Co. Donegal.
Contact Details: Constituency Office: (074) 916 5466. Mobile: (086) 821 8084. Email: brian.odomhnaill@oireachtas.ie.
Birth Place/Date: Letterkenny, 18 October 1977.
Marital Status: Single.
Education: Falcarragh Community School. University of Ulster (BSc Hons).
Occupation: Senator; former teacher.

Appointed to the Seanad in 2007 as one of the Taoiseach's nominees. Member, Donegal County Council, 2004–07. Elected to Údarás na Gaeltachta, 1999.

Michael Comiskey (FG)

Home Address: Leckaun, Co. Leitrim.
Contact Details: Constituency Office: (071) 916 4245. Mobile: (086) 230 4525. Email: michael.comiskey@oireachtas.ie; comiskey1@esatclear.ie.
Birth Place/Date: Manorhamilton, Co. Leitrim, 1 October 1953.
Marital Status: Married to Elizabeth McMorrow. Five sons.
Education: Manorhamilton Vocational School.
Occupation: Public representative; farmer

New senator. Unsuccessful Dáil candidate for Sligo–Leitrim in 2007 General Election.

Pat O'Neill (FG)

Home Address: Ballyredding, Bennettsbridge, Co. Kilkenny.
Contact Details: Seanad Office: (01) 618 3082. Mobile: (087) 277 1483. Email: pat.oneill@oireachtas.ie.
Birth Place/Date: Kilkenny, 14 November 1958.
Marital Status: Married to Brigid.
Education: Leaving Cert and green cert in Agriculture.
Occupation: Public representative; farmer.

New senator. Elected to Kilkenny County Council for Thomastown area in 2004 and re-elected in 2009.

Agricultural Panel

Jim Walsh (FF)

Home Address: Mountgarrett, New Ross, Co. Wexford.
Contact Details: Constituency Office: (051) 421771. Seanad Office: (01) 618 3763. Mobile: (086) 600 8155. Email: jim.walsh@oireachtas.ie.
Birth Place/Date: New Ross, 5 May 1947.
Marital Status: Married to Marie Furlong. One son, one daughter.
Education: CBS New Ross.
Occupation: Senator.

Member of the Agricultural Panel since 1997. Member, Wexford County Council, 1979–2004 (Chairman 1992–93). Member, New Ross UDC, 1974–2004 (Chairman nine times). Member, General Council of County Councils, 1979–2004. Chairman, Local Authority Members Association, 1997–2002. President, Irish Road Haulage Association, 1982–84.

Susan O'Keeffe (Lab)

Home Address: Kinnagrelly House, Collooney, Co. Sligo.
Contact Details: Email: susan.okeeffe @oireachtas.ie. Mobile: (085) 131 4084.
Birth Place/Date: Dublin, 18 September 1960.
Marital Status: Married. Three children.

Education: Convent of the Sacred Heart, Mount Anville, Dublin. UCC (BSc, Dairy and Food).
Occupation: Senator; journalist.

New senator. Unsuccessful candidate for Sligo–Leitrim in 2011 General Election and in 2009 European Parliament elections in Ireland North-West. Her reporting on beef industry for ITV programme *World in Action* in 1991 led to the Hamilton Tribunal of Inquiry and she was the only one prosecuted as a result, for refusing to reveal sources.

Denis O'Donovan (FF)

Home Address: 9 Beacon Hill, Bantry, Co. Cork.
Contact Details: Constituency Office: (027) 53840. Seanad Office: (01) 618 4479. Mobile: (087) 254 3806. Email: denis.odonovan@oireachtas.ie.
Birth Place/Date: Bantry, Co. Cork, 23 July 1955.
Marital Status: Separated. Three sons, one daughter.
Education: Bantry Secondary School. Carrignavar Secondary College. UCC (BCL).
Occupation: Senator; solicitor.

Leas-Chathaoirleach of the Seanad. First appointed to Seanad as a Taoiseach's nominee from 1989–93 and elected to the Industrial Panel 1997–2002 and 2007–11. TD for Cork South-West 2002–07. Member of Cork County Council, 1985–2003; Chairman, 1989–90.

Paschal Mooney (FF)

Home Address: Carrick Road, Drumshanbo, Co. Leitrim.
Contact Details: Seanad Office: (01) 618 3148. Email: paschal.mooney@oireachtas.ie.
Birth Place/Date: Dublin, 14 October 1947.
Marital Status: Married to Shiela Baldrey. Three sons, two daughters.
Education: Drumshanbo N.S. Presentation Brothers, Carrick-on-Shannon. Camden Institute, London.
Occupation: Journalist/broadcaster; senator.

First elected to the Seanad (Cultural and Educational Panel) in 1987 and subsequent elections, but lost seat in 2007. Re-elected to the Agricultural Panel at by-election in January 2010.

Elected (5 Seats)

Deirdre Clune (FG)	10th count
Thomas Byrne (FF)	13th count
Labhrás Ó Murchú (FF)*	13th count
John Gilroy (Lab)	14th count
Michael Mullins (FG)	14th count
Quota	178.667

Candidates

Name	(County, Party)	Vote (1st Pref)
Nominating Bodies Sub-Panel		
Boyhan, Victor	Dún Laoghaire, Ind	44
Delaney, Conor	Tipperary, FG	16
Hogan, Nicholas	Offaly, FG	27
Irish, Anne-Maria	Kilkenny, FG	25
Kennedy, Pat	Limerick, FG	32
McCartain, John	Leitrim, FG	68
Mullins, Michael	Galway, FG	78
O'Dea, Jim	Dublin, FG	11
Ó Murchú, Labhrás	Tipperary, FF	104
Ormonde, Ann	Dublin, FF	66
Quinlan, Hilary	Waterford, FG	47
Walsh, Seamus	Galway, FF	86
Oireachtas Sub-Panel		
Byrne, Thomas	Meath, FF	129
Clune, Deirdre	Cork, FG	103
Gilroy, John	Cork, Lab	157
Quinn, Liam	Offaly, FG	23
Tormey, Bill	Dublin, FG	49

Deirdre Clune (FG)

Home Address: 144 Blackrock Road, Cork.
Contact Details: Constituency Office: (021) 489 0000. Mobile: (087) 238 7539. Email: deirdre.clune@oireachtas.ie.
Birth Place/Date: Cork, June 1959.
Marital Status: Married to Conor Clune. Four sons.
Education: Ursuline Convent, Blackrock, Cork. UCC (BE; Diploma in Management for Engineers; Higher Diploma in Environmental Engineering).
Occupation: Public representative; civil engineer.

New senator. She was TD for Cork South-Central from 1997 to 2002 and again from 2007 to 2011, when she lost her seat in the general election. Member, Cork City Council 1999–2007. Lord Mayor 2005–06. Daughter of Peter Barry, former Tánaiste, Government Minister and TD for Cork constituencies 1969–87.

Thomas Byrne (FF)

Home Address: 42 The Boulevard, Grange Rath, Colpe, Co. Meath.
Contact Details: Seanad Office: (01) 618 3310. Mobile: (086) 603 8886. Email: thomas.byrne@oireachtas.ie.
Birth Place/Date: Drogheda, Co. Louth, 1 June 1977.

Cultural and Educational Panel

Marital Status: Married to Ann Hunt. One son, two daughters.
Education: St Mary's Diocesan School. TCD (LLB). Law Society of Ireland. State Bar of New York.
Occupation: Public representative; formerly solicitor.

New senator. TD for Meath East 2007–11 but lost his seat in the 2011 General Election. Fianna Fáil Seanad spokesperson on Public Expenditure and Financial Sector Reform.

Labhrás Ó Murchú (FF)

Home Address: An Bóithrín Glas, Caiseal Mumhan, Co. Thiobraid Árann.
Contact Details: Seanad Office: (01) 618 4018. Mobile: (087) 252 8747. Email: labhras.omurchu@oireachtas.ie.
Birth Place/Date: Cashel, Co. Tipperary, 14 August 1939.
Marital Status: Married to Una Ronan.
Education: Cashel CBS.
Occupation: Director General, Comhaltas Ceoltóirí Éireann.

First elected to the Seanad in 1997. National Chairman of the Irish Family History Foundation. National Chairman of Fondúireacht an Phiarsaigh.

John Gilroy (Lab)

Home Address: 9 Hazelwood Court, Glanmire, Co. Cork.
Contact Details: Seanad Office: (01) 618 3089. Mobile: (087) 279 9608. Email: john.gilroy@oireachtas.ie; johngilroy01@gmail.com.
Birth Place/Date: Athboy, Co. Meath, 20 July 1967.
Marital Status: Married to Marion. One son, one daughter.
Education: Our Lady's Hospital, Cork (Certificate in Psychiatric Nursing).
Occupation: Psychiatric nurse.

New senator. Unsuccessful candidate in Cork North-Central in the 2011 General Election. Elected to Cork County Council 2004 and 2009.

Michael Mullins (FG)

Home Address: Cleaghmore, Ballinasloe, Co. Galway.
Contact Details: Constituency Office: (090) 964 2728. Mobile: (087) 2607405. Email: michael.mullins@oireachtas.ie.
Birth Place/Date: Galway, 22 February 1953.
Marital Status: Married to Mary Lyne.
Education: Woodlawn N.S. St Joseph's College, Garbally Park, Ballinasloe. Irish Management Institute. Institute of Personnel and Development.
Occupation: Senator; former human resources manager.

New senator. Member of Galway County Council for Ballinasloe area since 1985; Chairperson 1992–93 and 2006–07.

Elected (9 Seats)

Jimmy Harte (Lab)	22nd count
Mary White (FF)*	25th count
Averil Power (FF)	25th count
Marc MacSharry*	25th count
Imelda Henry (FG)	29th count
Paul Coghlan (FG)*	31st count
Catherine Noone (FG)	33rd count
Colm Burke (FG)	33rd count
Kathryn Reilly (SF)	33rd count
Quota	106.701

Candidates

Name	(County, Party)	Vote (1st Pref)

Nominating Bodies Sub-Panel

Name	(County, Party)	Vote (1st Pref)
Burke, Colm	Cork, FG	40
Butler, Richard	Limerick, FG	21
Byrne, Danny	Dublin, FG	15
Casserly, Mel	Sligo, Ind	2
Clendennan, John	Offaly, FG	19
Coghlan, Paul	Kerry, FG	45
Crotty, Pat	Kilkenny, FG	6
Crowe, John	Clare, FG	36
Fitzgerald, David	Kilkenny, FG	8
Fortune, Tom	Wicklow, Lab	13
Hayden, Aideen	Dublin, Lab	27
Henry, Imelda	Sligo, FG	41
Higgins, Lorraine	Galway, Lab	41
Hynes, Pat	Galway, Ind	22
Keogh, Paul	Dublin, Ind	1
Kinsella, Michael	Wexford, FG	9
Leddin, Joe	Limerick, Lab	40
MacSharry, Marc	Sligo, FF	69
McGonigle, Laura	Cork, FG	21
McVitty, Peter	Cavan FG	40
Malone, Patrick	Louth FG	0
Nolan, Michael (Spike)	Kildare, FG	18
Noone, Catherine	Dublin, FG	33
O'Flynn, Kenneth	Cork, FF	24
Sheehan, Michael	Wexford, FF	12
White, Mary	Dublin, FF	78

Oireachtas Sub-Panel

Name	(County, Party)	Vote (1st Pref)
Boyle, Dan	Cork, GP	19
Breen, Gerry	Dublin, FG	21
Brophy, Colm	Dublin, FG	36
Burke, Peter	Westmeath, FG	21
Conlon, Margaret	Monaghan, FF	47
Harte, Jimmy	Donegal, Lab	70
McHugh, Tom	Galway, FG	29
Power, Averil	Dublin, FF	75
Reilly, Kathryn	Cavan, SF	73

Jimmy Harte (Lab)

Home Address: 3 Sylvan Park, Letterkenny.
Contact Details: Constituency Office: (074) 911 1005. Mobile: (087) 251 1037. Email: jimmy.harte@oireachtas.ie.
Birth Place/Date: Lifford, 27 February 1958.
Marital Status: Married to Mary Galligan. Two daughters, two sons.
Education: St Eunan's College, Letterkenny. UCD (BA in Psychology).
Occupation: Public representative; insurance broker.

New senator. Elected to Donegal County Council in 1999. Deputy Mayor of Letterkenny, 2010. Unsuccessful candidate in Donegal North-East in the 2011 General Election.

Mary White (FF)

Home Address: 6 Wyckham Park Road, Dundrum, Dublin 16.
Contact Details: Mobile: (086) 256 0533. Email: mwhite@oireachtas.ie.
Birth Place/Date: Dundalk, 7 October 1944.
Marital Status: Married to Padraic White. One daughter.
Education: Holy Family Convent, Newbridge, Co. Kildare. Bolton Street College of Technology. UCD (BA in Economics and Politics).

Industrial and Commercial Panel

Occupation: Senator; entrepreneur; co-founder of Lir Chocolates.

Senator since 2002, when first elected to the Industrial and Commercial Panel. Chairwoman of Gaisce, the President's Award, 1999–2001. Member, Fianna Fáil national executive. Former member, Higher Education Authority, and board of National College of Art and Design. Author of policy documents including 'A New Approach to Childcare', 'A New Approach to Ageing and Ageism' and 'What We Can do About Suicide in the New Ireland'.

Averil Power (FF)

Home Address: Bayside, Dublin 13.
Contact Details: Seanad Office: (01) 618 3156. Mobile: (086) 727 7770. Email: averil.power@oireachtas.ie; apowerff@gmail.com.
Birth Place/Date: Dublin, 26 July 1978.
Marital Status: Married to Fionnan Sheahan.
Education: TCD (BA in Business, Economics and Social Science).
Occupation: Policy adviser.

New senator. Unsuccessful candidate for Dublin North-East in the 2011 General Election. Fianna Fáil spokesperson on Education in the Seanad. Former president, TCD Students' Union.

Marc MacSharry (FF)

Home Address: Fatima, Pearse Road, Sligo.
Contact Details: Constituency Office: (071) 914 0049. Seanad Office: (01) 618 4221. Mobile: (086) 267 4764. Email: mmacsharry@oireachtas.ie.
Birth Place/Date: Dublin, 12 July 1973.
Marital Status: Married to Marie Murphy. One son, one daughter.
Education: St John's Marist Brothers, Sligo. Castleknock College, Dublin.
Occupation: Senator.

First elected to the Seanad in 2002. Fianna Fáil spokesperson in the Seanad on Health. Son of former Minister, EU Commissioner and Sligo TD 1969–88, Ray MacSharry.

Imelda Henry (FG)

Home Address: Riverside, Sligo.
Contact Details: Mobile: (087) 817 7777. Email: imelda.henry@oireachtas.ie.
Birth Place/Date: Sligo, 5 March 1967.
Marital Status: Married to Aiden. One son, one daughter.
Education: Ursuline College, Sligo. Secretarial and Business College, Dublin.
Occupation: Public representative.

New senator. Unsuccessful candidate for Sligo–Leitrim in the 2007 Dáil election and subsequent Seanad election. Elected to Sligo County Council in 2004 for the Strandhill area and re-elected in 2009.

Paul Coghlan (FG)

Home Address: Ballydowney, Killarney, Co. Kerry.
Contact Details: Constituency Office: (064) 663 1892. Mobile: (087) 221 7400. Email: paul.coghlan@oireachtas.ie.
Birth Place/Date: Killarney, June 1944.
Marital Status: Married to Peggy O'Shea. Two sons, three daughters.
Education: St Brendan's College, Killarney. De La Salle College, Waterford.
Occupation: Public representative; auctioneer; businessman.

Member of Seanad since 1997. Former member, Kerry County Council, 1991–97, and Killarney UDC. Former President, Killarney Chamber of Commerce.

Catherine Noone (FG)

Home Address: Eglinton Court, Donnybrook, Dublin 4.
Contact Details: Seanad Office: (01) 618 3127. Mobile: (087) 232 7433. Email: catherine.noone@oireachtas.ie.

Birth Place/Date: Claremorris, Mayo, 24 June 1976.
Marital Status: Single.
Education: NUI Galway (BA in Law and Italian). Law Society of Ireland.
Occupation: Senator; solicitor.

New senator. Elected to Dublin City Council in 2009.

Colm Burke (FG)

Home Address: Gleann Rua, 36 Farranlea Grove, Model Farm Road, Cork.
Contact Details: Constituency Office: (021) 434 8140. Mobile: (087) 259 2839. Email: colm.burke@oireachtas.ie.
Birth Place/Date: Cork, 17 January 1957.
Marital Status: Married to Mary McCaffrey.
Education: UCC (BCL).
Occupation: Solicitor.

New senator. Former member of the European Parliament, where he replaced Simon Coveney on the latter's re-election to the Dáil in 2007. Member, Cork City Council 1995–2007. Lord Mayor, 2003–04.

Kathryn Reilly (SF)

Home Address: Farragh, Ballyjamesduff, Co. Cavan.
Contact Details: Constituency Office: (049) 437 3510. Seanad Office: (01) 618 3171. Email: kathryn.reilly@oireachtas.ie.
Birth Place/Date: Cavan, 17 September 1988.
Marital Status: Single.
Education: Crosskeys N.S. Virginia Vocational School. DCU (BA Hons in Economics, Politics and Law). UCD (MEconSc in European Economic and Public Affairs).
Occupation: Economics adviser.

New senator. Former policy adviser to former Sinn Féin TD for Louth and party spokesperson on Finance, Arthur Morgan.

Labour Panel

Elected (11 Seats)

Maurice Cummins (FG)*	1st count
Fidelma Healy-Eames (FG)*	4th count
Marie Moloney (Lab)	6th count
David Cullinane (SF)	9th count
Tony Mulcahy (FG)	13th count
Cáit Keane (FG)	13th count
Terry Brennan (FG)	14th count
Darragh O'Brien (FF)	17th count
Terry Leyden (FF)*	17th count
Ned O'Sullivan (FF)	17th count
John Whelan (Lab)	17th count
Quota	88.834

Candidates

Name	(County, Party)	Vote (1st Pref)
Nominating Bodies Sub-Panel		
Brennan, Terry	Louth, FG	54
Campbell, Sirena	Meath, FG	33
Cassidy, Denie	Westmeath, FF	42
Cummins, Maurice	Waterford, FG	100
Feeny, Geraldine	Waterford, FF	44
Hanafin, John	Tipperary, FF	39
Leyden, Terry	Roscommon, FF	51
Moloney, Marie	Kerry, Lab	63
Nevin, Barry	Wicklow, Lab	37
O'Callaghan, Joe	Cork, FG	28
O'Reilly, ML	Dublin, Lab	14
O'Sullivan, Ned	Kerry, FF	55
Oireachtas Sub-Panel		
Cullinane, David	Waterford, SF	84
Donnelly, Frances	Kildare, Ind	37
Healy-Eames, Fidelma	Galway, FG	83
Keane, Cáit	Dublin, FG	44
Mulcahy, Tony	Clare, FG	64
Murnane O'Connor, Jennifer	Carlow, FF	38
O'Brien, Darragh	Dublin, FF	51
Richmond, Neale	Dublin, FG	39
Whelan, John	Laois, Lab	66

Maurice Cummins (FG)

Home Address: 34 Ursuline Court, Waterford.
Contact Details: Seanad Office: (01) 618 4206. Mobile: (087) 682 7737. Email: maurice.cummins@oireachtas.ie.
Birth Place/Date: Waterford, 25 February 1954.
Marital Status: Married to Anne O'Shea. One son, one daughter.
Education: De La Salle, Waterford.
Occupation: Public representative.

Leader of the Seanad. Member of the House since 2002. Member of Waterford City Council, 1991–2002. Mayor of Waterford, 1995–96.

Fidelma Healy-Eames (FG)

Home Address: Maree, Oranmore, Co. Galway.
Contact Details: Constituency Office: (091) 792 017. Mobile: (087) 677 6937. Email: fidelma.healyeames@oireachtas.ie.
Birth Place/Date: Moylough, Co. Galway, 14 July 1962.
Marital Status: Married to Michael Eames. One son, one daughter.
Education: Carysfort College, Blackrock, Co. Dublin.

Occupation: Public representative; businesswoman; formerly primary school teacher and lecturer.

Member of Seanad since 2007, after unsuccessfully contesting Galway West in previous three general elections. Member, Galway County Council, 2004–07.

Marie Moloney (Lab)

Home Address: Coolick, Kilcummin, Killarney, Co. Kerry.
Contact Details: Constituency Office: (064) 663 2034. Mobile: (086) 304 9422. Email: marie.moloney@oireachtas.ie.
Birth Place/Date: Kerry, 26 August 1958.
Marital Status: Married.
Education: Coolick N.S. Killarney Technical College.
Occupation: Full-time public representative.

New senator. Stood without success in Kerry South in 2011 General Election. Elected to Kerry County Council, 2009. Deputy Mayor of Kerry, 2010. Former assistant to Breeda Moynihan-Cronin, TD for Kerry South, 1992–2007.

David Cullinane (SF)

Home Address: 1 Maple Terrace, Lisduggan, Waterford.
Contact Details: Seanad Office: (01) 618 3176. Mobile: (086) 372 5152.

Email: david.cullinane@oireachtas.ie.
Birth Place/Date: Waterford City, 4 July 1974.
Marital Status: Married to Kathleen Funchion. One son.
Education: Diploma in Marketing and Business Management.
Occupation: Public representative.

New senator. Unsuccessful Sinn Féin candidate for Waterford in past three general elections. Elected to Waterford City Council, 2004 and 2009.

Tony Mulcahy (FG)

Home Address: 6 Tullyvarraga Crescent, Shannon, Co. Clare.
Contact Details: Seanad Office: (01) 618 3105. Mobile: (086) 243 6345. Email: tony.mulcahy@oireachtas.ie.
Birth Place/Date: Newcastle West, Co. Limerick, 12 April 1959.
Marital Status: Married to Carmel. Four children.
Education: Junior Cert. Qualified chef.
Occupation: Public representative; self-employed caterer.

New senator. Unsuccessful candidate for Clare in 2007 and 2011 Dáil elections. Represented Shannon area on Clare County Council from 1999. Member of Shannon Town Council, 1999–2011.

Cáit Keane (FG)

Home Address: 26 Rushbrook Court, Templeogue, Dublin 6W.
Contact Details: Seanad Office: (01) 618 3179. Mobile: (087) 811 7824. Email: cait.keane@oireachtas.ie.
Birth Place/Date: Galway, 24 September 1949.
Marital Status: Married to Sean. One son, two daughters.
Education: BA. MA. Diploma in Montessori Education. Diploma in Community Development.
Occupation: Public representative.

New senator. Progressive Democrats member of Dublin County Council and South Dublin County Council 1991–2008, when she joined Fine Gael; re-elected as FG councillor 2009. Unsuccessful FG candidate in Dublin South-West 2011 General Election; previously contested the 1992 and 1997 general elections and by-election in Dublin South Central as PD candidate.

Terry Brennan (FG)

Home Address: Ghan Road, Carlingford, Co. Louth.
Contact Details: Constituency Office: (042) 937 3348. Mobile: (087) 294 2956. Email: terry.brennan@oireachtas.ie.

Labour Panel

Birth Place/Date: Carlingford, Co. Louth, 24 May 1942.
Marital Status: Married.
Education: Leaving Cert. City & Guilds A.C.D.C.
Occupation: Public representative.

New senator. Member Louth County Council for Dundalk/Carlingford area from 1999 to election to Labour Panel.

Darragh O'Brien (FF)

Home Address: 49 Galtrim Grange, Malahide, Co. Dublin.
Contact Details: Seanad Office: (01) 618 3802. Mobile: (086) 251 9893. Email: darragh.obrien@oireachtas.ie.
Birth Place/Date: Malahide, Co. Dublin, 8 July 1974.
Marital Status: Married.
Education: Pobal Scoil Íosa, Malahide.
Occupation: Senator. Formerly financial manager with Friends First.

Former TD for Dublin North, 2007–11. He was appointed by the outgoing Taoiseach to the Seanad on 4 March 2011. Member, Fingal County Council, 2004–07. Vice-Chair of Public Accounts Committee in last Dáil.

Terry Leyden (FF)

Home Address: Castlecoote, Co. Roscommon.
Contact Details: Constituency Office: (090) 662 6422. Mobile: (087) 797 8922. Email: terry.leyden@oireachtas.ie.
Birth Place/Date: Roscommon, 1 October 1945.
Marital Status: Married to Mary O'Connor. Three daughters, one son.
Education: CBS Primary School, Roscommon Town. Vocational School, Roscommon. NUI Galway (Diploma in Politics, Sociology and Economics).
Occupation: Public representative.

Member of Seanad since 2002 and a Taoiseach's nominee briefly in 1992 after he lost the Dáil seat in Roscommon which he held from 1977–92. Minister of State in several Departments, 1982 and 1987–92. Member, Roscommon County Council, 1974–2003.

Ned O'Sullivan (FF)

Home Address: Cahirdown, Listowel, Co. Kerry.
Contact Details: Constituency Office: (068) 21831. Mobile: (087) 245 9290. Email: ned.osullivan@oireachtas.ie.
Birth Place/Date: Listowel, Co. Kerry, 25 November 1950.
Marital Status: Married to Madeleine Murphy. Three sons.
Education: UCD (BA; HDip in Education). St Patrick's College of Education, Drumcondra, Dublin.
Occupation: Public representative; businessman. Formerly primary and secondary teacher.

First elected to Seanad in 2007. Member, Kerry County Council ,1991–2007. Mayor of Kerry, 2004. Member, Listowel Town Council, 1985–2007.

John Whelan (Lab)

Home Address: Cremorgan, Timahoe, Portlaoise, Co. Laois.
Contact Details: Constituency Office: (057) 863 4047. Seanad Office: (01) 618 3244. Mobile: (087) 250 9663. Email: john.whelan@oireachtas.ie.
Birth Place/Date: Portlaoise, 24 March 1961.
Marital Status: Married to Grazyna Rekosiewicz. Two daughters, one son.
Education: St Paul's CBS, Monasterevin, Co. Kildare. St Ignatius Rice College, Dún Laoghaire. St Paul's Secondary School, Monasterevin.
Occupation: Public representative; journalist.

New senator. Unsuccessful candidate in Laois–Offaly in 2011 General Election. Former Editor of *Leinster Leader*, *Leinster Express*, *Offaly Express* and Managing Editor of the Voice group of local newspapers.

Elected (3 Seats)

Rónán Mullen (Ind)*	24th count
John Crown (Ind)	24th count
Feargal Quinn (Ind)*	24th count
Electorate	102,000
Valid Poll	33,831
Quota	8,458

Candidate	Votes (1st Pref)
Canning, Thomas 'Paul'	354
Cowley, Matthias	57
Coyle, James	307
Crown, John	4,703
Doorley, James	547
Healy, Paddy	947
Kelleher, Declan	3,771
Kennedy, John	279
Keogh, Helen	1,362
Langan, Mick	129
Lynam, Paul	476
McCurtin, David	262
Molloy, Mick	484
Mooney, Peter	547
Mullen, Rónán	6,459
Ó Broin, Eoin	490
Ó Brolcháin, Niall	718
Ó Cadhla, Diarmaid	182
O'Connell, Donncha	1,629
O'Connor, Regina	1,101
O'Donnell, Francis 'Frank'	199
O'Donoghue, James	154
O'Shea Farren, Linda	1,083
O'Sullivan, Bernadine	2,028
Price, Brendan	671
Quinn, Feargal	4,591
Sullivan, Daniel	193

Rónán Mullen (Ind)

Home Address: Ahascragh, Ballinasloe, Co. Galway.
Contact Details: Seanad Office: (01) 618 3930. Mobile: (087) 244 6911. Email: ronan.mullen@oireachtas.ie.
Birth Place/Date: Ballinasloe, Co. Galway, 13 October 1970.
Marital Status: Single.
Education: Kilglass N.S. Holy Rosary College, Mountbellew, Co. Galway. NUI Galway (BA). Dublin City University (MA Journalism). King's Inns (Barrister-at-Law).
Occupation: Senator; lecturer.

First elected to NUI panel in 2007. Member of board of directors, Daughters of Charity Community Services (for Dublin's Inner City); member of board of directors, CEIST (trustees of 112 voluntary secondary schools nationwide). Law and Communications lecturer in Institute of Technology, Blanchardstown. Former President, NUI Galway Students' Union, 1991–92.

John Crown (Ind)

Home Address: 270 Merrion Road, Dublin 4.
Contact Details: Seanad Office: (01) 618 3260. Mobile: (087) 264 7767. Email: john.crown@oireachtas.ie.

Birth Place/Date: Brooklyn, New York City, 1 March 1957.
Marital Status: Divorced. Two daughters, one son.
Education: Synge Street. Terenure College. UCD (MB; BCh; BAO; BSc; MBA).
Occupation: Physician/oncologist.

New senator. Consultant in St Vincent's Hospital, Dublin since 1993. Founder of Ireland's first national cancer treatment research group, ICORG, 1997. Professor in cancer research, UCD and DCU.

Feargal Quinn (Ind)

Home Address: Sutton Cross, Dublin 13.
Contact Details: Seanad Office: (01) 618 3222. Mobile: (087) 686 5215. Email: himself@feargalquinn.ie.
Birth Place/Date: Dublin, 27 November 1936.
Marital Status: Married to Denise Prendergast. Three sons, two daughters.
Education: Newbridge College, Kildare. UCD (BComm).
Occupation: Founder of Superquinn.

Senator; elected to NUI panel at every election since 1993. Vice-Chairman, EuroCommerce. Adjunct Professor, NUI Galway. Former chairman of An Post; Irish Management Institute president; finance committee of Dublin Archdiocese; Marketing Institute of Ireland president. Holds three honorary doctorates and received a Papal Knighthood in 1994.

University of Dublin

Elected (3 Seats)

David Norris (Ind)*	1st count
Ivana Bacik (Lab)*	10th count
Sean Barrett (Ind)	18th count

Electorate	53,583
Total Valid Poll	15,557
Quota	3,890

Candidate	Votes (1st Pref)
Bacik, Ivana	2,982
Barrett, Sean	1,051
Coleman, Marc	772
Connolly, Bart	72
Cox, Maeve	174
Dudgeon, Jeffrey	205
Frost, Dermot	178
Gueret, Maurice	822
Hanan, Robin	406
McDonagh, Rosaleen	446
McGovern, Iggy	397
Martin, David	194
Norris, David	5,623
O'Malley, Fiona	441
Priestley, William	258
Quinn, Graham	131
Sheehan, Dermot	49
Williams, Tony	1,336

David Norris (Ind)

Home Address: 18 North Great George's Street, Dublin 1.
Contact Details: Seanad Office: (01) 618 3104. Email: david.norris@oireachtas.ie.
Birth Place/Date: Leopoldville, Belgian Congo, July 1944.
Marital Status: Single.
Education: St Andrew's College, The High School, Dublin. TCD (BA; MA).
Occupation: Public representative.

First elected to Dublin University Panel in 1987. Candidate for the Presidency, 2011. Chairman of James Joyce Cultural Centre, Dublin and of North Great George's Street Preservation Society, Dublin. Senior lecturer in English department, TCD, 1968–96. Campaigner for homosexual law reform.

Ivana Bacik (Lab)

Home Address: Portobello, Dublin 8.
Contact Details: Seanad Office: (01) 618 3136. Mobile: (086) 813 3751. Email: ivana.bacik@oireachtas.ie.
Birth Place/Date: London, 25 May 1968.
Marital Status: Co-habiting with partner Alan Saul. Two children.
Education: Alexandra College, Dublin. TCD (LLB). London School of Economics (LLM). King's Inns Dublin. ICSL, 1992.
Occupation: Reid Professor of Criminal Law, TCD; barrister.

Leader of the Labour Party in the Seanad, she was first elected in 2007. Stood unsuccessfully in the 2011 General Election in Dún Laoghaire constituency; the 2009 by-election in Dublin South Central; and the 2004 European Parliament elections. Former president, TCD Students' Union, 1989–90, when taken to court by SPUC for providing information on abortion. Lectures and publishes on criminology, feminism and human rights issues.

Sean Barrett (Ind)

Home Address: Maynooth, Co. Kildare.
Contact Details: Seanad Office: (01) 618 3264. TCD Office: (01) 896 1523. Email: sdcbarrett@gmail.com; seand.barrett@oireachtas.ie.
Birth Place/Date: Cork, 1944.
Marital Status: Married to Dr Maeve O'Brien. One daughter.
Education: UCD (BA; PhD). McMasters University, Canada (MA).
Occupation: Senator; senior lecturer of Economics.

New senator. Previously contested the Dublin University Panel in 1997 and 2002. Economics lecturer in TCD since 1977, specialising in transport, especially aviation, and tourism. Former director of Bord Fáilte. Member of National Economic and Social Council since 2005.

Nominated (11 Seats)

Eamonn Coghlan (Ind)

Jim D'Arcy (FG)

Aideen Hayden (Lab)

Lorraine Higgins (Lab)

Fiach Mac Conghail (Ind)

Martin McAleese (Ind)

Mary Moran (Lab)

Mary Ann O'Brien (Ind)

Marie-Louise O'Donnell (Ind)

Jillian van Turnhout (Ind)

Katherine Zappone (Ind)

Eamonn Coghlan (Ind)

Home Address: 5 Homeleigh, Porterstown, Dublin 15.
Contact Details: Seanad Office: (01) 618 3027. Email: eamonn.coghlan@oireachtas.ie.
Birth Place/Date: Dublin, 21 November 1952.
Marital Status: Married to Yvonne. Three sons, one daughter.
Education: Villanova University, USA (BSc in Marketing and Communications).
Occupation: Public representative; marketing consultant.

New senator. World Champion 5000m, 1983; and World Indoor Champion 1500m, 1979. Held indoor mile world record four times. Competed in Olympics in 1976, 1980 and 1988. Director of the Crumlin Children's Medical and Research Foundation.

Jim D'Arcy (FG)

Home Address: 12 Sandygrove Close, Blackrock, Dundalk, Co. Louth.
Contact Details: Seanad Office: (01) 618 3059. Mobile: (087) 686 4582. Email: jim.darcy@oireachtas.ie.
Birth Place/Date: Drogheda, 20 July 1954.
Marital Status: Separated.

Education: St Patrick's College, Drumcondra. Open University (BA Hons; Diploma in European Humanities).
Occupation: Public representative. Formerly teacher.

New senator. Unsuccessful candidate in Louth in 2007 General Election. Member of Louth County Council from 1999 and of Dundalk Town Council from 2004; Chairperson Louth County Council 2009–10.

Aideen Hayden (Lab)

Home Address: Upper Albert Road, Glenageary, Co. Dublin.
Contact Details: Seanad Office: (01) 618 3178. Mobile: (087) 231 1921. Email: aideenhayden@gmail.com; aideen.hayden@oireachtas.ie.
Birth Place/Date: Carlow, 1959.
Marital Status: Married to Chris O'Malley. Two daughters.
Education: UCD (BA). Incorporated Law Society.
Occupation: Public representative.

New senator. Unsuccessful candidate on Industrial and Commercial Panel 2011. Chairperson of housing charity Threshold since 1998.

Taoiseach's Nominees

Lorraine Higgins (Lab)

Home Address: Prospect, Athenry,
Co. Galway.
Contact Details: Seanad Office: (01) 618 3186.
Mobile: (087) 903 4883. Email:
lorraine.higgins@oireachtas.ie.
Birth Place/Date: Galway, 3 August 1979.
Marital Status: Single.
Education: NUI Galway (BA Hons in Political
and Social Science and History). King's Inns.
Occupation: Public representative; barrister.

New senator. Labour Party spokesperson in
Seanad on Foreign Affairs and Trade and on
Reform and Public Expenditure. Contested
the 2011 General Election in Galway East and
2009 local elections for Galway County
Council.

Fiach Mac Conghail (Ind)

Home Address: 3 Bóthar Emmet, Inse Chóir,
BÁC 8.
Contact Details: Seanad Office: (01) 618 3261.
Email: fiach.macconghail@oireachtas.ie.
Birth Place/Date: Dublin, 4 August 1964.
Marital Status: Married to Bríd Ní Neachtain.
Two daughters.
Education: Scoil Lorcáin. Scoil Dhún Chaoin.
Coláiste na Rinne. Coláiste Eoin. TCD.
Occupation: Public representative; director of
the Abbey Theatre.

New senator. Chairman of We the Citizens,
group seeking new ways of public decision-
making. Former adviser to Minister for Arts
2002–05. Artistic director of Project Arts
Centre 1992–99. Appointed director of Abbey
Theatre 2005.

Martin McAleese (Ind)

Home Address: Áras an Uachtaráin, Phoenix
Park, Dublin 8.
Contact Details: Seanad Office: (01) 618 3277.
Email: martin.mcaleese@oireachtas.ie.
Birth Place/Date: Belfast, 24 March 1951.
Marital Status: Married to Mary McAleese.
Two daughters, one son.
Education: Queen's University, Belfast (B.Sc
Hons Physics). TCD (BA; B. Dent. Sc; MA).
Notre Dame University, USA; University of
Ulster; HETAC (Hon. Doctorates of Laws).
DCU; DIT (Hon. Doctorates of Philosophy).
Occupation: Public representative; dental
surgeon.

New senator. Husband of President Mary
McAleese. Began his career as accountant
but later re-retrained as dentist. Credited with
behind-the-scenes role in Northern peace
process through contacts with Loyalist
groups.

Mary Moran (Lab)

Home Address: Haynestown Road,
Haggardstown, Dundalk, Co. Louth.
Contact Details: Seanad Office: (01) 618
3522. Mobile: (087) 169 4835. Email:
mary.moran@oireachtas.ie.
Birth Place/Date: Drogheda, Co. Louth, 28
June 1960.
Marital Status: Married to Damian Moran.
Three daughters, two sons.
Education: St Vincent's Secondary School,
Dundalk. UCD (BA in Music, English and
Philosophy). DKIT (MA in Music Technology).
Occupation: Public representative; secondary
teacher.

New senator. Unsuccessful candidate for
Louth in 2011 General Election. Member of
the parents' council and board of
management for St Mary's Special School,
Drumcar.

Mary Ann O'Brien (Ind)

Home Address: Griesebank house, Ballytore,
Co. Kildare.
Contact Details: Office: (045) 486 800.
Mobile: (087) 777 0011.
Email: maobrien@lilyobriens.ie.
Birth Place/Date: Waterford, 8 September
1960.
Marital Status: Married to Jonathan Irwin.

Education: Ursuline Convent, Waterford.
Occupation: Public representative; managing director.

New senator. Founder and head of Lily O'Brien's Chocolates and co-founder with her husband of the Jack and Jill Foundation, which helps the families of children with severe neurological problems.

Marie-Louise O'Donnell (Ind)

Home Address: 15 The Palms, Roebuck Road, Clonskeagh, Dublin 14.
Contact Details: Seanad Office: (01) 618 3635. Mobile: (087) 848 3620. Email: marielouise.odonnell@oireachtas.ie.
Birth Place/Date: Castlebar, Co. Mayo, 5 September 1952.
Marital Status: Single.
Education: Nottingham University (BA). Maynooth (M.Ed). UCD (MA, Modern Drama). Guildhall, London (LGSMD).
Occupation: Public representative; university lecturer; broadcaster.

New senator. Communications lecturer in Dublin City University. Former actor; involved in establishing Helix Theatre.

Jillian van Turnhout (Ind)

Home Address: Ísiltír, Slatecabin Lane, Dublin 18.
Contact Details: Seanad Office: (01) 618 3375. Mobile: (087) 233 3784. Email: jillian.vanturnhout@oireachtas.ie.
Birth Place/Date: Dublin, 29 March 1968.
Marital Status: Married.
Education: Graduate of Marketing.
Occupation: Public representative.

New senator. CEO of Children's Rights Alliance. Vice-Chair European Movement Ireland since 2008. Chief Commission, Irish Girl Guides, 2001–07. President, National Youth Council of Ireland, 1993–99.

Katherine Zappone (Ind)

Home Address: The Shanty, Glenaraneen, Brittas, Co. Dublin.
Contact Details: Mobile: (087) 233 3784. Seanad Office: (01) 618 3583. Email: katherine.zappone@oireachtas.ie.
Birth Place/Date: Spokane, Wa., USA, 25 November 1953.
Marital Status: Married to Dr Ann Louise Gilligan.
Education: Catholic University of America (MA). UCD (MBA). Boston College (PhD).
Occupation: Director, The Centre for Progressive Change.

New senator. Member of Irish Human Rights Commission. Former CEO of the National Women's Council of Ireland. First openly lesbian member of Oireachtas and first in a same-sex marriage.

Joan Collins (left) of the People Before Profit Alliance canvassing in Dublin. Photograph: Bryan O'Brien.

Leo Varadkar, Richard Bruton and Enda Kenny share a joke at the launch of Fine Gael's Fiscal Plan in their election headquarters in Dublin. Photograph: David Sleator.

The European Parliament

The seventh direct elections to the European Parliament were held in Ireland on 5 June 2009. Because of the expansion of the European Union into Eastern Europe, Ireland lost one seat and returned twelve members to the new parliament.

A redrawing of the four constituencies in the Republic saw a reduction in Dublin, which had three seats (compared to four in the 2004 European Parliament elections). Of the twelve Irish seats, Fine Gael won four, Fianna Fáil and Labour won three each, the Socialist Party won one and there was one Independent.

Dublin returned one Fine Gael, one Labour and one Socialist Party member. Ireland East returned one Fine Gael, one Labour and one Fianna Fáil member. In Ireland North-West the election returned one Independent, one Fianna Fáil and one Fine Gael member. Ireland South saw the election of one Fianna Fáil, one Fine Gael and one Labour member.

Two of those elected to the Dáil in the 2011 General Election, Joe Higgins of the Socialist Party and Alan Kelly of the Labour Party, were MEPs and handed on their seats in the European Parliament to people on their replacement lists. Paul Murphy replaced Higgins in Dublin while Phil Prendergast replaced Kelly in Ireland South. The end of the dual mandate means that people cannot be members of the Dáil and European Parliament at the same time.

By-elections to the European Parliament are not held in Ireland and sitting members are replaced by people on a list provided to returning officers before each election. The members of the replacement lists before the 2009 European elections were:

Dublin
Fine Gael: Naoise O'Muiri, Gerry O'Connell, Gerry Breen, Neale Richmond, John Kennedy.
Labour Party: Emer Costello, Aidan O'Sullivan, Mary Freehill, Desmond O'Toole, Loraine Mulligan, Ross Higgins.
Socialist Party: Clare Daly, Ruth Coppinger, Mick Murphy, Denis Keane, Paul Murphy (replaced Joe Higgins).

East
Fine Gael: John Paul Phelan, Liam Twomey, Marcella Corcoran Kennedy, Darren Scully, Michael O'Dowd.
Labour Party: Gerald Nash, Kevin Byrne, Sean Butler, Anne Ferris, Niamh McGowan, George Lawlor, Sean O'Brien.
Fianna Fáil: Thomas Byrne, Lisa McDonald, Jim Walsh, Gerry Bridgett.

North-West
Independents: Paudge Connolly, James Breen.
Fianna Fáil: Paschal Mooney, Pat O'Rourke, Terry Leyden, Gerald O'Connor.
Fine Gael: Joe O'Reilly, Mark Cooney, Peter Feeney, Michael Comiskey, Barry O'Neill, Sean McKiernan, Heather Humphreys.

South
Fianna Fáil: Ned O'Keeffe, John Hanafin, Michael Ahern, Mark Daly.
Fine Gael: Colm Burke, Paul Bradford, Dara Murphy, Mary Greene, Tom Berkery, Noel Harrington.
Labour Party: Arthur Spring, Phil Prendergast (replaced Alan Kelly), Joe Leddin, Virginia O'Dowd, Mark Khan.

Liam Aylward (East)

Fianna Fáil member. Born in Knockmoylon, Mullinavat, Co. Kilkenny, 27 September 1952. Laboratory technician. Member of the Dáil for Carlow–Kilkenny 1977–2007. Minister of State at: the Department of Forestry (1988–89); the Department of Energy (1989–92); the Department of Education (1992–94); and the Department of Agriculture (2002–04). Elected to the European Parliament 2004; re-elected in 2009. Committees: Agriculture and Rural Development; Delegation to the Euro–Latin American Parliamentary Assembly; Delegation for Relations with Mercosur countries.

Nessa Childers (East)

Labour Party member. Born in Dublin, 9 October 1956. BA in Psychology, TCD; post grad Dip in Psychology, UCD. Former psychoanalyst. Established the MSc course in Psychoanalytic Psychotherapy in TCD and was course director there. Elected to the European Parliament in 2009. Former councillor for Blackrock, Co. Dublin 2004–08. Committees: Environment, Public Health and Food Safety; Delegation for Relations with Japan.

Brian Crowley (South)

Fianna Fáil member. Born in Dublin, 4 March 1964. Diploma in Law, UCC. Senator (1993–94). Member of Council of State (1997–2004). Elected to the European Parliament 1994 and at all subsequent elections. Leader of the Fianna Fáil Group in the EP. Former president, Union for Europe of the Nations Group in the EP. Committees: Industry, Research and Energy; Delegation for Relations with the United States.

Proinsias De Rossa (Dublin)

Labour Party member. Born in Dublin, 15 May 1940. Member of Dáil Éireann 1982–2002. Former leader of The Workers' Party (1988–92) and Democratic Left (1992). Minister for Social Welfare 1994–97. Member of the European Parliament 1989–92 and since 1999. Vice-Chair of the European Parliament's Delegation to the Palestinian Legislative. Committees: Social Affairs and Employment; Petitions; Security and Defence. Co-author of EP's report on European Social Model 2006. Temporary Committees on: Equitable Life Inquiry; and the CIA's Extraordinary Renditions Programme. Member of the European Convention on the Future of Europe (2002–03) and Labour Party Delegation to the National Forum on Europe.

Pat 'the Cope' Gallagher (North-West)

Fianna Fáil member. Born in Burtonport, Co. Donegal, 10 March 1948. Former fish exporter; Minister of State. B.Comm, NUI Galway. TD for Donegal South-West 1981–97 and 2002–09. Member European Parliament 1994–2002 and 2004 to date. Minister of State at: the Department of Transport 2006–07; the Department of Communications, Marine and Natural Resources 2004–06; the Department of the Environment and Local Government 2002–04; the Department of the Marine 1987–89. Minister of State for Arts, Culture and the Gaeltacht 1989–94. Committees: Conference of Delegation Chairs; Fisheries; Chair of Delegation for Relations with Switzerland, Norway and EU–Iceland Joint Parliamentary Committee; and European Economic Area Joint Parliamentary Committee.

Marian Harkin (North-West)

Independent member. Born in Sligo, 26 November 1953. BSc, HDipEd, UCD. Secondary teacher. Independent TD for Sligo–Leitrim 2002–07. Chairperson, Council of the West. Elected to the European Parliament 2004, on second attempt; re-elected in 2009. Committees: Employment and Social Affairs; Delegation for Relations with the United States.

Jim Higgins (North-West)

Fine Gael member. Born in Ballyhaunis, Co. Mayo, 4 May 1945. Post-primary teacher. BA, HDipEd, NUI Galway. Member of the Dáil for Mayo 1987–2002. Senator: 1981, Taoiseach's nominee; 1983–87; 2002–07. Minister of State at: the Department of Finance 1995; the Department of Taoiseach and Government Chief Whip 1995–97. Committees: Parliament's Bureau; Quaestors; Transport and Tourism; Delegation to EU–Chile Joint Parliamentary Committee; Delegation to Euro–Latin American Parliamentary Assembly.

The European Parliament

Seán Kelly (South)

Fine Gael member. Born in Killarney, 26 April 1952. BEd, St Patrick's College of Education; BA, HDipEd, UCD; honorary doctorate, DIT. Former teacher. President of the GAA 2003–06. Chairman of the Irish Institute of Sport 2006–08. Elected to the European Parliament 2009. Committees: Regional Development; Delegation for Relations with the United States.

Mairead McGuinness (East)

Fine Gael member. Born in Drogheda, 13 June 1959. BAgrSc (Econ), UCD. Former journalist and broadcaster. Elected to the European Parliament in 2004; re-elected in 2009. Unsuccessful candidate in the 2007 General Election. Committees: Agriculture and Rural Development; Environment, Public Health and Food Safety; Petitions. Chairperson of Committee of Inquiry into the collapse of the Equitable Life Assurance Society.

Gay Mitchell (Dublin)

Fine Gael member. Born in Dublin, 30 December 1951. MSocSc Queen's University Belfast. Chartered secretary and administrator. Member of the Dáil for Dublin South-Central 1981–2007. Chairman, Committee of Public Accounts 1987–93. Chairman, Oireachtas European Affairs Committee 2002–04. Lord Mayor of Dublin 1992–93. Minister of State at the Departments of Taoiseach and Foreign Affairs, with responsibility for European Affairs, 1994–97. First elected to the European Parliament in 2004; re-elected in 2009. Committees: Development; Financial, Economic and Social Crisis; Vice-Chairman of the EU Delegation to the ACP–EU Joint Parliamentary Assembly.

Paul Murphy (Dublin)

Socialist Party member. Born in Dublin, 13 April 1983. BCL, UCD. Previously European Parliament Assistant to Joe Higgins, whom he replaced on the latter's election to the Dáil in 2011. Committees: Employment and Social Affairs; Petitions; Relations with Mercosur countries.

Phil Prendergast (South)

Labour Party member. Born in Kilkenny, 20 September 1959. Former nurse. Appointed to the European Parliament in 2011 to replace Alan Kelly after his election to the Dáil for Tipperary North in the 2011 General Election. Senator 2007–11. Member, Tipperary South Riding County Council 1999–2007. Committees: Internal Market and Consumer Protection; Delegation for Relations with the United States.

An election to the European Parliament was held on 5 June 2009. The Republic of Ireland results are summarised on this page and details of the counts in each of the constituencies are given on the following pages.

Dublin

Elected

Gay Mitchell (FG)*
Proinsias De Rossa (Lab)*
Joe Higgins (SP)

	Number	%
Seats	3	
Electorate	812,465	
Total Poll	412,684	
Turnout		50.79
Spoiled	6,054	
Total Valid Poll	406,630	
Quota	101,658	
Candidates	10	

Voting by Party

1st Pref	Number	%	Gain/Loss
Fine Gael	96,715	23.78	4.65
Labour	83,471	20.53	-2.00
Fianna Fáil	74,302	18.27	-7.31
Sinn Féin	47,928	11.79	-2.53
Green Party	19,086	4.69	-4.89
Others	85,128	20.94	12.09

	Quotas	Seats
Fine Gael	1.0	1
Labour	0.8	1
Fianna Fáil	0.7	–
Sinn Féin	0.5	–
Green Party	0.2	–
Others	0.8	1

Note: Joe Higgins was replaced by Paul Murphy after Higgins won a seat for Dublin West in the 2011 General Election.

East

Elected

Mairead McGuinness (FG)*
Nessa Childers (Lab)*
Liam Aylward (FF)*

	Number	%
Seats	3	
Electorate	778,502	
Total Poll	442,291	
Turnout		56.81
Spoiled	13,042	
Total Valid Poll	429,249	
Quota	107,313	
Candidates	11	

Voting by Party

1st Pref	Number	%	Gain/Loss
Fine Gael	172,217	40.12	-0.43
Labour	78,338	18.25	5.20
Fianna Fáil	105,778	24.64	-0.44
Sinn Féin	47,499	11.07	2.38
Green Party	0	0.00	-5.64
Others	25,417	5.92	-1.07

	Quotas	Seats
Fine Gael	1.6	1
Labour	0.7	1
Fianna Fáil	1.0	1
Sinn Féin	0.4	–
Green Party	0.0	–
Others	0.2	–

North-West

Elected

Marian Harkin (Ind)*
Pat 'the Cope' Gallagher (FF)*
Jim Higgins (FG)*

	Number	%
Seats	3	
Electorate	805,626	
Total Poll	510,982	
Turnout		63.43
Spoiled	15,675	
Total Valid Poll	495,307	
Quota	123,827	
Candidates	13	

Voting by Party

1st Pref	Number	%	Gain/Loss
Fine Gael	117,657	23.75	-0.20
Labour	28,708	5.80	2.49
Fianna Fáil	125,628	25.36	-1.74
Sinn Féin	45,515	9.19	-6.31
Green Party	0	0.00	0.00
Others	177,799	35.90	5.77

	Quotas	Seats
Fine Gael	1.0	1
Labour	0.2	–
Fianna Fáil	1.0	1
Sinn Féin	0.4	–
Green Party	0.0	–
Others	1.4	1

South

Elected

Brian Crowley (FF)*
Seán Kelly (FG)
Alan Kelly (Lab)

	Number	%
Seats	3	
Electorate	823,652	
Total Poll	509,963	
Turnout		61.91
Spoiled	11,836	
Total Valid Poll	498,127	
Quota	124,532	
Candidates	10	

Voting by Party

1st Pref	Number	%	Gain/Loss
Fine Gael	146,300	29.37	4.81
Labour	64,152	12.88	8.75
Fianna Fáil	134,854	27.07	-13.95
Sinn Féin	64,671	12.98	6.24
Green Party	15,499	3.11	0.86
Others	72,651	14.58	-6.72

	Quotas	Seats
Fine Gael	1.2	1
Labour	0.5	1
Fianna Fáil	1.1	1
Sinn Féin	0.5	–
Green Party	0.1	–
Others	0.6	–

Note: Alan Kelly was replaced by Phil Prendergast after Kelly won a seat for Tipperary North in the 2011 General Election.

Dublin

Seats 3
Quota 101,658

Candidate		COUNT 1	Distribution of Simons, Sweeney votes — 2	Distribution of Byrne votes — 3	Distribution of De Búrca votes — 4	Distribution of Mitchell surplus — 5	Distribution of McKenna votes — 6	Distribution of McDonald votes — 7
Byrne, Eibhlin	(FF)	18,956	(+492) 19,448					
De Búrca, Déirdre	(GP)	19,086	(+1,140) 20,226	(+1,765) 21,991				
De Rossa, Prionsias*	(Lab)	83,471	(+1,746) 85,217	(+2,057) 87,274	(+7,032) 94,306	(+1,330) 95,636	(+7,589) 103,225	
Higgins, Joe	(SP)	50,510	(+1,947) 52,457	(+581) 53,038	(+2,078) 55,116	(+235) 55,351	(+4,814) 60,165	(+22,201) 82,366
McDonald, Mary Lou*	(SF)	47,928	(+2,169) 50,097	(+883) 50,980	(+1,467) 52,447	(+82) 52,529	(+2,900) 55,429	
McKenna, Patricia	(Ind)	17,521	(+4,002) 21,523	(+857) 22,380	(+2,833) 25,213	(+423) 25,636		
Mitchell, Gay*	(FG)	96,715	(+2,383) 99,098	(+1,712) 100,810	(+3,603) 104,413			
Ryan, Eoin*	(FF)	55,346	(+971) 56,317	(+9,888) 66,205	(+2,312) 68,517	(+605) 69,122	(+2,408) 71,530	(+5,426) 76,956
Simons, Caroline	(Lib)	13,514						
Sweeney, Emmanuel	(Ind)	3,583						
NON-TRANSFERABLE			2,247	1,705	2,666	80	7,925	27,802

Seats 3 Quota 107,313		Distribution of **McGuinness** surplus	Distribution of **Garvey, Grealy, Tallon** votes	Distribution of **O'Malley** votes	Distribution of **Sharkey** votes	Distribution of **Byrne** votes	Distribution **Funchion** votes
COUNT	1	2	3	4	5	6	7
Aylward, Liam* (FF)	74,666	(+200) 74,866	(+258) 75,124	(+1,171) 76,295	(+749) 77,044	(+22,192) 99,236	(+4,369) 103,605
Byrne, Thomas (FF)	31,112	(+152) 31,264	(+216) 31,480	(+796) 32,276	(+1,107) 33,383		
Childers, Nessa (Lab)	78,338	(+576) 78,914	(+1,231) 80,145	(+4,053) 84,198	(+2,456) 86,654	(+2,701) 89,355	(+12,865) 102,220
Funchion, Kathleen (SF)	26,567	(+80) 26,647	(+485) 27,132	(+2,173) 29,305	(+13,780) 43,085	(+1,337) 44,422	
Garvey, Paddy (Ind)	2,934	(+11) 2,945					
Grealy, Micheál E (Ind)	1,514	(+9) 1,523					
McGuinness, Mairead* (FG)	110,366						
O'Malley, Raymond (Lib)	18,557	(+171) 18,728	(+668) 19,396				
Phelan, John Paul (FG)	61,851	(+1,739) 63,590	(+579) 64,169	(+3,803) 67,972	(+1,636) 69,608	(+1,238) 70,846	(+6,114) 76,960
Sharkey, Tomás (SF)	20,932	(+102) 21,034	(+427) 21,461	(+2,493) 23,954			
Tallon, Jim (Ind)	2,412	(+13) 2,425					
NON-TRANSFERABLE		0	3,029	4,907	4,226	5,915	21,074

Seats 3
Quota 123,827

Candidate	Party	1	Distribution of Higgins, King, McCullagh, McNamara, Ó Luain votes		Distribution of O'Keeffe votes		Distribution of O'Reilly votes		Distribution of Mooney votes		Distribution of Mac Lochlainn votes	
COUNT		1	2		3		4		5		6	
Gallagher, Pat 'the Cope'	(FF)	82,643	(+2,037)	84,680	(+1,162)	85,842	(+1,872)	87,714	(+24,908)	112,622	(+8,308)	120,930
Ganley, Declan	(Lib)	67,638	(+2,287)	69,925	(+2,550)	72,475	(+1,519)	73,994	(+1,711)	75,705	(+8,572)	84,277
Harkin, Marian*	(Ind)	84,813	(+5,125)	89,938	(+9,623)	99,561	(+4,381)	103,942	(+8,268)	112,210	(+9,462)	121,672
Higgins, Jim*	(FG)	80,093	(+2,364)	82,457	(+4,140)	86,597	(+24,536)	111,133	(+2,677)	113,810	(+6,375)	120,185
Higgins, John Francis	(Ind)	3,030										
King, Thomas	(Ind)	1,124										
Mac Lochlainn, Pádraig	(SF)	45,515	(+1,898)	47,413	(+2,812)	50,225	(+2,159)	52,384	(+2,353)	54,737		
McCullagh, Noel	(Ind)	1,940										
McNamara, Michael	(Ind)	12,744										
Mooney, Paschal	(FF)	42,985	(+1,734)	44,719	(+968)	45,687	(+2,015)	47,702				
O'Keeffe, Susan	(Lab)	28,708	(+2,468)	31,176								
Ó Luain, Fiachra	(Ind)	6,510										
O'Reilly, Joe	(FG)	37,564	(+1,290)	38,854	(+3,496)	42,350						
NON-TRANSFERABLE				6,145		6,425		5,868		7,785		22,020

Seats 3
Quota 124,532

COUNT	1	Distribution of Sexton, Stafford votes 2		Distribution of Boyle votes 3		Distribution of O'Keeffe votes 4		Distribution of Crowley surplus 5		Distribution of Burke votes 6		Distribution of Kelly surplus 7		Distribution of Ferris votes 8	
Boyle, Dan (GP)	15,499	(+751)	16,250												
Burke, Colm (FG)	53,721	(+896)	54,617	(+2,573)	57,190	(+694)	57,884	(+770)	58,654						
Crowley, Brian* (FF)	118,258	(+1,367)	119,625	(+2,779)	122,404	(+10,006)	132,410								
Ferris, Toiréasa (SF)	64,671	(+1,190)	65,861	(+1,443)	67,304	(+992)	68,296	(+999)	69,295	(+4,094)	73,389	(+1,091)	74,480		
Kelly, Alan (Lab)	64,152	(+1,969)	66,121	(+3,562)	69,683	(+626)	70,309	(+682)	70,991	(+7,660)	78,651	(+5,270)	83,921	(+21,676)	105,597
Kelly, Seán (FG)	92,579	(+1,851)	94,430	(+1,723)	96,153	(+1,329)	97,482	(+912)	98,394	(+36,318)	134,712				
O'Keeffe, Ned (FF)	16,596	(+300)	16,896	(+228)	17,124										
Sexton, Maurice (Ind)	2,474														
Sinnott, Kathy (Ind)	58,485	(+3,572)	62,057	(+2,238)	64,295	(+1,223)	65,518	(+1,402)	66,920	(+4,429)	71,349	(+3,819)	75,168	(+19,966)	95,134
Stafford, Alexander (Ind)	11,692														
NON-TRANSFERABLE			2,270		1,704		2,254		3,113		6,153		0		32,838

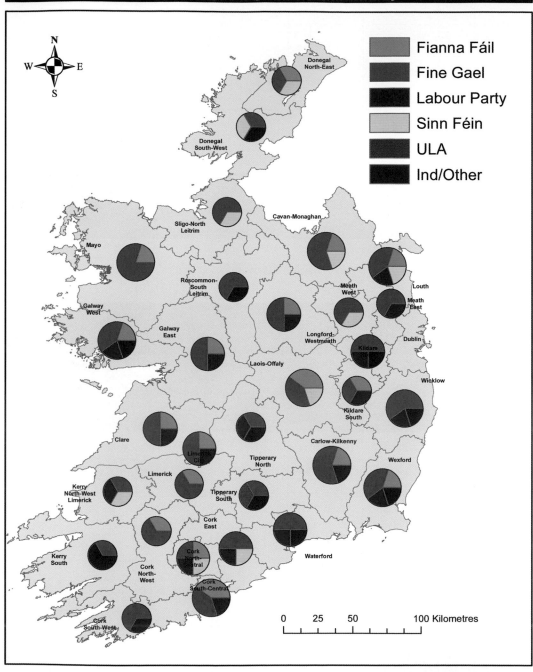

31st Dáil Election Results
Seats by Party and Constituency

Legend:
- Fianna Fáil
- Fine Gael
- Labour Party
- Sinn Féin
- ULA
- Ind/Other

© Houses of the Oireachtas Service 2011
© Ordnance Survey Ireland/Government
   of Ireland
Copyright Permit No. MP 002511

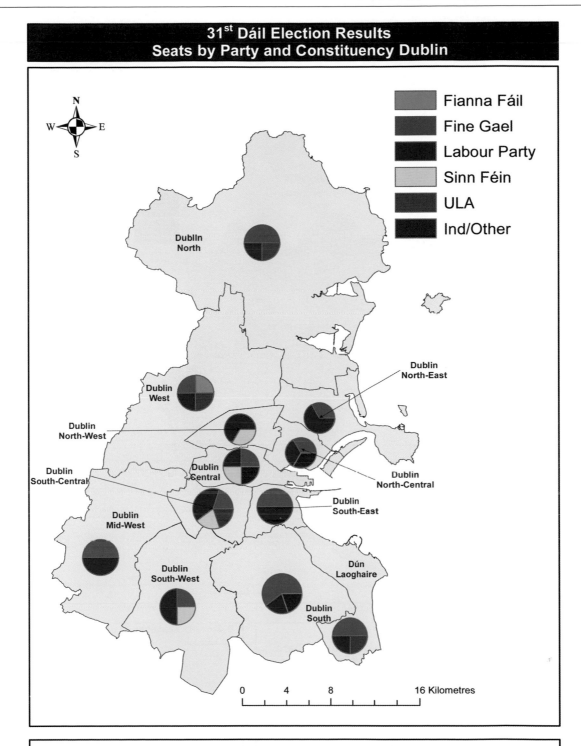

**31st Dáil Election Results
Seats by Party and Constituency Dublin**

Fianna Fáil
Fine Gael
Labour Party
Sinn Féin
ULA
Ind/Other

Dublin North

Dublin West

Dublin North-West

Dublin North-East

Dublin South-Central

Dublin Central

Dublin North-Central

Dublin Mid-West

Dublin South-East

Dublin South-West

Dún Laoghaire

Dublin South

0   4   8   16 Kilometres

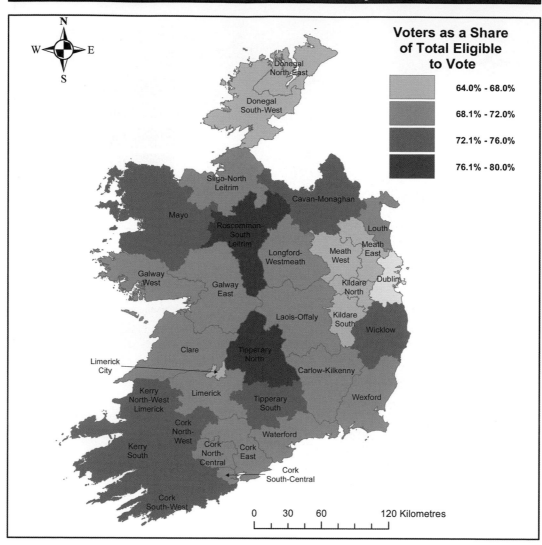

**31st Dáil Election Results
Turnout by Constituency**

**Voters as a Share
of Total Eligible
to Vote**

64.0% - 68.0%

68.1% - 72.0%

72.1% - 76.0%

76.1% - 80.0%

0   30   60   120 Kilometres

Ordnance Survey *Ireland*

**Oireachtas Library
& Research Service**
Seirbhís Leabharlainne & Taighde an Oireachtais
Houses of the Oireachtas
Tithe an Oireachtais

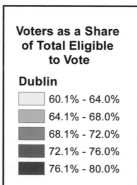

**Voters as a Share
of Total Eligible
to Vote**

Dublin

60.1% - 64.0%

64.1% - 68.0%

68.1% - 72.0%

72.1% - 76.0%

76.1% - 80.0%

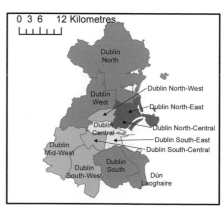

0 3 6   12 Kilometres

Dublin North

Dublin North-West

Dublin North-East

Dublin West

Dublin Central

Dublin North-Central

Dublin South-East

Dublin South-Central

Dublin Mid-West

Dublin South-West

Dublin South

Dún Laoghaire

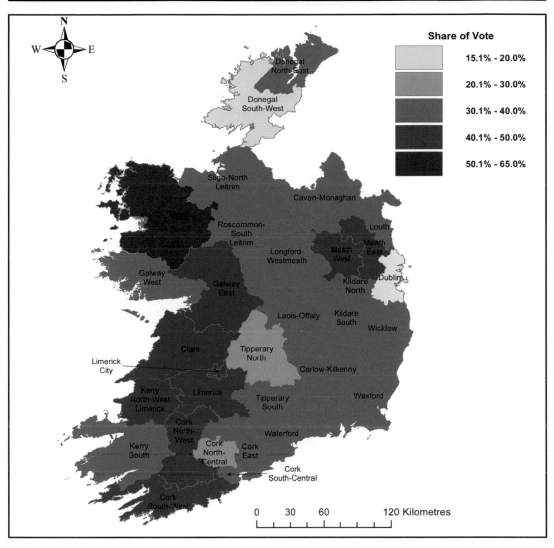

31st Dáil Election Results
Fine Gael Share of First Preference Vote by Constituency

Share of Vote

- 15.1% - 20.0%
- 20.1% - 30.0%
- 30.1% - 40.0%
- 40.1% - 50.0%
- 50.1% - 65.0%

0   30   60   120 Kilometres

© Houses of the Oireachtas
Service 2011
© Ordnance Survey Ireland/
Government of Ireland
Copyright Permit No. MP 002511

Ordnance Survey Ireland
OSi

Oireachtas Library & Research Service
Seirbhís Leabharlainne & Taighde an Oireachtais
Houses of the Oireachtas
Tithe an Oireachtais

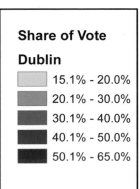

Share of Vote

Dublin

- 15.1% - 20.0%
- 20.1% - 30.0%
- 30.1% - 40.0%
- 40.1% - 50.0%
- 50.1% - 65.0%

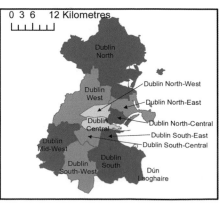

0 3 6   12 Kilometres

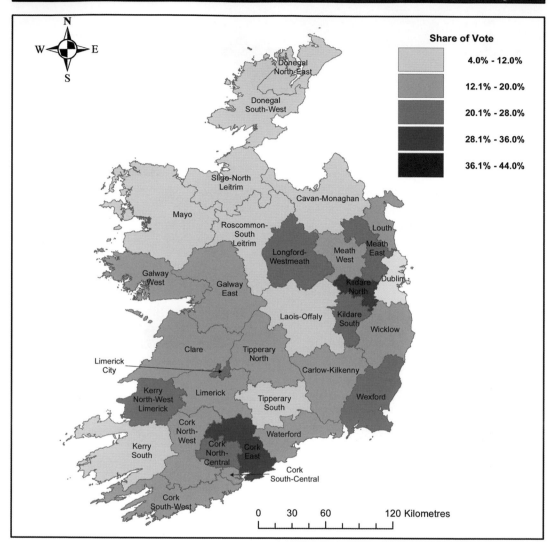

**31ˢᵗ Dáil Election Results
Labour Party Share of First Preference Vote by Constituency**

Share of Vote

- 4.0% - 12.0%
- 12.1% - 20.0%
- 20.1% - 28.0%
- 28.1% - 36.0%
- 36.1% - 44.0%

0 30 60 120 Kilometres

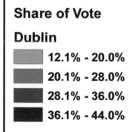

Share of Vote

Dublin

- 12.1% - 20.0%
- 20.1% - 28.0%
- 28.1% - 36.0%
- 36.1% - 44.0%

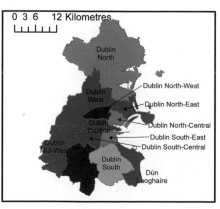

0 3 6 12 Kilometres

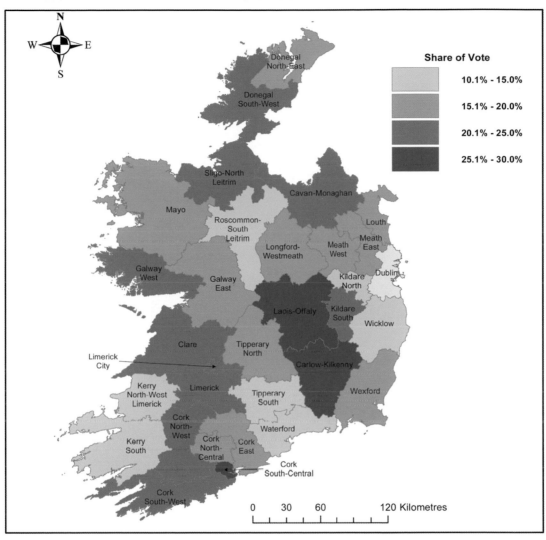

31st Dáil Election Results
Fianna Fáil Share of First Preference Vote by Constituency

Share of Vote

- 10.1% - 15.0%
- 15.1% - 20.0%
- 20.1% - 25.0%
- 25.1% - 30.0%

0   30   60   120 Kilometres

Share of Vote

Dublin

- 5.1% - 10.0%
- 10.1% - 15.0%
- 15.1% - 20.0%
- 20.1% - 25.0%
- 25.1% - 30.0%

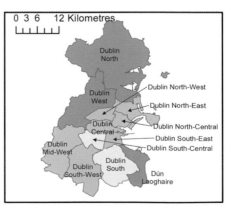

0 3 6   12 Kilometres

Dublin North
Dublin North-West
Dublin North-East
Dublin North-Central
Dublin West
Dublin Central
Dublin South-East
Dublin South-Central
Dublin Mid-West
Dublin South-West
Dublin South
Dún Laoghaire

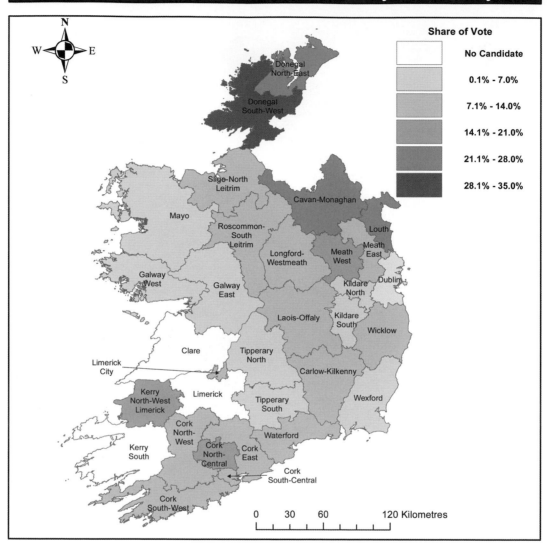

31st Dáil Election Results
Sinn Féin Share of First Preference Vote by Constituency

Share of Vote

No Candidate

0.1% - 7.0%

7.1% - 14.0%

14.1% - 21.0%

21.1% - 28.0%

28.1% - 35.0%

0   30   60   120 Kilometres

© Houses of the Oireachtas
Service 2011
© Ordnance Survey Ireland/
Government of Ireland
Copyright Permit No. MP 002511

Ordnance
Survey
Ireland

Oireachtas Library
& Research Service
Seirbhís Leabharlainne & Taighde an Oireachtais
Houses of the Oireachtas
Tithe an Oireachtais

Share of Vote

Dublin

No Candidate

0.1% - 7.0%

7.1% - 14.0%

14.1% - 21.0%

21.1% - 28.0%

28.1% - 35.0%

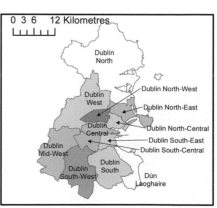

31ˢᵗ Dáil Election Results
United Left Alliance Share of First Preference Vote by Constituency

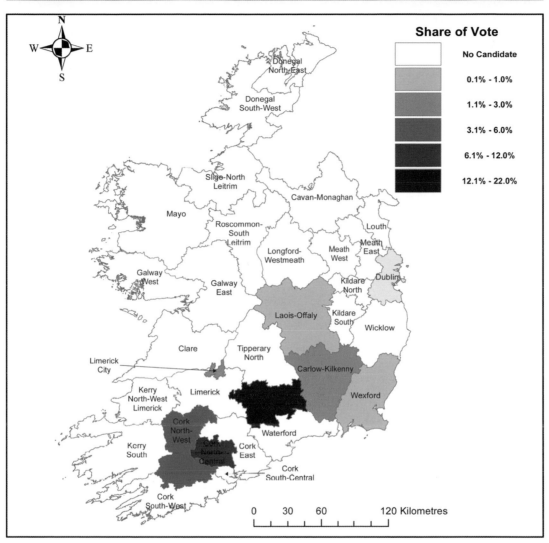

Share of Vote

- No Candidate
- 0.1% - 1.0%
- 1.1% - 3.0%
- 3.1% - 6.0%
- 6.1% - 12.0%
- 12.1% - 22.0%

0   30   60   120 Kilometres

Share of Vote

Dublin

- No Candidate
- 0.1% - 1.0%
- 1.1% - 3.0%
- 3.1% - 6.0%
- 6.1% - 12.0%
- 12.1% - 22.0%

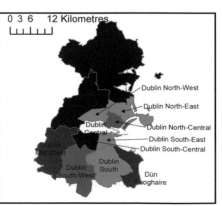

0 3 6   12 Kilometres

- Dublin North-West
- Dublin North-East
- Dublin North-Central
- Dublin South-East
- Dublin South-Central

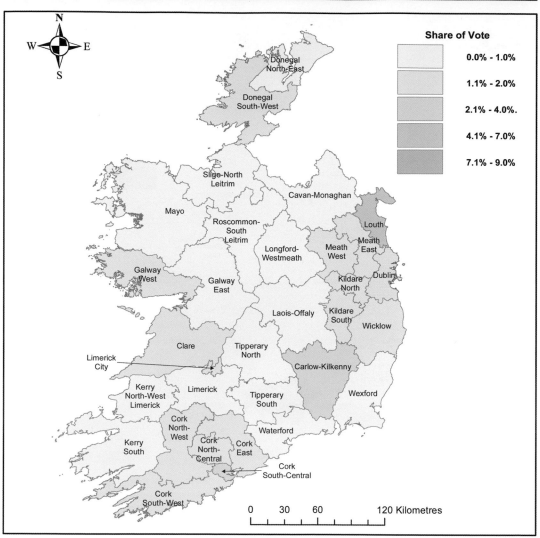

31st Dáil Election Results
Green Party Share of First Preference Vote by Constituency

Share of Vote

- 0.0% - 1.0%
- 1.1% - 2.0%
- 2.1% - 4.0%.
- 4.1% - 7.0%
- 7.1% - 9.0%

0   30   60   120 Kilometres

© Houses of the Oireachtas
Service 2011
© Ordnance Survey Ireland/
Government of Ireland
Copyright Permit No. MP 002511

Ordnance Survey Ireland
OSi

Oireachtas Library
& Research Service
Seirbhís Leabharlainne & Taighde an Oireachtais
Houses of the Oireachtas
Tithe an Oireachtais

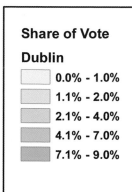

Share of Vote
Dublin

- 0.0% - 1.0%
- 1.1% - 2.0%
- 2.1% - 4.0%
- 4.1% - 7.0%
- 7.1% - 9.0%

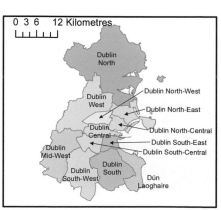

0 3 6   12 Kilometres

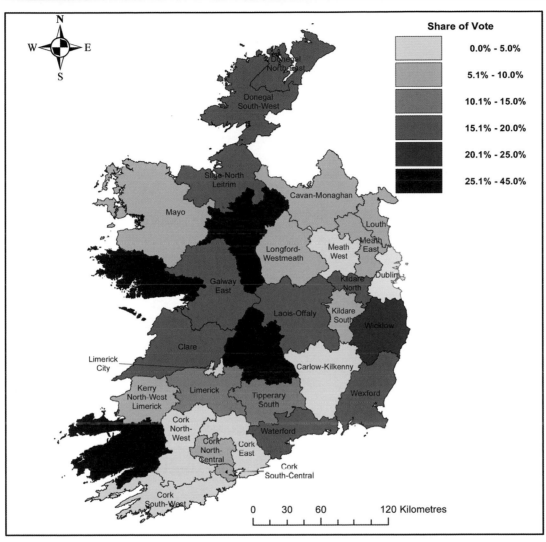

31st Dáil Election Results
Independents/Others Share of First Preference Vote by Constituency

Share of Vote

- 0.0% - 5.0%
- 5.1% - 10.0%
- 10.1% - 15.0%
- 15.1% - 20.0%
- 20.1% - 25.0%
- 25.1% - 45.0%

0 30 60 120 Kilometres

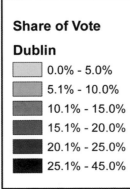

Share of Vote
Dublin

- 0.0% - 5.0%
- 5.1% - 10.0%
- 10.1% - 15.0%
- 15.1% - 20.0%
- 20.1% - 25.0%
- 25.1% - 45.0%

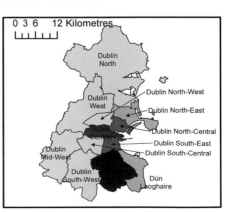

0 3 6 12 Kilometres

31st Dáil Election Results
Number of Female TDs by Constituency

No. of Female TDs

| | 0 |
| | 1 |

Labharlanna Fhine Gall

© Houses of the Oireachtas
Service 2011
© Ordnance Survey Ireland/
Government of Ireland
Copyright Permit No. MP 002511

Ordnance Survey Ireland
OSi

Oireachtas Library
& Research Service
Seirbhís Leabharlainne & Taighde an Oireachtais
Houses of the Oireachtas
Tithe an Oireachtais

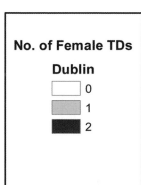

No. of Female TDs

Dublin

	0
	1
	2

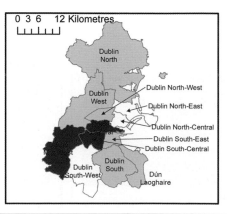

Index

Date	Subject	Electorate	Total Poll	%	Spoiled Votes	%	Total Valid Poll	%	Yes Votes	%	No Votes	%	% of Elect. Yes	% of Elect. No
1/7/37	Constitution	1,775,055	1,346,207	75.8	134,157	10.0	1,212,050	68.3	685,105	56.5	526,945	43.5	38.6	29.7
17/6/59	Straight Vote	1,678,450	979,531	58.4	39,220	4.0	940,311	56.0	453,322	48.2	486,989	51.8	27.0	29.0
16/10/68	Formation of Dáil Consts	1,717,389	1,129,477	65.8	48,489	4.3	1,080,988	62.9	424,185	39.2	656,803	60.8	24.7	38.2
16/10/68	Straight Vote	1,717,389	1,129,606	65.8	48,212	4.3	1,081,394	63.0	423,496	39.2	657,898	60.8	24.7	38.3
10/5/72	EEC Membership	1,783,604	1,264,278	70.9	10,497	0.8	1,253,781	70.3	1,041,890	83.1	211,891	16.9	58.4	11.9
7/12/72	Voting Age	1,783,604	903,439	50.7	47,089	5.2	856,350	48.0	724,836	84.6	131,514	15.4	40.6	7.4
7/12/72	Position of RC Church	1,783,604	903,669	50.7	49,326	5.5	854,343	47.9	721,003	84.4	133,340	15.6	40.4	7.5
5/7/79	Adoption	2,179,466	623,476	28.6	15,517	2.5	607,959	27.9	601,694	99.0	6,265	1.0	27.6	0.3
5/7/79	Seanad University Seats	2,179,466	622,646	28.6	24,562	3.9	598,084	27.4	552,600	92.4	45,484	7.6	25.4	2.1
7/9/83	Protection of Unborn	2,358,651	1,265,994	53.7	8,625	0.7	1,257,369	53.3	841,233	66.9	416,136	33.1	35.7	17.6
14/6/84	Voting for Non-citizens	2,399,257	1,138,895	47.5	40,162	3.5	1,098,733	45.8	828,483	75.4	270,250	24.6	34.5	11.3
26/6/86	Divorce	2,436,836	1,482,644	60.8	8,522	0.6	1,474,122	60.5	538,279	36.5	935,843	63.5	22.1	38.4
24/5/87	Single European Act	2,461,790	1,085,304	44.1	4,904	0.5	1,080,400	43.9	755,423	69.9	324,977	30.1	30.7	13.2
18/6/92	Maastricht Treaty	2,542,840	1,457,219	57.3	7,488	0.5	1,449,731	57.0	1,001,076	69.1	448,655	30.9	39.4	17.6
25/11/92	Right to Life	2,542,841	1,733,309	68.2	81,835	4.7	1,651,474	64.9	572,177	34.6	1,079,297	65.4	22.5	42.4
25/11/92	Travel	2,542,841	1,733,821	68.2	74,454	4.3	1,659,367	65.3	1,035,308	62.4	624,059	37.6	40.7	24.5
25/11/92	Information	2,542,841	1,732,433	68.1	74,494	4.3	1,657,939	65.2	992,833	59.9	665,106	40.1	39.0	26.2
24/11/95	Divorce	2,628,834	1,633,942	62.2	5,372	0.3	1,628,570	62.0	818,842	50.3	809,728	49.7	31.1	30.8
28/11/96	Bail	2,659,895	777,586	29.2	2,878	0.4	774,708	29.1	579,740	74.8	194,968	25.2	21.8	7.3
30/10/97	Cabinet Confidentiality	2,688,316	1,268,043	47.2	66,091	5.2	1,201,952	44.71	632,777	52.6	569,175	47.4	23.5	21.2
22/5/98	Amsterdam Treaty	2,747,088	1,543,930	56.2	33,228	2.2	1,510,702	55.0	932,632	61.7	578,070	38.3	33.9	21.0
22/5/98	Northern Ireland	2,747,088	1,545,395	56.3	17,064	1.1	1,528,331	55.6	1,442,583	94.4	85,748	5.6	52.5	3.1
11/6/99	Local Govt	2,791,415	1,425,881	51.1	109,066	7.6	1,316,815	47.2	1,024,850	77.8	291,965	22.2	36.7	10.5
7/6/01	Death penalty	2,867,960	997,885	34.8	14,480	1.5	983,405	34.3	610,455	62.1	372,950	37.9	21.3	13.0
7/6/01	Int. Criminal Court	2,867,960	997,565	34.8	17,819	1.8	979,746	34.2	628,695	64.2	350,963	35.8	21.9	12.2
7/6/01	Nice Treaty 1	2,867,960	997,826	34.8	14,887	1.5	982,939	34.3	453,461	46.1	529,478	53.9	15.8	18.5
6/3/02	Abortion	2,923,918	1,254,175	42.9	6,649	0.5	1,247,526	42.7	618,485	49.6	629,041	50.4	21.2	21.5
19/10/02	Nice Treaty 2	2,923,918	1,446,588	49.5	5,384*	0.4	1,441,204	49.3	906,317	63.0	534,887	37.0	31.0	18.3
11/06/04	Citizenship	3,041,688	1,823,434	60.0	20,219	1.1	1,803,215	59.0	1,427,520	79.2	375,695	20.8	49.6	12.4
12/6/08	Lisbon Treaty 1	3,051,278	1,621,037	53.13	6,171	0.38	1,614,866	52.92	752,451	46.06	862,415	53.40	24.66	28.26
2/10/09	Lisbon Treaty 2	3,078,032	1,816,098	59.00	7,224	0.40	1,808,874	58.77	1,214,268	67.13	594,606	32.87	39.45	19.32

*Spoilt votes reduced due to use of electronic voting in seven constituencies.

General Elections 1923–2011 (Party Seats and % of First-Preference Votes)

Year of election	Total Seats	Fianna Fáil (Anti-Treaty in 1923)		Fine Gael (Cumann na nGaedheal to 1933)		Labour		Sinn Féin		Farmers	
		Seats	% Votes	Seats	% Votes	Seats	% Votes	Seats	% Votes	Seats	% Votes
1923	153	44	27.6	63	38.9	14	12.4			15	10.6
June 1927	153	44	26.1	47†	27.5	22	13.8	5	3.6	11	8.9
Sept 1927	153	57	35.2	62†	38.7	13	9.5			6	6.4
1932	153	72	44.5	57†	35.3	7	7.7			4	2.1
1933	153	77†	49.7	48	30.5	8	5.7				
1937	138	69†	45.2	48	34.8	13	10.3				
1938	138	77†	51.9	45	33.3	9	10.0				

		Fianna Fáil		Fine Gael		Labour		Sinn Féin		Clann na Talmhan	
1943	138	67†	41.9	32	23.1	17	15.7			14	10.3
1944	138	76†	48.9	30	20.5	12††	11.5			11	10.8
1948	147	68†	41.9	31	19.8	19††	11.3			7	5.3
1951	147	69†	46.3	40	25.7	16	11.4			6	2.9
1954	147	65	43.4	50	32.0	19†	12.0			5	3.1
1957	147	78	48.3	40	26.6	12†	9.1	4	5.4	3	2.4
1961	144	70	43.8	47	32.0	16†	11.6			2	1.5
1965	144	72	47.8	47	33.9	22†	15.4				
1969	144	75†	45.7	50	34.1	18	17.0				
1973	144	69†	46.2	54	35.1	19	13.7				
1977	148	84	50.6	43	30.5	17†	11.6				

		Fianna Fáil		Fine Gael		Labour		Sinn Féin		Progressive Democrats	
1981	166	78	45.3	65	36.5	15	9.9				
Feb 1982	166	81†	47.3	63	37.3	15	9.1				
Nov 1982	166	75	45.2	70	39.2	16	9.4				
1987	166	81	44.2	51†	27.1	12	6.4			14	11.9
1989	166	77	44.2	55	29.3	15	9.5			6	5.5
1992	166	68	39.1	45	24.5	33	19.3			10	4.7
1997	166	77	39.3	54	28.0	17	10.4	1	2.5	4	4.7

		Fianna Fáil		Fine Gael		Labour		Sinn Féin		Progressive Democrats	
2002	166	81	41.5	31	22.5	21†	10.8	5	6.5	8	4.0
2007	166	78†	41.6	51	27.3	20	10.1	4	6.9	2	2.7
2011	166	20†	17.4	76	36.1	37	19.4	14	9.9		

** Other parties

1981	Socialist Labour Party 1
1987	Democratic Socialist Party 1
1989	Democratic Socialist Party 1
1997	Socialist Party 1
2002	Socialist Party 1

† includes outgoing Ceann Comhairle returned without contest
†† In 1943 Labour divided into Labour and National Labour and re-merged in 1950

National League		Centre Party (later merged with Fine Gael)		Other Parties** and Independents		Taoiseach (President of Executive Council to 1937)	Government
Seats	% Votes	Seats	% Votes	Seats	% Votes		
				17	10.5	W.T. Cosgrave	Cumann na nGaedhael
8	7.3			16	12.8	W.T. Cosgrave	Cumann na nGaedhael
2	1.3			13	8.9	W.T. Cosgrave	Cumann na nGaedhael
				13	10.4	Éamon de Valera	FF
		11	9.1	9	5	Éamon de Valera	FF
				8	9.7	Éamon de Valera	FF
				7	4.8	Éamon de Valera	FF

Clann na Poblachta		National Progressive Democrats		Other Parties** and Independents		Taoiseach	Government
				8	9	Éamon de Valera	FF
				9	8.3	Éamon de Valera	FF
10	13.2			12	8.5	John A. Costello	FG/ Lab/National Labour/ Clann na Poblachta/Clann na Talmhan/Inds
2	4.1			14	9.6	Éamon de Valera	FF
3	3.8			5	5.7	John A. Costello	FG/ Lab/ Clann na Talmhan
1	1.7			9	6.5	Éamon de Valera to 1959/ Seán Lemass	FF
1	1.2	2	1.0	6	8.9	Seán Lemass	FF
				3	2.9	Seán Lemass to 1966/ Jack Lynch	FF
				1	3.2	Jack Lynch	FF
				2	5.0	Liam Cosgrave	FG/Lab
				4	7.3	Jack Lynch to 1979/ Charles Haughey	FF

Green Party		SFWP/WP/ Democratic Left		Other Parties** and Independents		Taoiseach	Government
		1	1.7	7	6.6	Garret FitzGerald	FG/Lab
		3	2.2	4	4.1	Charles Haughey	FF
		2	3.1	3	3.1	Garret FitzGerald	FG/Lab
		4	3.8	4	6.6	Charles Haughey	FF
1	1.5	7	5	5	5.0	Charles Haughey to 1992/ Albert Reynolds	FF/PD
1	1.4	4	2.8	5	8.2	Albert Reynolds to 1994/ John Bruton	FF/PD FG/Lab/DL
2	2.8	4	2.5	7	9.8	Bertie Ahern	FF/PD

Green Party		United Left Alliance		Other Parties** and Independents		Taoiseach	Government
6	3.8			14	10.9	Bertie Ahern	FF/PD
5	4.7			5	6.7	Bertie Ahern to 2008/ Brian Cowen	FF/GP/PD
		5	2.6	14	12.6	Enda Kenny	FG/Lab